The Jossey-Bass Nonprofit Sector Series also includes:

THE NEW-YORK HISTORICAL SOCIETY

THE NEW-YORK HISTORICAL SOCIETY

Lessons from One Nonprofit's Long Struggle for Survival

Kevin M. Guthrie

Foreword by William G. Bowen

Jossey-Bass Publishers
San Francisco

27708

Substantial discounts on bulk quantities of Jossey-Bass books are available to corporations, professional associations, and other organizations. For details and discount information, contact the special sales department at Jossey-Bass Inc., Publishers: (415) 433-1740; Fax (800) 605-2665.

For sales outside the United States, please contact your local Simon & Schuster International Office.

 Manufactured in the United States of America on Lyons Falls Pathfinder Tradebook. This paper is acid-free and 100 percent totally chlorine-free.

Opening epigraph in Chapter One is from William H. Honan, "Historical Society to Close Library," *New York Times*, 4 February, 1993. Copyright © 1993 by The New York Times Company. Reprinted by permission.

Table 3.1 and Table 10.1 are from I. Kennedy and C. Schneider, *Historical Capital Market Returns* (Boston: Cambridge Associates, 1994). Reproduced by permission of Cambridge Associates, Inc.

Documents and materials from The New-York Historical Society are used with permission.

Library of Congress Cataloging-in-Publication Data

Guthrie, Kevin M.
    The New-York Historical Society: lessons from one nonprofit's long struggle for survival/ Kevin M. Guthrie.
        p. cm.—(The Jossey-Bass nonprofit sector series)
    Includes bibliographical references (p.   ) and index.
    ISBN 0-7879-0187-3 (acid-free paper)
    1. New-York Historical Society. 2. Nonprofit organizations—United States—Case studies. I. Title. II. Series.
    F116.N77G88   1996
    974.7'006—dc20
                                                                                              95-23655
                                                                                              CIP

HB Printing   10 9 8 7 6 5 4 3 2 1   FIRST EDITION

CONTENTS

PART TWO: ANALYSES AND LESSONS FOR NONPROFITS   149

APPENDIXES   183

FIGURES AND TABLES

Figures

Tables

FOREWORD

This is a study of the evolution over almost two centuries of The New-York Historical Society (N-YHS), a venerable institution founded before the Metropolitan Museum of Art and, for that matter, before almost any of the other American libraries and museums that are of consequence today. In late 1993 and early 1994, the Society attracted a great deal of attention in the New York press—not, unfortunately, because of new accomplishments but rather because of recurring threats to its very existence and because of controversy over deaccessioning and some of the other steps it has taken or contemplated in an effort to survive.

There have been many expressions of astonishment that a nonprofit institution with such unparalleled collections could have come to such a pass. The Society owns materials documenting the early history of America (and especially New York) that are among the greatest in the world, as well as an impressive array of paintings and museum objects. How can an institution with assets valued at $1 to $2 billion face bankruptcy?

Kevin Guthrie's fascinating case study answers this question, as well as many others concerning the successes and travails of the Society. To the best of my knowledge, no other study examines in such rich detail the path followed by a major nonprofit institution that consistently failed to find its way. As one commentator on an early draft of the manuscript observed sagely, the real surprise is not that the Society is now in trouble but that it is still here at all—given the difficulties it has faced in defining its mission, the recurring disputes concerning its "elitism" and openness, and the nature of its governing structure.

It is hard to imagine a problem that a nonprofit cultural institution, dependent almost exclusively on an endowment and on contributed income, could confront that the N-YHS has not had to face—often more than once! Careful examination of what happened to the Society over its long history, of decisions made and not made, of changing circumstances and unchanging policies, is extraordinarily illuminating for anyone interested in the well-being of nonprofit institutions. That is precisely why The Andrew W. Mellon Foundation decided to sponsor this study.[1]

Readers will want to draw their own conclusions from the chronicle of events and personalities that makes up the first and largest part of the book, which concludes with an analysis of the options available to the Society at the present time. Though some of the problems the Society has confronted have been idiosyncratic, most have not been. In the second part of the book, Guthrie provides his own commentary on such basic questions as how one distinguishes between financial and cultural assets and the confusions that can result from failure to understand this key distinction. He also writes perceptively about the uses and abuses of endowment and about lessons for the governance of institutions such as the Society. Lurking not far below the surface are interesting issues of public policy, including the role played by the New York State attorney general and the effects of intense media coverage.

In praising the book, I realize full well that I am hardly an unbiased commentator. It was, after all, at my urging that the study was carried out. But I have certainly had no second thoughts about that decision. I have learned a great deal from this detailed account of the long history of efforts by committed people to preserve an important part of the nation's heritage. We are reminded, among other things, of the dangers of looking too hard for villains and of suspecting, perhaps unconsciously, that "evil" (or at least self-serving behavior) was somehow at the root of problems not readily explained in other ways. In truth, the greater dangers are failures to understand basic propositions, reluctance to take what may appear to be negative actions, and perhaps even too much faith that, as the leader of another organization in trouble once put it, "the Lord will provide."

This is not, then, an exposé. It is, rather, an effort to understand why well-intentioned people, including some very able individuals, were unable to correct problems that were rooted in decisions made years earlier—in some instances, more than a century before. I have been very impressed by the determined efforts of the two most recent full-time directors, Barbara Debs and Betsy Gotbaum, to rescue the situation—albeit by pursuing quite different strategies. The problems they have encountered are hardly indictments of them or of other able individuals who have served on the board of the Society.

Still, the serious dilemmas the Society faces have not been resolved. It is our hope that recognition of the long shadows cast by decisions made generations ago concerning mission, scope of the collections, and funding patterns, combined with a large dose of realism, will yet lead to solutions designed to preserve the irreplaceable treasures that the Society owns and for which it continues to be responsible. Even more, we hope that this account will have preventive value—that it will alert leaders and trustees of other nonprofits to emerging problems that can be addressed most successfully if detected at earlier stages in their development.

It remains only to introduce the author and then let him tell his story. The Mellon Foundation engaged Kevin Guthrie to participate in its research program on nonprofit institutions because of his unusual combination of talents. After earning an undergraduate degree at Princeton University in engineering, Guthrie developed a software product that he and his associates marketed aggressively in a traditional entrepreneurial mode. He then enrolled in Columbia Business School, where he earned his M.B.A. in 1990. Since the Foundation was particularly interested in how best to disentangle, present, and analyze financial data for nonprofits, many of which were small and "entrepreneurial," Guthrie's mix of training and experience seemed appropriate.

In the course of this project, Guthrie also repeatedly demonstrated certain personal qualities that proved essential to the success of the study—above all, persistence, good humor, openness, the ability to earn trust, and an abundant capacity to work long hours. It was just as well that he did not really know what he was getting into when he embarked on this study—a more knowledgeable person might have declined the honor! As it was, Guthrie's ability to see things through fresh eyes proved extremely valuable. All of us who have worked with him at the Foundation have learned from him ("Don't take the Jaguar" will remain one of his legacies; see Chapter Nine). On behalf of the Foundation, I am delighted to record here our appreciation to him for his tireless efforts to understand the story of The New-York Historical Society and then to present it in an interesting and instructive way.

New York, New York William G. Bowen
November 1995 *President*
  The Andrew W. Mellon Foundation

Note

1. The Foundation has also sponsored a companion study of five independent research libraries, conducted by Jed Bergman (1995). Each of these studies adds value to the other in that, considered together, they help the reader differentiate problems and circumstances peculiar to individual institutions from those that are more universal.

For my parents, with affection and gratitude.

PREFACE

If you are reading these words, it is likely that you have heard of The New-York Historical Society (N-YHS). Even if you recognize nothing more than the odd hyphen in the institution's name, you know more than I did when, as a member of The Mellon Foundation's research staff, I attended a meeting with the Society's top leadership in the fall of 1992. When William G. Bowen invited me to that meeting, he said that the Society's situation had the potential to be a very interesting case study of the types of problems faced by institutions in the non-profit sector.

As I heard about the Society's various problems for the first time—its budget deficits, the inadequacy of its endowment, the virtual absence of earned income—I thought a case study of the Society would be much like others I had worked on during my first six months at the Foundation. Although these studies began with a brief qualitative history of each organization, they were focused primarily on financial issues. We were particularly interested in identifying trends in key financial indicators, such as a change in the dependence on a particular revenue source or unusually rapid growth of a certain class of expenditures. Our plan at the time was to assemble and then compare a group of these financial histories in the hope of identifying financial predictors of success and failure in the non-profit sector. Armed with an M.B.A., nearly ten years of experience as an entrepreneur, and facility with computer spreadsheet programs, I was well suited for such work.

It is impossible to encapsulate briefly what has happened at the Society since that meeting. There have been three leadership transitions. The Society was closed because of financial difficulties. Dispersal of its collections seemed likely. An outside advisory committee recommended that the Society be saved but offered a controversial prescription that included sales of collections, substantial development of real estate in a historic district along Central Park West, and significant capital and annual support from the public sector. Later, a potential affiliation with New York University, negotiated over several months by officers of the two entities, was rejected by the Society's Board of Trustees, eventually leading to the resignations of the Society's co-chairmen of the board. No one could have anticipated what has taken place in a very short time, and William Bowen's original characterization of this case as "potentially interesting" would have to be regarded as an understatement.

As one would expect, the New York media have pursued this story with gusto, sometimes even becoming a part of the drama. Thus I have had the opportunity to study the history of a venerable institution while it was simultaneously embroiled in public controversy. This unusual situation has allowed me to learn a great deal not only about the Society but also about how public perceptions are formed. Suffice it to say that for every piece of information conveyed in a newspaper article, there is perhaps a hundred times as much background that never surfaces. Although much of the background is of tangential relevance, some of it is critical to understanding the principal issues. This book tells, as they say, "the rest of the story."

Many times during the writing of this book, I struggled to make progress. When I sought the advice of friends and colleagues, they often encouraged me to focus on my audience: "Think about who will read this book," they would say. It was good advice. Reflecting on it now, I realize that how I actually acted on this advice has changed over time. That evolution explains not only the structure of this study but also its potential importance.

At first, I thought mainly of the Society's new director, Betsy Gotbaum, and the Society's Board of Trustees. If this study could give them a clearer understanding of the many difficult issues their institution faces, that would be a real service. Later, as controversy enveloped the Society and the opinions of important stakeholders—such as donors, foundation leaders, and public officials—were being shaped by incomplete information, I hoped to provide at least some historical and conceptual framework for their decisions. These objectives guided the preparation of Part One, which focuses on the Society's history and options for the future.

Part One contains eight chapters. Chapter One serves as an introduction to the institution, and Chapters Two through Seven chronicle the Society's history from 1804 to 1994. The story divides most naturally by periods of leadership. Chapter Eight describes the major issues facing the Society today and presents a series of six options that could be pursued, ranging from continuing to operate as an independent entity to total dissolution.

The historical narrative ends with the appointment of Betsy Gotbaum as the Society's new executive director in the summer of 1994. Although the story continues to evolve daily—the Society staged a major reopening in May 1995—I did not think it appropriate to write about a new administration just getting started.

The most remarkable aspect of the story of the Society is the astonishing range of issues it illuminates. Many transcend the idiosyncrasies of the Society's situation; they are faced by managers and board members of all nonprofit institutions. Part Two of the book, which has three chapters, summarizes these broader lessons. Chapter Nine discusses both the financial and nonfinancial "valuations" of nonprofit collections and their implications. Chapter Ten addresses the distinction between unrestricted and restricted funds and principles of endowment management. Finally, Chapter Eleven examines the importance of effective governance.

As a person who began this study with no experience in the nonprofit sector, I can say that this case taught me more than any single job experience and was richer by far than any for-profit case I studied in business school. As I prepare to move on to new endeavors, I take with me a new appreciation of the serious challenges that nonprofit institutions face, as well as a deep respect for the volunteers and trustees who will have to play a key role if these obstacles are to be overcome.

Acknowledgments

In conducting the research for the early history of the Society, I relied heavily on two secondary sources, *Knickerbocker Birthday,* by Robert W. G. Vail, and *Scholars and Gentlemen,* by Pamela Spence Richards. These books deserve special mention because they played such an important role in helping me develop an understanding of the historical underpinnings of the Society's problems.

On a more personal level, I must say that this book would not have been possible without help from a great many people. My feelings of gratitude for their support are incalculable.

First, I must express my most profound appreciation to William G. Bowen. His patient encouragement, wise counsel, and skillful editing of the manuscript kept me moving (albeit slowly!). Beyond his many contributions to this book, however, I cannot overstate my good fortune in having had the opportunity to work closely with him. He sets a standard of effectiveness, leadership, and integrity that raises the level of performance of everyone around him.

I have many colleagues at The Andrew W. Mellon Foundation to thank. Jed Bergman helped develop the conceptual foundations for the financial analysis in this study, using them in his own research on five major independent research libraries. Our common "mandated obsessions" provided a fertile field not only for productive work but also for friendship. Liz Breyer helped research prevailing attitudes among art museum professionals regarding deaccessioning for Chapter Ten. Liz Duffy, whose many projects keep her at the office late at night, was my frequent dinner companion. Her comments on initial drafts of all chapters were always right and proved extremely valuable—especially her restructuring of Chapter Two. Idana Goldberg, who joined the Foundation after I was deep in the writing phase of the project, provided helpful encouragement in its final stages. Tom Nygren contributed to every aspect of this book's development, from conception to final product. James Shulman, my friend and office-mate during most of the writing of the final manuscript, has endured much. His willingness to discuss and debate an endless stream of hypotheses played a vital role in the shaping of Part Two. Finally, Perry van der Meer offered valuable editing advice and helped with primary research on the Society's earliest days, while Kamla Motihar, the Foundation's librarian, and her assistant Linda Ng, helped me find and sort through literally hundreds of newspaper articles.

Members of the Foundation's program staff also deserve special mention. Rachel Bellow, the Foundation's program officer for arts and culture, helped me to synthesize the Society's history into the major themes presented in Chapter Eight. In addition, her experience working with cultural institutions provided depth to the ideas presented in Chapters Nine and Eleven. Henry Drewry, a former N-YHS board member, read a draft of Chapter Six and helped ensure that my recent analysis was on the right track. Rich Ekman, the Foundation's secretary—and the program officer responsible for grants to this territory—was an important mentor on historical scholarship and a pleasure to work with throughout this long process. He also offered many helpful comments that improved the manuscript. Finally, Tish Emerson provided wise counsel on many late nights, Dennis Sullivan offered moral support, and Harriet Zuckerman gave advice on my first thirty pages, which got me launched.

From the present and past at the N-YHS, I must thank Bill Carson, Barbara Debs, Stewart Desmond, Bobby Goelet, Betsy Gotbaum, Ed Norris, Miner Warner, Pug Winokur, and Phil Zimmerman for their willingness to talk candidly with me, to read drafts of chapters, and to make their files available. Marcus McCorison, former director of the American Antiquarian Society, also read a draft of the manuscript. This book would not have been the same without their cooperation and insights.

Finally, I would like to thank Sari, my wife, for putting up with my crazy schedule and for putting up with me. I am truly rich to have her as my partner and best friend.

New York, New York   Kevin M. Guthrie
November 1995

THE AUTHOR

Kevin M. Guthrie is the executive director of JSTOR, an independent non-profit organization recently established with the assistance of The Andrew W. Mellon Foundation to help the scholarly community take advantage of advances in information technology. Previously, he was a research associate at The Andrew W. Mellon Foundation. He earned his master's degree in business administration from Columbia University, where he was a Samuel Bronfman Fellow. He is the cofounder of CCSports Associates, Inc., a video products and computer software consulting firm specializing in sports applications. Earlier, he received his bachelor's degree cum laude from Princeton University, majoring in civil engineering.

THE NEW-YORK HISTORICAL SOCIETY

PART ONE

AGAINST ALL ODDS: THE STORY OF THE NEW-YORK HISTORICAL SOCIETY

CHAPTER ONE

CRISIS IN THE HEADLINES

Historical Society to Close Library

The board of the New-York Historical Society voted yesterday to shut down the institution's library on Feb. 19. All public programs are to be canceled, with the exception of a traveling show of 90 Audubon watercolors that had long been planned, and 41 staff members will be dismissed; a skeleton crew of 35 will be left to handle security, conservation and disposition of the collections.

NEW YORK TIMES, FEB. 4, 1993

To many people, the news was a shock. Following the closing of the Society's museum just five weeks before, the shutting of the library was tantamount to a for-profit business's filing for bankruptcy protection. Hard as it was to believe, the Society's museum and library holdings, arguably the single greatest collection of materials documenting early American and New York life, were at risk of being broken up and dispersed.

Reaction to the news was swift and unanimous. Six hundred scholars at forty campuses across the nation signed a petition urging New York's city and state officials to "keep the collections intact and available to New Yorkers." the *New York Times* ran an editorial calling for "responsible stewardship of so irreplaceable a part of the city's 'memory.'" And New York's governor, Mario Cuomo, issued a statement in support of the Society, calling it "a vital part of the cultural heritage of New York State."

Founded in 1804 to collect and preserve materials relating to the early history of New York and the United States, The New-York Historical Society is home to one of the nation's most distinguished research libraries. Its collections include approximately eight hundred thousand volumes and more than three million manuscripts, maps, photographs, prints, and architectural drawings that collectively provide an unparalleled picture of the early history of New York. But it is not just a library. The Society's museum is New York's oldest, predating the founding

3

of the Metropolitan Museum of Art by nearly seventy years. The art holdings have grown to a collection of over 1.6 million objects, including world-renowned Hudson River School paintings, an extensive collection of Tiffany glasswork, and 433 of the 435 original watercolors used for John J. Audubon's classic work, *Birds of America.*

With such highly esteemed collections and seemingly broad support, how could the Society be in such trouble? Although the answer to that question is complex—indeed, searching for answers to it is the central purpose of this book—the catalyst for the Society's crisis was really quite simple. After many years of operating deficits that had eroded the Society's capital base, there were insufficient fungible resources to pay the day-to-day operating costs of the institution. In other words, the Society had run out of cash. Generating cash and, more important, recurring cash flow would be essential if the Society was to survive. A special advisory committee, which included prestigious specialists adept at turning around troubled for-profit companies, was assembled to evaluate alternatives and to try to craft a workable solution.

The outcry that had led to the appointment of the advisory committee was "public" in every respect, and articles appeared in the New York press that attempted to explain the reasons for the Society's problems. In general, these articles emphasized the Society's reputation as an elitist institution, its inability to engage both its surrounding community and the general public in its collections and programs, and the magnitude of its financial difficulties. A *New York Times* article headlined "Is This the End for New York's Attic?" laid much of the blame on the Society's board of trustees, describing a "depressing saga of crisis management."[1] It emphasized the erosion of the Society's endowment in the 1980s and the failure of trustees and administrators to focus on an attainable mission. The article asserted that the Society's "mission statement was so vague that it could serve for the Smithsonian Institution" and pointed out that one of the key tasks for the advisory committee was to "accomplish in the next several weeks what the trustees did not when there was time: to articulate, once and for all, a clear mission for the Society."

There were disparaging articles in other papers as well. An article in the *New York Observer,* headlined "New-York Historical Society Rattling Toward Disintegration," was particularly critical of Society management.[2] It asserted that during the late 1980s, the Society "continued to wrack up annual deficits of $2 million a year and . . . had to 'invade' the . . . relatively small endowment to cover expenses." It quoted an unnamed member of the advisory committee, who wondered, "How can it be that year in and year out they were dissipating the endowment without any sign of improvement? It makes you wonder what was going on."

Déjà Vu?

This was not the first time that crisis had enveloped the Society. In 1988, a similar public controversy developed after the Society laid off one-fourth of its employees and announced plans to sell roughly forty European paintings.

The Society's decision to sell some of its art drew sharp criticism from the professional museum community. Richard Oldenberg, director of the Museum of Modern Art, said, "If you start cannibalizing your collections, for whatever worthy purpose, it's an abdication of responsibility by the people running the place."[3] Regarding the use of proceeds from those sales, representatives of the Society admitted that "under some limited circumstances, . . . the interest made from investment of the proceeds could be used for some operating costs."[4] Museum professionals considered that plan unethical and a violation of accepted museum practice. Peter C. Marzio, then president of the Association of Art Museum Directors, said, "The spirit of any deaccession"—the art world term for selling works from a museum collection—"is to improve the permanent collection. That's the only reason for deaccession."[5]

The Society's problems did not end with the criticisms of layoffs and deaccessioning. In the days following these announcements, a two-year-old confidential trustees' report detailing horrendous conditions at an off-site storage facility was obtained by the *New York Times*. Apparently, some paintings had been damaged or had been allowed to deteriorate as a result of the poor storage environment in a New Jersey warehouse. The resulting *Times* exposé attracted the attention of the New York State attorney general, who launched an investigation into "whether the art collection is being properly cared for and what legal consequences that may have."[6]

The firestorm of public criticism spread rapidly. The *New York Times* published an article headed "Museum's Downfall: Raiding Endowment to Pay for Growth," which described the circumstances that led to the erosion of the Society's endowment and criticized the role played by the Society's board, especially in the area of fundraising.[7] *New York* magazine weighed in days later with "Plundering the Past: The Decline of the New-York Historical Society."[8] That article attacked every aspect of the Society's operations, including its long history of deficits, the deterioration of and decision to sell parts of the collection, and its continuing image as "a sleepy, self-involved, closed fraternity of friends who thought that keeping trouble outside its . . . doors was the same as having none."

The mounting public controversy debilitated the Society. Less than one month after the announced layoffs, the Society's director resigned and his chief deputy was dismissed. In a step that would be repeated during the 1993 crisis, a blue-ribbon advisory committee composed of influential business people and arts administrators was convened to conduct a comprehensive analysis of the Society's mission, operations, and future prospects.

The Causes

Of course, the simplest and presumptive explanation for the Society's failures—and the one generally accepted by most observers who know little more than what they read in the newspapers—is that the Society had been poorly managed and improperly governed. Someone must be responsible. However, the rush to fix blame can have highly undesirable consequences. Most important, it can deflect attention from the root causes of difficulty and lead one to believe that problems will be solved by replacing a chief executive and restructuring membership on a board of trustees.

The fact that the Society suffered two very similar crises in such a short period of time should make one wonder whether the Society's problems were more deeply seated—more structural—than the newspaper article criticisms suggested. After all, the Society was effectively reborn in 1988. Not only did the Society hire a new director, but ten new members were added to the board of trustees. Between 1988 and 1993, experienced leadership with a track record of success executed a plan devised by a blue-ribbon committee under the microscope of intense public scrutiny. Nonetheless, the result was, once again, financial crisis, harsh criticism, and the threat that the Society's collections would be dispersed. There must be more to the story.

How Far Back?

Any attempt to uncover the root causes of the Society's problems clearly requires an investigation of its history. But how far back need one go? Very far, actually. Many of the Society's present problems have ancient antecedents.

Consider the criticism that the Society has acted as an elitist private club. In January 1917, one of the Society's members stood up at a meeting and declared the Society "dead and moribund." She said: "I have been attending the meetings of the New-York Historical Society for nearly three years, and have not heard one new or advanced scientific thought, although many distinguished scholars have visited the city."[9] The accusations shook the normally staid Society, and the resulting controversy, which was covered in the New York papers, eventually resulted in, yes, the convening of an outside advisory committee to investigate the Society's affairs. The following quote appeared in the *New York Times:* "Outsiders can only say that . . . there isn't much evidence . . . to indicate that the New-York Historical Society is an organization notable for either industry or enterprise—not much to show that it is toiling successfully either to acquire or to diffuse knowledge of the kind of which it is supposed to be the ardent finder and distributor."[10]

What about other Society problems, such as the lack of public awareness of its priceless collections? In 1993, an editorial appeared in the *New York Times* criticizing Society leadership for, in effect, poor marketing of the collections, stating that the Society's trustees "failed . . . to proclaim its treasures to the mass of New Yorkers—who might then have made keeping the institution alive a priority."[11] Ninety-four years earlier, in 1899, an article in the *New York Herald* made a very similar claim:

> While the superb collections of two sister societies are nobly housed in the great museums of Art and Natural History, where all the world may enjoy them, darkness and neglect have been the portion of the great aggregation of books, pictures, antiquities and memorials of great men and of stirring events that for nearly a century has been in process of collection by the New-York Historical Society. Apart from a very limited number of persons interested in antiquarian lore, the existence of this great collection has been unrecognized, and when the time comes that it can be worthily displayed, the people of New York will marvel how it has happened that treasures so worthy of civic pride have so long remained hidden from popular view. By some strange freak of progress this great museum remained, as it were, stranded by the upward current of the city's growth and has for many years lain forgotten and neglected in what was once the centre of wealth and culture.[12]

Just as these criticisms of the Society's activities have historical precedents, so do doubts about the Society's viability as an institution. In 1825, the Society faced a debt that threatened its very existence. The issues the Society faced then were remarkably similar to those it would face 168 years later:

> The committee confesses its entire inability to devise any means to liquidate a debt of this magnitude. Every possible economy was used to save further expense. The position of Sub-Librarian was abolished and the library closed; . . . it had been suggested that [several libraries in the city] combine to form one great public library but nothing came of this proposal. . . . It was proposed that the Society sell its library to pay its debts. This, of course, raised a storm of protest both in and out of the Society and it was suggested that the Society might not have the legal right to sell gifts. . . . The Society's situation was indeed desperate.[13]

The Society's problems are not new. Even under the best of circumstances they would not be easy to solve. Two hundred years of institutional inertia is not reversed quickly. But the depth of the historical roots of these difficulties also has implications for the scope of this study. Because fundamental questions about the viability of the Society have existed since its earliest days, this narrative must start at the beginning: 1804. That is indeed where Chapter Two begins.

Notes

1. Kimmelman (1993a).
2. Bagli (1993).
3. McGill (1988b).
4. McGill (1988d).
5. McGill (1988b).
6. McGill (1988g).
7. McGill (1988h).
8. Larson (1988).
9. "Tells Historical Society It Is Dead" (1917).
10. "Dry Bones Were Shaken Up" (1917).
11. "Cleaning Out New York's 'Attic'" (1993).
12. "Hidden Treasures" (1899).
13. Vail (1954, pp. 63–68).

CHAPTER TWO

THE FORMATIVE YEARS, 1804–1920

Humble Beginnings, 1804–1857

On November 20, 1804, a merchant named John Pintard gathered a group of ten prominent New Yorkers and established an organization with a mission "to collect and preserve whatever may relate to the natural, civil, or ecclesiastical History of the United States in general and of this State in particular."[1] With this broad statement of mission, The New-York Historical Society (N-YHS) was born.

Among the Society's earliest activities were canvassing for new members (for a $10 initiation fee and $2 annual dues),[2] educating the public on the importance of historical records and their preservation (by sponsoring lectures on history by prominent New Yorkers), and collecting whatever items people would donate. In an 1805 appeal "To the Public," which was distributed directly to prominent citizens and printed in the *New-York Herald*, the Society explained the importance of accurate historical documentation: "For without the aid of historic records and authentic documents, history will be nothing more than a well-combined series of ingenious conjectures and amusing fables."[3] It then requested donations to help it record authentic history, asking for "Manuscripts, Records, Pamphlets, and Books relative to the History of this Country." A long and varied list of desired materials followed, ranging from items such as copies of laws and records to more unusual items such as proceedings from ecclesiastical conventions and narratives of Indian wars.

The breadth of the Society's appeal seems ambitious—"Our inquiries are not limited to a single State or district, but extend to the whole Continent"—but as only the second institution of its kind in the small nation, so comprehensive an agenda was understandable. The population of the entire United States in 1804 was only about six million people, the population of New York State approximately six hundred thousand, and the population of New York City just seventy-five thousand. Consequently, at that time, the Society's agenda was not overly aggressive; in fact, its first appeals resulted in just a trickle of donations.

The library got its real start in 1809 when Pintard sold his own book and manuscript collection to the Society. With the nucleus of a collection established, the Society was incorporated in the State of New York on February 10, 1809.[4] Still, none of the eleven founders endowed the new Society financially, and it operated on a shoestring. Fortunately, New York City Mayor DeWitt Clinton was one of the Society's founders. For the first five years of its existence, meetings were held rent-free in a room at City Hall. As the Society's collection grew, however, the cost of maintaining the library quickly outpaced revenues. In March 1810, the Society turned to the state assembly for relief. This initial request for funds was rejected, but when the Society petitioned the state for assistance four years later, it was more successful; an 1814 bill sponsored by DeWitt Clinton (who had been elected New York State senator) passed, granting the Society the right to raise, by means of a lottery, $12,000 to support its activities.

With money borrowed against projected income from the lottery, the Society published a library catalog and a second volume describing its collections. By 1823, the Society had accumulated a debt of $8,000, but still no lottery had taken place, and prospects for one had dissolved. The debt set the stage for a major financial crisis that forced the Society to consider sale of its collections. The following auction notice, signed by the executive committee of the Society, appeared in the *New York Commercial Advertiser* under the headline "Sale of Very Valuable Books":

> The undersigned, . . . a committee with full powers, appointed by the New York Historical Society for the purpose of extricating said Society from its pecuniary embarrassments, find themselves compelled, very reluctantly, to offer for sale the choice and rare Library of that institution. . . . The undersigned very sincerely and earnestly hope that such steps will be taken by some of the Literary Institutions of this city, in order to prevent the scattering of that valuable collection of Books, and its thus being lost to this city and state.[5]

The Society's difficulties attracted the attention of state government officials, including DeWitt Clinton, who had been elected governor of New York. In his address to the legislature in 1826, Governor Clinton recommended that "the resuscitation of this Society and a liberal provision for its extended usefulness are measures worthy of . . . adoption."[6] On March 1, 1827, the legislature passed a bill, appropriating $5,000 to rescue the Society. With the receipt of the state funds, the Society was saved, at least for the immediate future.

To add to its financial problems during the first part of the century, the Society also found itself in a nearly constant search for a permanent home. In the period between 1809 and 1857, when it was finally able to construct its own building, the Society moved five times. In addition, the collections were twice crated and moved to safeguard against enemy bombardment. Somehow, despite this adversity, the Society managed to become a leader among American historical societies. Its library was growing at a faster rate than the Massachusetts Historical Society and was nearly the same size as that of the wealthier American Antiquarian Society.[7]

Membership in the Society also increased during this period. Between 1843 and 1849, nearly a thousand new members were added to its rolls. In his report to members, the chairman of the executive committee referred to "the prosperous condition and flattering prospects of the Society. . . . The stated meetings continue to be well attended and are popular and useful." These lectures played a primary role in stabilizing the Society's financial condition in the late 1830s.[8]

This relative prosperity allowed the Society to embark on a building campaign in the hope of securing, for the first time, a permanent and fireproof shelter for its rapidly growing and valuable collections. Two attempts to secure state or city funding for this initiative failed, and the Society concentrated its efforts on raising funds from private sources. By 1854, enough money had been raised to purchase a lot at the corner of Eleventh Street and Second Avenue, and three years later, the Society's first building was completed.

Going Its Own Way, 1857–1900

The completion of the new building, one of the few fire-safe depositories in New York City, made the Society a most attractive place for the protection and public display of valuable materials of all types. In the decade between 1858 and 1867, the Society's collection of art grew significantly through both donations and purchases. In 1858, the Society received the entire New York Gallery of the Fine Arts, including the collection of Luman Reed, one of America's foremost early-nineteenth-century patrons of the fine arts. In 1860, the Society raised $60,000 through public subscription to purchase the Abbott collection of Egyptian artifacts, which included three mummies and was at that time the greatest Egyptian collection in America. In 1863, the Society raised $4,000 to purchase

433 of the original watercolor paintings used to print *Birds of America,* by John James Audubon, from Audubon's widow.[9] And in 1867, Thomas J. Bryan gave the Society his collection of 381 works, mostly of European art. Collections such as these made the Society, prior to the opening of the Metropolitan Museum of Art in 1872, the most important art museum in the city.

During this period, the Society's library collection also grew. Under the direction of George Moore (1849–1876), the library expanded from twenty-five thousand volumes in 1857 to over sixty thousand in 1872. These figures do not include the considerable growth in other items, such as manuscripts, maps, and newspapers. This remarkable growth took place without a clearly defined acquisitions policy; no policy had been written that superseded the original broad appeal to the public. The Society basically accepted anything and everything it was given.

Such a broad acquisitions policy and the considerable growth in the Society's collections reflected the priorities of Frederic De Peyster, then president of the Society (1864–1866, 1873–1882). De Peyster saw an "opportunity to inaugurate a new power in the social progress of the nation, one of the grandest that has ever been offered."[10] To fulfill this vision, De Peyster encouraged growth in both the art and library collections because he believed that the Society should be a "center of intellectual light for the city and state."[11]

But the growth in the Society's collections and the expansion of the Society's goals did not come without cost. This transformation of the Society into an art gallery, library, and educational institution introduced competing purposes and emphases in the Society's mission that would prove very difficult to manage. Moreover, from a more immediate and practical standpoint, art galleries had not been incorporated in the original plans of the new building. The rapid growth of both the library and the museum collections put particular strain on library users and librarians because of a lack of space for books and limited desk room.[12]

Short of space to store and display its increasingly valuable holdings, the Society once again petitioned the state for assistance. In response, the New York State legislature set aside building sites for the Society in Central Park in both 1862 and 1868. Unfortunately, funds for construction of a building on those sites could not be raised, and the Society was unable to secure the Central Park locations (the latter parcel became the site of the Metropolitan Museum of Art). Interestingly, although the Society still wanted to move, no record exists of any further attempts by the Society to secure city or state assistance.[13]

Despite the space difficulties, the Society was highly regarded by both scholars and the popular press during this era. Even though access to the collections was restricted, there were few libraries competing with it to serve the intellectual needs of scholars and historians. Moreover, the perceived quality of a library, then even more than now, was highly dependent on the number of volumes in its care, and New Yorkers could point with pride to the size and growth of the Society's collections. Finally, the Society's reputation was enhanced by the public's respect for its officers and lecturers, such as the well-known historians George Bancroft and J. Romeyn Brodhead.[14]

The final quarter of the nineteenth century was a defining period for the Society. Although its library was among the largest and fastest-growing in the nation and its art collection was the finest in New York City, its external environment was changing at a rate so fast and in ways so profound that maintaining that standing would be a difficult challenge. The United States was entering the industrial age, a time of enormous political, economic, and social change. Because of the nature and the permanence of these changes, the Society's strategic choices would prove to have long-lasting impact. Unfortunately, the Society entered this dynamic period both undercapitalized and under new leadership (George Moore left in 1876 to run the Lenox Library). The decisions reached during this time, particularly regarding the Society's relationship to its professional peers, the public, and local government, made it difficult for the Society to maintain its preeminent position in city life.

It was after Moore left in 1876 that the Society first fell out of pace with its peer institutions. During the 1880s and 1890s, there was a strong movement toward professionalization of historical study and improvements in library service. In 1876, the American Library Association was founded; the Society was one of only two libraries in the city that did not join immediately. In fact, it did not join the association until 1910, thirty-four years after its founding.[15]

Other events further distanced the Society from the professional establishment. The founding of the American Historical Association in 1884 gave voice to a growing rift between professional historians and members of the older historical societies. James Franklin Jameson, a pioneer in the professionalization movement, decried historical societies as "few, feeble and mostly myopic."[16] Without Moore, a professional librarian and respected historian, at its helm, the Society was unable to bridge the growing gap between these communities; consequently, its reputation suffered.

The lack of focused leadership during this period was due in part to a change in the distribution of responsibilities among professional and volunteer leadership at the Society. Because the Society was a membership organization, the position of its official leader, the librarian, was an elected office. Until the end of Moore's tenure, the elected librarian and the full-time professional working in the library were one and the same. For some unknown reason, William Kelby, who would have been Moore's natural successor to assume both posts, chose not to run for election as the librarian and remained the Society's assistant librarian. Kelby's reluctance to stand for election meant that for the first time, the society's chief executive was a volunteer. The three librarians who succeeded Moore were all elected volunteers. To outsiders, the placement of responsibility for the library in the hands of a nonprofessional just as comparable institutions were becoming more professionalized further undermined the Society's credibility.[17]

Another development that cast the Society further outside the circle of professionalized libraries was its identification with the growth of patriotic and genealogical organizations. During the late 1800s, New York was a center of genealogical activity. Kelby himself was the official examiner of membership applications for the Sons of the Revolution in the state of New York. The growth of genealogical organizations in New York City was at least partly in response to the changing ethnic makeup of the city. By 1890, fully 80 percent of New York City's population was either born abroad or first-generation American. Many "native" New Yorkers (who were in fact just descendants of earlier immigrants) began to feel that their "way of life" was threatened. With membership in an organization to prove their descent from the city and country's founders, the old families could set themselves apart from the masses. Although it was natural that the Society's library, with its early collection of records and manuscripts, would be helpful in genealogical research, "it was unquestionably due to Kelby's particular enthusiasm for the subject that . . . the Society became one of the city's chief centers of genealogical research."[18]

The Society's movement away from the professional community and toward the amateur genealogists severely damaged its reputation. Whereas it had been highly regarded in the 1850s and 1860s, by the late nineteenth century, the Society was unknown to most New Yorkers. Those who were aware of it viewed it as a "quaint backwater of the city, serving not the historian (much less the interested amateur or inquirer) but a small circle of Knickerbocker families who descended from the founders."[19]

Although the Society's reputation suffered under Kelby, its collections continued to grow. By 1900, the library had amassed over one hundred thousand volumes. Unfortunately, the library's capacity to absorb these new materials was limited. Not only was the library's space overburdened, but the printed catalog listed only a quarter of the Society's book titles. Because it had chosen not to involve itself with the library associations, the Society was slow to adopt the tools available to manage its ever-increasing collection. For example, the shelving system, which had been adequate for a library of fifteen thousand titles, had become completely overwhelmed. Books were sometimes assigned to shelves based not on subject but on where they would fit.[20]

It was not just the library that was overflowing. The Society could also no longer accommodate its growing art collection. An article in the local press stated that "the building . . . was not intended for displaying a large collection of paintings. . . . Four-fifths [of the Society's paintings] are distributed about in dark corridors, galleries and corners, where for want of light they cannot be satisfactorily examined, even during the sunniest days of the year."[21]

The Society continued to accept all donations of art and books, even though it was unable either to store or to catalog them. This policy was to have long-term implications. The Society was building a huge backlog of uncataloged items, creating a future liability that would inevitably have to be addressed.

Critical choices were also made during this pivotal era concerning relations with the New York state and city governments. Early in its history, the Society depended on the city and state for various kinds of assistance. Indeed, as mentioned earlier, were it not for the timely actions of DeWitt Clinton (as mayor of New York city, then as state senator, and finally as governor), the Society would probably not have survived its first twenty-five years. But the Society's inability to raise the money needed to erect a building on the two parcels of land the city offered in the 1860s had a profound and long-lasting impact. First, the land offered by the city in 1868 became the site of a new major cultural museum, the Metropolitan Museum of Art, which the Society came to regard as "its great competitor."[22] Second, and perhaps more important, this turn of events launched the Society on a trajectory that did not include an ongoing relationship with the public sector; the Society committed itself to pursuing only private financial contributions to support its annual operations.

Why the Society abandoned efforts to raise funds from the city and state is not entirely clear, although it is possible that widespread corruption in city politics during that era played a role.[23] Still, by spurning public support, the Society chose a direction that ran counter to a trend being established by other cultural institutions in the city. The Metropolitan Museum of Art and the American Museum of Natural History, for example, made arrangements whereby the city provided grounds, building, and maintenance while the trustees retained ownership of the collections and stewardship of the institution. In the late 1800s, nearly all free circulating libraries either were municipally supported or soon to become so. After 1911, when the Lenox and Astor libraries became a part of the New York Public Library, only The New-York Historical Society, the New York Society, and Mercantile Libraries remained completely private.[24]

The Society's choice of an independent path was consequential. In the short run, it meant that the Society had to purchase land for its present site on Central Park West at a cost of $286,000, nearly all of its available resources. Not only did this purchase leave the Society without the money to erect a new, larger building, but it also limited the Society's ability to maintain and exhibit its collections. As one journalist at the time explained, the Society "has put all its money in a lot . . . where it is hoped some day to erect a building. Meantime it cannot afford a railing to keep back people . . . nor even a guardian to see that [art works] are not carried off."[25] Without sufficient funds, the Society effectively closed itself off from the public. This only tarnished further its already faded reputation in the city.

The Society's retreat from a partnership with the city had other long-range implications. When the Lenox Library acquired the esteemed Emmet Collection of Revolutionary War materials in 1896, it was "a personal grief [to Kelby] that the fine Emmet collection, which would have rounded out [the Society's] newspaper files for the last century, should have passed to the Lenox Library and be destined to be swallowed up by that Leviathan, the new Public Library."[26] With the city aligned with and supporting the New York Public Library and the Metropolitan Museum of Art, institutions that the Society considered its prime adversaries, it is easy to imagine how it became a matter of institutional pride that the Society could support itself without governmental assistance. The Society chose not to petition the city or state for operating support again for more than one hundred years, when it was forced to do so by its crises in the late 1980s. The decisions that the Society made in the late nineteenth century to go its own way continue to have effects. By forging a path of its own, the Society took the first steps away from a position of prominence in the city's culture.

Public Collections, Private Club, 1900–1921

During the early 1900s, the Society again confronted an issue that had dominated its life in its earliest days: how to house its growing collections. The Second Avenue building had long outlived its capacity to serve the Society's purposes, and the new site on Central Park West was only that—a site. All efforts were directed toward raising the money needed to finance the construction of a building.

During this time, the Society was led by Robert Hendre Kelby, the brother of William Kelby. The most important achievement of his tenure was securing the support of Henry Dexter, a New York businessman, in the cause of building the Society's new home. Dexter's gift of $200,000 initiated construction in 1904, and the central portion of the building was completed and furnished in 1908 at a total cost of $421,150.

The prospect of a new building engendered hope among New Yorkers that the Society would play a greater role in providing service to the public. During the capital campaign for the building, prior to actual construction, an editorial in the *New York Times* glowed: "With proper facilities for the display of interesting objects and greater convenience of access, throngs of people would enter its doors where now but few stray in. . . . The project certainly ought to possess interest with everyone who knows anything whatever of the splendid history of which this island has been the centre . . . events that should become familiar in the recollections of every American citizen."[27]

To some extent, as happened in 1857 when the Society moved into its Second Avenue home, moving to Central Park West did breathe new life into the Society. The executive committee ended the policy of requiring visitors to be introduced by a member, and attendance at the Society increased. Moreover, interest in the new building spurred donations of books, manuscripts, and art, although this was a mixed blessing as the growth of the Society's backlog of uncataloged items accelerated.

But the promise of public service would not soon be realized, at least not during the tenure of Robert Kelby. Despite some improvements, Kelby seemed to have little interest in having the Society play an active public service role. For example, although funds had been made available by the executive committee to hire two additional staff members at the library, there is no evidence that Kelby hired anyone. During the period between 1903 and 1912, the Society added more than sixty thousand volumes to its library and one hundred fifty paintings to its museum collections. Attempting to process this great influx of material was a staff of four: Kelby; his assistants, Alexander J. Wall and William Hildebrand; and the janitor, Charles Washbourn.[28] This inflow of materials added to a collection that already numbered more than a quarter of a million volumes and was nowhere near to being fully cataloged. It simply was not possible for such a small staff to provide service at the level of a top professional research library. Looking back on this period, Dixon Ryan Fox, president of the New York State Historical Association and a former Columbia University history professor, observed, "The reputation of the Society for gracious public service, frankly, was not high. . . . There was a feeling all too prevalent that it was not and probably could not be a public institution in any real sense."[29]

There are several reasons why the Society accomplished little in the way of public service under Robert Kelby. First, Kelby had been with the Society for more than forty years and was in declining health. Even when he was healthy, he did not encourage widespread use of the library. When asked by users if, like the New York Public Library, the Society library might open on Sundays, Kelby's customary response was "No, we go to Church on Sundays."[30] Second, like his brother William, Robert Kelby had a strong interest in genealogy and seemed more interested in making the library available to amateur genealogists than in making it more useful to professional scholars and the public. Third, and perhaps most important, although the Society had managed to erect a new building, it was unable to raise the funds needed to build the north and south wings as planned. The Society once again found itself in a structure too small to house its large and rapidly growing collections. Whatever energy management possessed was directed at the inadequacy of the physical plant and on finding the means to purchase the adjacent lots and finish the building.

Kelby's lack of demonstrated interest in serving the public finally caught up with the Society in the latter part of his tenure. In January 1917, May Van Rensselaer stood up at a Society meeting and declared that the Society was nothing more than an "old men's club" and that instead of being in the front rank of American historical societies and libraries, it was "dead and moribund." Though Van Rensselaer's motives were somewhat suspect,[31] she did raise a series of legitimate points that struck a chord with the press. Most resonant of these criticisms were those regarding the Society's lack of popular appeal and deficient public services. The *New York Times* quoted a scholar who admitted that the Society's collections were magnificent but added: "It would be very helpful if these collections were intelligently cataloged." The article went on to say that the Society "has collections of great size, but nobody seems to be profiting from them to any extent."[32]

The Society's leadership was shaken by the accusations and moved to control the damage. John Abeel Weekes, president of the Society, assured the press that "the most careful consideration is being given to Mrs. Van Rensselaer's suggestions for educational work and in making the collections more available for strangers."[33] Weekes established a special committee to investigate the situation and appointed to it, in addition to members of the Society's executive board, Worthington C. Ford of the Massachusetts Historical Society, John W. Jordan of the Pennsylvania Historical Society, and Clarence S. Brigham of the American Antiquarian Society. This committee was to conduct a complete evaluation of the Society's building, collection, and staff.

The report of the special committee was completed in less than a month, and its recommendations were released to the membership in a circular dated February 5, 1917. The conclusions of the committee contained only one significant criticism: that the Society had not done an adequate job of publicizing its holdings, facilities, and activities to the membership, the press, and the public. Other than that failing, the report stated that the Society's officers were doing the best job that could be expected considering the Society's lack of funds. Brigham, of the American Antiquarian Society, stated that "if certain work has not been done . . . it is because the officers have not been provided with the necessary means to fulfill these obligations."[34] Responsibility for the Society's lack of resources was ascribed to the large capital investments the Society had made in new facilities, rather than to the failure by leadership to raise the necessary funds. Apparently, at that time, it was not part of an officer's job to secure those means.

Even though the report was generally uncritical of Society management, the publicity surrounding the Van Rensselaer incident did have an impact. In April

1917, the Society began publishing the *Quarterly Bulletin* (after 1946, it was called *The New-York Historical Society Quarterly*), its first effort to publicize its collections. In addition, the Society hired three new staff members by year-end. Most significant, the latter part of the decade saw the gradual handing over of leadership of the Society library to Alexander J. Wall, a man who would take a far more active role in presiding over the Society than his predecessors.

Notes

1. This quote is from the Society's original Constitution, which is reprinted in its entirety in Appendix A.
2. These amounts are not as high as one might suppose. According to a "composite commodity price index" compiled by John J. McCusker, professor of history and economics at Trinity University, the $10 initiation fee is the equivalent of around $110 in 1991 dollars, and the $2 annual dues equates to $22 per year. For a discussion of the techniques used to develop this index, see McCusker (1992, tab. A-2, pp. 323–332).
3. The entire appeal "To The Public" is reprinted in Appendix B.
4. The act of incorporation recognized the Society "by the name of 'The New-York Historical Society,' and by such name they and their successors forever hereafter shall and may have succession." That is how the Society came to have the hyphen in its name, which has never been dropped (Vail, 1954, p. 34).
5. "Sale of Very Valuable Books" (1825).
6. Vail (1954, p. 67).
7. Richards (1984, p. 23).
8. Vail (1954, p. 90).
9. The collection is now estimated to be worth approximately $100 million.
10. Vail (1954, p. 33).
11. During Moore's tenure, improvements were made in the areas of cataloging, publications, and hours of operation, but despite De Peyster's vision of the Society as a cultural center serving the wider populace, the collections remained essentially unavailable to the public. As had been the case since the Society's inception, use of the library was restricted to readers introduced by a member.
12. Richards (1984, p. 30).
13. Richards (1984, p. 33).
14. Richards (1984, p. 41).
15. Richards (1984, p. 45).
16. Richards (1984, p. 44).
17. Richards (1984, p. 45).
18. Richards (1984, p. 49).
19. Richards (1984, p. 50).
20. Richards (1984, p. 38).
21. Vail (1954, p. 157).
22. Vail (1954, p. 119).
23. Richards (1984, p. 33).
24. Richards (1984, p. 34).

25. Walker (1896).
26. New-York Historical Society minutes, Nov. 1, 1898, cited in Richards (1984, p. 63).
27. Vail (1954, p. 175).
28. Richards (1984, p. 192).
29. Fox (1937).
30. Richards (1984, p. 59).
31. Van Rensselaer later led an effort to displace the board and take over management of the Society. When this endeavor failed, she founded the Society of Patriotic New Yorkers, an organization with a rigid system for membership depending on ancestry. That organization later became the Museum of the City of New York.
32. "Dry Bones Were Shaken Up" (1917).
33. "Historical Society to Take on New Life" (1917).
34. Richards (1984, p. 62).

CHAPTER THREE

PROFESSIONALIZATION AND POSTWAR EXPANSION, 1921–1959

Alexander J. Wall Builds a Professional Institution, 1921–1944

A staff member since the age of fourteen, Alexander J. Wall had been Robert Kelby's assistant for more than twenty years and was therefore intimately familiar with the library and its holdings. Even more than his knowledge of the collections, it was Wall's personality and charisma that had the most impact on the Society. One biographer observed that "few people enjoyed a party with companionable friends more than he did" and that "this quality was a predominant reason for his success in life."[1] Considering Wall's nature, it is not surprising that following his installation as librarian, the Society took steps to become both more open to the public and more active in issues of importance to a broader segment of its potential constituents.

One of the many successes of Wall's tenure was bridging the gap between the historical societies and the scholarly community, something that previous Society leaders had failed to accomplish. With a particular passion for preservation, Wall led historical society professionals in urging the federal government to establish a national archive. In addition, Wall's dedication to this cause led to his later involvement as one of the organizers of the American Association for State and Local History. Wall's interests were not confined to historical preservation; he also actively cultivated relationships with the academic community. In

1925, he established a $300 New-York Historical Society Scholarship at Columbia "to encourage further study and investigation in the field of history." Although the scholarship was discontinued due to lack of funds in 1933, it represented the first step in the Society's relationship with Columbia, a relationship that eventually led to Wall's appointment as an associate in history, teaching a seminar titled Resources and Methods of an American Historical Society. Wall's simultaneous roles as a spokesperson for historical professionals and as a scholar teaching at a respected university helped propel The New-York Historical Society into the mainstream of professional library and scholarly activity.

During his tenure, Wall encountered the natural contradictions faced by a library trying to serve both a relatively exclusive community (scholars) and the wider populace. Wall's efforts to resolve this tension emphasized the importance of education in bringing history to a broad audience. For the Society, this approach had both practical and philosophical implications. In 1928, the state legislature approved Wall's petition to modify the Society's act of incorporation to include language specifically recognizing its educational mission. This step was more than a legalistic gesture; gifts and bequests to educational institutions were not subject to state taxes. But Wall's motivation was not just financial; he believed strongly in the Society's educational responsibility. In an article published in the *New-York Historical Society Quarterly* in April 1938, Wall wrote, "Historical societies should have an important place in education. In the past we have failed to achieve this position primarily because we have been too ready to believe that historical investigation belonged to the few and that those who entered our portals treaded on holy ground. . . . But times have changed and people no longer have to knock at our doors for they should be open. And our work should be an inspiration to interest the many in the satisfying and unending joy of research and investigation."[2] The *Quarterly* was one vehicle Wall relied on to "interest the many." Conceived by Wall primarily to publicize the work of the Society, the *Quarterly* enjoyed a solid reputation in the field of historical society journals. As its editor, Wall also used the *Quarterly* to publicize his position on issues of importance to the Society and to the profession, as well as to publish some of the library's treasures that were not appropriate for inclusion in more formal publications of the library's collections.[3]

If the *Quarterly* was Wall's effort to take the Society to the people, Wall's educational programs emphasized bringing people to the Society. He and his assistant, Dorothy Barck, who was appointed librarian in 1942, shared a desire to encourage historical interests in young people. In 1945, Barck established two undergraduate internships in library training that were filled by students from nearby colleges and universities. Such programs, along with general encouragement offered to young readers, bore fruit early in the postwar period, when there was a noticeable increase in the number of undergraduates, high school students, and even grammar school students using the library. Barck wrote in the 1945 annual report that this trend was "heartily to be encouraged, and we welcome young people who are genuinely interested in research."[4]

Wall's efforts to open up the Society did not go unnoticed. Dixon Ryan Fox, president of the New York State Historical Association and an outspoken critic of the Society under Robert Kelby, said that "the atmosphere of exclusiveness and self-content" at the Society had been dispelled not only by Wall's "intelligent sympathy" with all serious scholars but also by his "concern for popular education" and the fact that the Society "gladly welcomed school children and casual visitors."[5]

Wall's leadership of the library moved the Society beyond the mistakes of the late 1800s and helped position the institution to play a more significant public service role. Still, that progress might not have been possible were it not for two other developments that helped make Wall's tenure a period of prosperity and professionalism: first, in April 1935, Mary Gardiner Thompson, daughter of David Thompson (the former president of the New York Life Insurance Company), died, leaving over $4.5 million to the Society between 1935 and 1942;[6] and second, a reorganization of the Society's governance and management structure gave the Society an institutional framework commensurate with its increasing size and stature.

The Thompson bequest could not have come at a better time. In the beginning of 1935, "the wingless building was jammed . . . almost beyond endurance," and resources remained tight. With a limited endowment and only seven professional staff members, "there seemed little hope for the enlargement of [the Society's] activities or for the raising of the hopelessly large sum needed to complete the building."[7] Furthermore, the Society's endowment was largely invested in real estate, and the Depression had made collection of rent and mortgage payments difficult.

The Thompson bequest, equivalent to $54 million in 1993 dollars,[8] gave the Society financial breathing room for the first time in its history. More than one-third of the bequest—$1.7 million—was used to renovate the central building, build two new wings, and construct a fifteen-tier bookstack at the rear of the building. The remainder of the funds was placed in permanent endowment. Moreover, the completion of the building, which was closed for nearly two years, from May 1, 1937, to March 29, 1939, gave the Society's leadership time to reflect on its mission and policies. What resulted were several steps taken to professionalize the management of the institution.

One area that was badly in need of improvement was the cataloging, shelving, and classification of library collections. As was mentioned previously, the Society's cataloging and shelving had been inadequate even in the Second Avenue building. There had been little improvement since that time. When the library moved to the new building in 1908, books were shelved using the same system. In fact, "the card catalog, primarily accessible by author, was the same one instituted . . . in 1859."[9] The renovation of the central building and the reinstallation of the collections provided an opportunity for modernization.

In 1940, the Society adopted the Library of Congress classification system for new acquisitions and started a new card catalog that followed American Library Association rules. Though this step was an improvement, it created another problem: there were now two card catalogs, one for acquisitions made prior to 1940 and one for acquisitions made after that year. This dual system, along with the Society's backlog of uncataloged items, made it very difficult for users (and librarians) to access, much less comprehend, what items were in the collection. The fact that during the reshelving process, library management "discovered" a number of rare books for which there had been no records at the Society exemplifies this problem and makes one wonder whether similar discoveries might still be made at the Society.

Reorganization took place at a higher level as well. For its entire 122-year history, the Society had been a membership organization with an executive committee responsible for conducting its affairs. Participation by the membership had dwindled over the years, to the point that few members attended the meetings, and election of the Society's officers was effectively done by proxy. Given these circumstances, and the substantial endowment generated by the Thompson bequest, it was decided that the Society ought to update its governance structure to put it on par with its peer organizations.

On November 18, 1937, the last general meeting of the membership was called to approve a change to the organization's by-laws establishing a board of trustees and placing complete control of the Society's affairs with that board. Also approved at the meeting was a change in the chief executive officer's title from librarian to director. Although the responsibilities of the position did not change (the librarian had always run the day-to-day affairs of the Society), the change in title finally gave recognition to the fact that the Society was more than just a library. As director, Wall was now clearly accountable for the success of the museum as well as the library. In contrast to organizations like the Massachusetts Historical Society and the American Antiquarian Society, which had divested themselves of museum collections and were focused on their roles as research libraries, the Society chose to continue to pursue the challenging objective of supporting both endeavors.

The Society had never been thought of as having two distinct parts. Since its inception, it had been organized as a single entity. Although the original by-laws of the Society mentioned that the librarian was to be responsible for the museum (or "cabinet," as it was called), the cabinet was considered to be just another part of the library and had always been of secondary significance.

With the addition of prized museum collections in the late nineteenth century, however, the museum side of the Society grew in importance. That trend continued as more important paintings and museum artifacts were added to the collections, to the point that by the late 1930s, Wall believed that the library could not survive without the museum. Writing in the *Quarterly*, Wall asserted that the "scholarship part of the historical society's work would be likely to have a bare cupboard if not coupled with a popular museum and a program of public education."[10] He went on to suggest that exploiting the fundraising potential of the museum collections and historical artifacts was "the best way to gain financial support as we are judged by those whose fortune it is to endow, by what we do for the people as a whole, and not by the service we render scholars alone."[11]

Wall recognized the importance of the museum; he also knew that operating a popular museum required different management processes than running a scholarly library. In 1937, Wall created a separate and distinct museum department, thus allowing the museum to pursue its mission free of entanglements with the library. In addition, the realignment gave Wall a structural mechanism for evaluating and making resource allocation decisions between the two entities. But balancing the two was a complex task that required the attention of a highly skilled manager. Wall was, for the most part, successful; but as is so often the case, the solution to one problem created another. The programs and operations of the Society could be compromised if it were ever without the forceful leadership required to balance the competing demands of the two departments.

The story of Alexander Wall's tenure and its successes would not be complete without mention of George Zabriskie, who served as treasurer of the Society (1929–1939) and then president of its Board of Trustees (1939–1946). As treasurer from 1929 to 1939, Zabriskie oversaw a period of enormous highs and lows in the Society's finances. During his tenure, he managed to hold the Society's real estate investments together during the Great Depression and then prudently invested the Thompson bequest. As noted earlier, the Thompson bequest was used both to pay for the construction of the new building and to establish the Society's endowment.

During Zabriskie's tenure as board president, the Society accomplished a great deal in a short period of time. Within approximately two years, the building was finished and renovated; the by-laws were changed, establishing a self-perpetuating board of trustees; and a distinct museum department was established. In addition, the Society's endowment, which had grown to $4.3 million, comfortably supported its operating budget. By 1943, investment income had grown to $201,000, an amount far in excess of the Society's total operating expenditures of $168,000.[12] It is safe to say that these developments would not have been possible without a close working relationship between the board and the professional staff and, in particular, Zabriskie and Wall.

The closeness of Zabriskie and Wall's working relationship was evident when, after the Society closed for construction in 1937, the two men embarked on a European trip (at Zabriskie's expense) to research the best uses of natural lighting in gallery spaces. They visited fifty European museums and returned with many ideas that were implemented in the new building. When the building's new skylights were installed, they were considered the best in the country, and museum executives frequently came to the Society to study them.[13] The Zabriskie-Wall partnership was a high-water mark in the Society's history that would prove difficult to attain again.

On April 15, 1944, Alexander Wall died at the age of fifty-nine. The progress made at the Society during his tenure, particularly after the Thompson bequest, had established the Society as a leader among historical societies. The significant income from the endowment had made it possible for the Society to expand its operations; between 1935 and 1943, total operating expenditures increased 163 percent, from $64,000 to $168,000.[14] Much of these increases came in the form of increased compensation and the hiring of additional staff. Total compensation and benefits, the Society's largest expenditure category, grew 215 percent, from $40,000 to $125,000, over the same time period. Part of this figure was Wall's salary, which at the time of his death was $16,000 ($157,000 in 1993 dollars). The Society's growth during Wall's tenure made his position one of the most prestigious historical society directorships in the country.

The Difficult Postwar Years of R.W.G. Vail, 1944–1950

During the Society's first 140 years, it had always hired an internal candidate as the new chief executive (who had been the librarian through 1938 but was now the director). For the first time in its history, the Society looked outside for a replacement. Why the Society conducted an outside search cannot be known, but there are several possible explanations. One explanation could be that it was an indication of the success of Alexander Wall in professionalizing the Society. Another possibility might be that the Society needed to find a leader of high prestige and stature—someone to enhance even further the esteemed position the Society had staked out for itself. There is yet another possible explanation, dependent on a certain degree of speculation, that the Society searched externally because the most qualified inside candidate was a woman.

Over the course of the Society's history (except for the relatively brief period during which Robert Kelby chose not to be librarian), the assistant librarian had always ascended to the role of librarian. To carry on that tradition within the new organization structure, the likely choice for the position of director would have been the standing librarian. But Wall, who was ahead of his time in so many ways, had entrusted the position of librarian to Dorothy Barck, the first woman in the history of the Society to hold such a high office. Even though Barck had served the Society for twenty-four years, she was not chosen to be the director. This break from the traditional succession process, for whatever reason, altered the power balance among departments within the Society, a development that would have repercussions in terms of both leadership and direction in the years to come.

The job of leading the Society had become complicated. Balancing the sometimes competing demands of the museum and the library, in terms of both finances and focus, represented a formidable challenge. After a two-month search, the Board hired Robert W. G. Vail to succeed Wall as director. By hiring Vail, the board signaled that the library, not the museum, was of primary importance, for Vail's professional background was exclusively as a librarian.

Vail came to the Society from the New York State Library, where he had served as librarian since 1940. His previous experiences included a two-year stint as the librarian at the Minnesota Historical Society and nine years as the librarian at the American Antiquarian Society. Did Vail's experience prepare him for the complexities of the Society and for managing its two valuable and growing collections? Perhaps not. Vail's primary focus appears to have been scholarship and the publication of collections, not administration. In *The Collections and Programs of the American Antiquarian Society: A 175th Anniversary Guide*, a single sentence is devoted to Vail's nine-year tenure from 1930 to 1939. It reads: "While in office, he [Vail] completed Sabin's *Bibliotecha Americana* (volumes 22–29), picking up where Wilberforce Eames of the New York Public Library had left off."[15] Further, LeRoy Kimball, the Society's president, wrote that Vail "just can't help delving and writing, and there is reason to believe he will be most unhappy unless he keeps his hand in way up to the elbow. For him, research and writing are part of his days— and nights."[16]

The professionalization of the Society in the Wall era set the stage for growth, but effectively managing that growth would have posed a formidable challenge for even the most highly skilled professional administrator. For Vail, the difficulty of managing the Society would be compounded by a need to balance his passion for research against the growing demands of a job that would require strong and focused leadership.

The years immediately following World War II turned out to be difficult ones for the Society. Revenues, which were highly dependent on the return from investments, were not growing at the same pace as expenditures, and in 1945 the Society ran a deficit. For an organization that was becoming accustomed to annual surpluses, the late 1940s were a period of forced self-assessment. In the annual report of 1946, Vail lamented that income was lagging and that there were insufficient funds to give staff the raises they deserved. As a cost-saving measure, Society management cut the workweek by five hours. In 1947, the revenue woes continued. Vail wrote, "In order to improve our service to scholars . . . we should have an additional annual income of $50,000 for the next 20 years to use in building our collections and cataloguing our treasured possessions."[17]

A close look at the Society's finances during this period highlights the very different mind-set that existed during this era regarding deficits. Put simply, deficits were not to be tolerated. Instead of waiting for mounting deficits to force cuts, management made cuts to avert deficits. Figure 3.1 shows the Society's operating balances during Vail's tenure. After an initial deficit in 1945, the Society actually ran moderate and increasing surpluses in the years between 1946 and 1950.

Nevertheless, the fear of recurring deficits exerted discipline on the Society. In the 1948 annual report, Vail wrote: "Although we have weathered this year successfully, we fear that our future may be endangered unless we economize and so it has been found necessary drastically to cut our budget for the coming year." These budget cuts resulted in the elimination of five positions, including the curator of paintings and sculpture.

While pressures were mounting to gain control of the Society's finances, efforts were still being made to expand the scope of services the Society offered. One reason for this expansion was the return from war service of Alexander Wall Jr.,

FIGURE 3.1.   OPERATING SURPLUS/DEFICIT, 1944–1959.

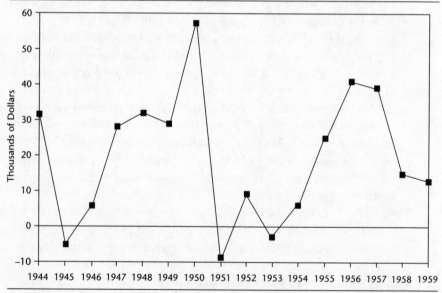

Source: New-York Historical Society annual reports; see also Table C.3–2 in Appendix C.

the son of the late director. In 1946, he returned to his position as director of education and public relations; shortly thereafter, he was named assistant director of the Society. This development, which placed Wall next in line to succeed Vail, was at least partially the result of the power vacuum created when Dorothy Barck, the librarian, was not named either director or assistant director.

With the assistant director now representing education, not the library, as had traditionally been the case, the Society's education initiatives became an area of increasing emphasis. In the annual report of 1946, the outgoing president of the Society said the Society hoped, even in the midst of a very difficult economic environment, "to continue and to expand its efforts to make American history a vital part of the education and entertainment of the young people of our schools." Special programs brought thousands of elementary school students to the Society, and a traveling exhibit toured New York City high schools. The Society tracked and proudly reported the exposure it received from these initiatives; the annual report for 1946 noted that approximately eighty-six thousand students were introduced to the Society through the traveling exhibits during the course of the year.

The Society's expansion resulted in small deficits in 1951 and 1953. Under pressure to balance the budget, Vail reminded the board of trustees of the need for more income. He emphasized the need for funds for the purchase of new materials for the library, museum, and art gallery and pointed out that if the Society hoped to give "adequate service" to its "ever-increasing clientele," it "must have better salaries and more trained people."

Despite Vail's pleas, there is little evidence to suggest that significant efforts were made to develop new revenue sources. The Society remained almost exclusively dependent on investment income to fund its operations (see Figure 3.2). For example, although the education programs provided a clear public service, no effort was made to involve the city or state government in defraying the cost of these services. Neither was there any attempt to raise private contributed income.

The expansion of the education department complicated further the task of managing the Society. Already wrestling with the demands of coordinating the museum and library, the Society's management now had to fold a more aggressive public education program into its overall mission. From the annual reports of the late 1940s and early 1950s, it is not entirely clear that the leadership of the Society was comfortable with integrating these purposes. For example, at the same time that initiatives were under way to introduce thousands of schoolchildren to the library through tours run by the education director, Vail, at a meeting of New York City librarians in 1948, "called for the elimination of student and popular use of research libraries."[18] In each successive year, the Society reported on the successes of the school education program and the growing number of students coming to the Society, even while a sign over the Reading Room read "Adults Only."

FIGURE 3.2. COMPONENTS OF OPERATING INCOME, 1944–1959.

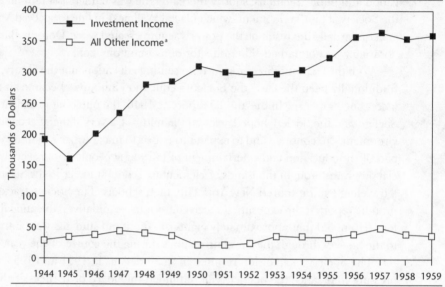

a Includes gifts, grants, contributions, net rentals, and earned income.

Source: New-York Historical Society annual reports; see also Table C.3–2 in Appendix C.

One possible reason that the public education program proved so appealing is that its success was easy to measure (by tracking, for example, how many students benefited from the Society's holdings). There seemed to be pressure, during this time, to provide quantitative measures of the Society's successes. During Vail's tenure, the Society's annual report began to include a statistical appendix that tracked many of the Society's services. It gave a wide variety of specific facts and figures about the Society, including such measures as the number of elementary, intermediate, and high school students who toured the Society, the number of readers who used the library, and the number of volumes requested from library staff. But statistical measures such as these do not fully convey the basic value and importance of a research library. In an attempt to quantify the library's essential output, the Society began to report the number of publications in which the author acknowledged the Society for its assistance. This number, reported annually from 1952 to 1975, averaged 60 publications per year. The year of the fewest acknowledgments was 1956, with 35, and the year with the most was 1975, with 108.

Although these statistical measures helped document the range of services being offered, the self-esteem of the institution continued to depend largely on the size and quality of its holdings. Moreover, members of the board of trustees considered themselves collectors first and saw the role of the Society primarily as a repository of important material. Consequently, great emphasis was placed on acquisitions, and most of each annual report was devoted to descriptions of items purchased by or donated to the Society during the year.

Emphasis on acquisitions was not, in and of itself, a bad thing; quite the contrary. The Society's collections were its chief asset. But an emphasis on acquisitions, particularly to the extent that quantity was regarded as important, could be dangerous. As mentioned earlier, the Society had a long history of accepting anything and everything that was given to it with little regard for the quality of the gift, the institution's capacity to absorb it, or the relevance of the gift to the Society's mission.

Donald Shelley, the art and museum curator during this period, called for a more focused acquisitions policy. As he put it, "The Society continually tried to make accessible to the public . . . accumulations which had nothing to do with American or New York history." Further, he called for "a detailed survey and analysis of our actual holdings" to "reveal the strengths and weaknesses which must henceforth determine the direction of our development." By 1947, Shelley believed that the Society had made some progress: "As the year closes, consideration is being given to the possibility of showing our European paintings elsewhere, thus . . . enabling us to devote ourselves entirely to early American art. Certainly such a solution will help us better to meet present-day competition from sister art institutions specializing in the same or related fields." In 1948, a list of 634 paintings was circulated among various cultural institutions in the city, including the Metropolitan Museum of Art.[19] No museums took the Society up on its offer, however, and in 1949, Shelley's position was eliminated in the course of financial cutbacks. There were no further attempts to loan or donate the pictures for the duration of Vail's tenure.

The need for a focused acquisitions policy was not limited to the museum; the library still had not taken steps to refine its collections policy. The library's appetite for acquisitions of all kinds led to a situation in which, like the museum, it held materials that did not fall within its mission, even though that mission was defined very broadly. But the Society did not take steps to cull out-of-scope materials. The struggle to become current in the cataloging of its ever-increasing collection was deemed more important. However, just keeping pace with the massive inflows on a current basis proved difficult, and the Society did not even begin to deal with its huge backlog, which the 1945 annual report estimated at "a hundred years of uncatalogued books."

In the 1947 annual report, the librarian wrote that the library needed to hire a dozen catalogers, and Vail pointed out that "the circumstances of history have left us with amazingly rich resources but without adequate funds for their preparation and processing. Most of the library still lacks adequate cataloguing." Signaling the importance of cataloging to the Society's long-term success, Vail hired additional catalogers in the library even as five staff positions elsewhere in the Society were eliminated. Vail wrote: "Since it is the chief function of the Society to give aid to American historical students and writers through our library, that department has been somewhat enlarged so that we may provide better Reading Room service and begin the task of processing our century-old backlog of uncatalogued books."

As the Society entered the 1950s, it was emerging from a difficult period in which its aspirations had begun to exceed its financial resources. Its already difficult mandate to operate both a library and a museum was exacerbated by pressures to provide educational programming to the public. Committed to avoiding operating deficits, the Society held down salaries and even laid off some employees. The financial squeeze strained what management regarded as its core mission and forced the Society to make difficult strategic decisions. Cuts were made in some areas to divert resources to more important initiatives. What remained to be seen was whether these decisions were part of a fundamental strategic change— a reframing of the Society's goals, objectives, and mission—or merely isolated reactions to the specific problems of a particular time.

Golden Years, 1950–1960

It would not take long for the answer to become clear. Just when the Society was being forced to narrow its programmatic focus, relief came on the revenue side from the extraordinary performance of the financial markets. Beginning in 1949, the stock market offered tremendous returns for investors. Over the period from 1949 to 1958, the average annual compound rate of return for stocks was 17.9 percent. Out of those ten years, there were only three years when the total real return averaged less than 10 percent: 1953, 1956, and 1957 (see Table 3.1). On the plus side, there were some truly remarkable years: 1954, 1955, and 1958.[20]

It is clear from the annual reports that management's mood mirrored the performance of the market. During the difficult period of the late 1940s, stock market returns were poor. By 1952, after four years of annual returns in the markets that averaged nearly 20 percent, the worries and concerns of the late 1940s had disappeared. In his 1952 report to the board, Vail wrote, "We are proud that an ever-growing clientele comes to us for the aid our trained staff can supply from our rich historical treasures. . . . Our affairs are in good order and each year we are better able to bring a knowledge of America's history, aims and ideals to our

TABLE 3.1.   AVERAGE ANNUAL MARKET RETURNS, 1949–1959.

Year	Nominal Return from Stocks (%)	Real Return from Stocks (%)
1949	18.0	21.0
1950	30.4	24.5
1951	24.5	17.1
1952	18.3	17.3
1953	–1.0	–1.6
1954	52.1	53.4
1955	31.3	31.1
1956	6.6	3.6
1957	–10.8	–13.4
1958	43.2	40.9
1959	11.9	10.3

Source: Kennedy and Schneider, 1994, pp. 19, 29. Used by permission of Cambridge Associates, Inc.

people and especially to those new citizens who want so much to understand their adopted country and their new loyalties and responsibilities." In addition to the more positive tone prevalent in Vail's statement, note also that management's focus had once again broadened beyond the service of scholars and researchers. The goal of public education had recaptured its place of importance on the Society's agenda. Indeed, despite his earlier statements, Vail wrote in 1953 that "an educational institution such as ours, to be worth its salt, must have a vigorous and growing program of service to the community and to the nation."

The performance of the markets had an extremely positive impact on the endowment, the Society's primary revenue source (see Figure 3.3). Between 1947 and 1959, the nominal market value of the endowment grew at an average rate of 7 percent per year and an average real rate of 4.5 percent per year.[21] By 1959, the market value of the endowment had grown to approximately $10.7 million.

Because of the Society's improving financial prospects, decisions regarding what services the Society would provide no longer represented a zero-sum game. The library, the museum, and the education program could all benefit from this improving environment. The periodic pressures to narrow the focus of the Society's acquisitions policy faded in this climate. In a review of gifts received in 1952, Vail thanked the public for "current materials" and expressed gratitude "to those with a strong sense of the swift march of time, who gave us, for preservation here, the ephemeral productions of today." Furthermore, in the librarian's report of 1953, Dorothy Barck wrote: "The library continues to procure, preserve and make usable records relating to varied phases of the history of New York and of the U.S. in general, and of the whole continent." She continued, "Interesting and varied additions were made in 1953 to all of these categories . . . and their use by students

FIGURE 3.3.   ENDOWMENT GROWTH, NOMINAL AND REAL, 1947–1959.

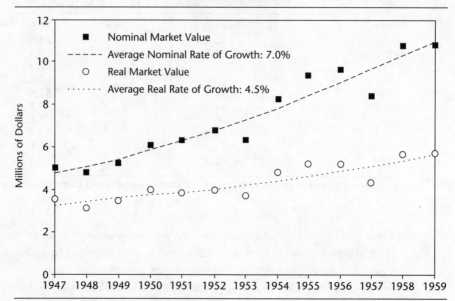

Source: New-York Historical Society annual reports; see also Table C.3–2 in Appendix C.

. . . justifies the Founders' wisdom in establishing the library on a very broad foundation." The Society was reasserting its broad mission, not only in terms of its willingness to accept materials from across the continent but also in its desire not to restrict its collections to any specific time period. Together with the notion that its constituency was more than just the researchers who used its library and now included "new and old citizens of New York," the Society's inclusive acquisitions policy constituted a real expansion of its mission that would require a growing revenue base to sustain.

The extraordinary and consistent performance of the markets in the early 1950s offered Society management the financial resources necessary to fulfill its promises. In addition, it was management's good fortune that the Society's improved prospects coincided with its 150th anniversary, a development that made the Sesquicentennial a real cause for celebration. At the celebratory dinner in May 1954, Fenwick Beekman, the Society's president, delivered the keynote address. In it, Beekman expressed the Society's renewed self-confidence: "After 150 years of vicissitudes, I can report that the Society is in fortunate circumstances: owning a fine building and with land on which to expand, sufficient endowment to provide for a modest education program, a fine museum collection illustrating life in early America and especially in New York City . . . Contributions to the endowment have allowed the Society to carry on its functions without making special appeals to the public or calling on the city for aid. We hope this can be continued." Speaking of the Society's challenge to expand its level of service, Beekman remarked, "Greater stress is now laid upon educating the public . . . The museum has been expanded and rearranged so that it is more efficient in illustrating the story that is to be told. . . . The Society's storerooms are bursting once more with contents, for our friends have been generous with their gifts, awaiting the day when the building can be enlarged."[22]

In the 1954 annual report, Vail echoed Beekman's confidence in the Society's prospects. Vail wrote that the Society's "record of increased service to the world of scholarship is cause for congratulation but it is also a challenge to greater service in the years ahead, for as the need grows, we must grow with it." This spirit set the tone for the duration of Vail's tenure. The period was characterized by glowing annual reports documenting the many services the Society was able to provide and the many items the Society had acquired.

But what had really changed between the late 1940s and the late 1950s to engender such expansive thoughts in the minds of Society leadership? Actually, very little. For example, the Society had made little headway in processing its monstrous cataloging backlog. In his address, Beekman attempted to turn the backlog into an unusual kind of asset, saying that "the fact that the stacks contain a large amount of uncatalogued, original documents makes it a 'treasure-trove' and consequently a challenge to a research student."[23] In addition, the sources of the Society's income had not been diversified—in 1956, fully 94 percent of its income came from the yield on investments—even though the services it was providing were serving a wider audience. Finally, the Society's acquisitions policy was, if anything, even less focused, with calls for people to donate current ephemera. What *had* changed was the size of the Society's revenue stream, a development that was, for practical purposes, outside the Society's control. The fundamental problems facing the Society remained, but they lay hidden beneath the growth of the Society's endowment and the resulting increases in spendable investment returns.

Since investment income continued to grow for the rest of Vail's tenure, balancing the annual budget was never a problem. In fact, the Society took the commendable step of beginning to save for the future by establishing three board-designated restricted funds: an accumulated surplus fund, a pension fund, and an accessions fund. By 1959, the balances in each of these funds were as follows: accumulated surplus, $221,000; pensions, $66,000; accessions, $8,000.

Still, even in the midst of this period of positive prospects for the Society, there was evidence that management was aware of the fundamental long-term issues and problems the institution faced (for example, how to pay for the education component of its mission and how to cope with the cataloging backlog). Beekman hinted that he was struggling with how best to resolve the education question in his Sesquicentennial address. His idea for a possible solution bordered on the clairvoyant, considering the options considered by the Society in the 1990s:

> That is all very well, but is it enough? Should we not look ahead and plan for the future by expanding in this part of our endeavors through entering the field of higher education where the unique library material which we control may be employed to the greatest advantage? This, I believe (and it must be taken as a personal opinion), can be accomplished through the Society associating itself with some university, or universities. . . . I say "associated" for it would not be judicious for the Society to lose any of its individuality or autonomy. This plan, if it might be carried out, would, I think, be of advantage to both parties. Such an association would result in common use of facilities, there would be less duplication of library objects, and the introduction of rare items of source material for common use would be of inestimable value for all concerned. Most important for us, however, is that the Society would enter a university atmosphere, with its stimulus and encouragement for original work, which no individual organization can alone attain.[24]

Beekman may have claimed that this was just his personal opinion, but because he was the president, it was taken seriously. Not long after this speech, in 1955, the Society joined forces with the Extension Division of the School of General Studies at City College of New York to offer a survey course in American art that would be taught at the Society. The class was to meet on Saturday mornings at 10:00 A.M. Unfortunately, the class was undersubscribed and was canceled. Beekman retired from the presidency later that year, and his idea for an affiliation with a university was retired with him. The possibility of an affiliation with an institution of higher learning would not be seriously pursued again until the late 1980s.

Another fundamental problem that remained hidden during this era of confidence and expansion was the need to gain professional control of the collections. As was mentioned previously, gifts were accepted and acquisitions made with very little regard for either the Society's mission or the comparative strengths or weaknesses of the collections. In terms of cataloging these accessions, it was all the Society could do to keep pace with the annual inflow. Virtually nothing was done about the cataloging backlog.

By the latter part of the 1950s, the long-term impact of the lack of a collections policy was brought to the Society's attention, even though management took no immediate steps to resolve it. In 1956, the Society commissioned a study, carried out by Lawrence C. Wroth, the librarian of the John Carter Brown Library at Brown University, asking for "a candid report of Wroth's personal views of our library, which we believe to be one of the greatest general American collections." The 1956 annual report did not discuss Wroth's findings, stating only that the report had been completed and was under study. That brief comment would prove to be the last direct reference to Wroth's report during Vail's tenure. Interestingly, though, in the same annual report, LeRoy Kimball, the Society's president, wrote: "We might remind ourselves that the Society is the second oldest historical society with a continuing existence in this country." He then discussed the Society's original constitution and broad statement of mission and said, "We have lived up to a large extent to these objects, possibly too well. There is perhaps a penalty for being first in some things."

It is no surprise that the Society's top leadership chose not to discuss Wroth's study in the annual reports. The study was highly critical of the library's huge cataloging backlog and its lack of attention to this area. In addition, Wroth criticized the Society for its "unchecked, uncritical accumulation of materials" and its lack of either a collections or an acquisitions policy.[25]

Even though its conclusions were not publicly acknowledged, the study did seem to have an impact on management. As the 1950s (and Vail's tenure) drew to a close, the Society showed renewed concern for both proper cataloging and the need to focus its collections. In the 1958 annual report, James Heslin, the librarian, described the Society's new cataloging initiative: "This heralds the beginning of a concentrated effort to catalog all the material which is not, at present, so cataloged. We believe that this is a project of great importance in terms of the more efficient use of the resources of the library." In 1959, Vail wrote that a review of the Society's collecting policies had improved its gift and purchase routines. Furthermore, he expressed that "these changes are the result of our realization that other collection agencies have grown up since we were founded a century and a half ago when, for lack of other specialized libraries and museums, we had taken the whole world as our province."

As Vail prepared to step down, 4 years after the Wroth report, 49 years after the formal establishment of the New York Public Library's research collections, more than 75 years after the birth of the Metropolitan Museum of Art, and 155 years after its own founding, the New-York Historical Society began to think about narrowing its broad reach.

Notes

1. Richards (1984, p. 68).
2. Wall (1938, p. 66).
3. Richards (1984, p. 77).
4. Richards (1984, p. 86).

5. Richards (1984, p. 72).
6. Thompson left her estate to be divided equally among six New York institutions: the Children's Aid Society, the New York Association for Improving the Condition of the Poor, The New-York Historical Society, the Society of the New York Hospital, the Presbyterian Hospital in the City of New York, and the Trustees of Columbia College in the City of New York.
7. Vail (1954, p. 239).
8. Present value was calculated using an official GDP price deflator (U.S. Bureau of Economic Analysis, 1994, pp. 104–107). The deflator is used throughout this book to calculate present values.
9. Richards (1984, p. 87).
10. Wall (1938, p. 65).
11. Wall (1938, pp. 64–65).
12. For these data, see Table C.3–1. Financial data were compiled from the Society's annual reports. Appendix C presents these data in tabular format, and Appendix D summarizes key assumptions made to keep the data comparable over time.
13. Vail (1954, p. 243).
14. See Table C.3–1 in Appendix C.
15. McCorison (1992, p. 23).
16. Kimball (1944, p. 166).
17. This and all other unattributed quotations in this chapter are taken from New-York Historical Society annual reports.
18. Richards (1984, p. 90).
19. Christiansen (1994).
20. Kennedy and Schneider (1994, pp. 19, 29).
21. To obtain the average annual rate of increase, a least-squares regression line was fitted to the natural log of the values being averaged. This methodology is used throughout the book to estimate growth rates for a variety of financial indicators, including revenues and expenditures. To take into account economywide trends in prices when calculating these growth rates, the government's GDP price deflator is used.
22. Beekman (1954, p. 211).
23. Beekman (1954, p. 102).
24. Beekman (1955).
25. New-York Historical Society (1959, p. 1).

CHAPTER FOUR

THE TURNING TIDE, 1960–1982

The Last of the Easy Years, 1960–1970

On April 1, 1960, James J. Heslin was named director of the Society, a position he would hold for twenty-two years. His tenure can be divided into two distinct periods: a relatively prosperous period from 1960 to 1969, when investment returns were strong and inflation was relatively modest, and a much more difficult period from 1970 to 1982, when poor performance of the financial markets and limited public and private support constrained revenues at the same time that inflation drove up expenses. In addition to these external factors, the two periods are also identifiable by a change in the leadership of the Society's board of trustees. For most of the 1960s, Frederick B. Adams Jr. was president of the board; succeeding him was Robert G. Goelet.

Like his predecessors, Heslin was a librarian by training. After receiving his Ph.D. in American history from Boston University in 1952, Heslin received a master's degree in library service from Columbia University in 1954. Heslin then served as assistant director of libraries at the University of Buffalo, the position he held when he was hired by the Society to be its librarian in 1956. He was promoted to assistant, then associate director of the Society between 1956 and 1960. Because Heslin had been Vail's deputy, the transition to new leadership was smooth and relatively uneventful. Not surprisingly, the issues that emerged toward the end of Vail's tenure—acquisitions policy and cataloging—dominated Heslin's early years in office.

In his first annual report as director and librarian in 1960, Heslin quoted a Society librarian's report originally published in the Society's *Proceedings* in 1843: "The Librarian would now urge upon the Society, as the first object of attention, the preparation of a new and methodical catalog of the whole collection. The library, although generally in excellent preservation, and so far as mere arrangements are concerned, conveniently dispersed, is almost inaccessible to general use from the want of one." Bringing the argument up-to-date, Heslin continued: "It is impossible to pursue our acquisitions with any certainty unless we possess the means of regular periodical examination" of the collections, a process "only afforded by a catalog." He dutifully reported progress on the catalog in annual reports from the early 1960s, noting that "the importance of the catalog was second only to the richness of the collections themselves."

In the January 1962 *Quarterly,* Heslin wrote an article titled "Library Acquisition Policy of The New-York Historical Society." The article reviewed briefly the history of the Society's collections policies and pointed out precedents for narrowing the scope of the collections. As examples, Heslin referred to the Society's extensive collection of natural history specimens, which were donated to the Lyceum of Natural History in 1829, and the Society's collection of Egyptian antiquities, which was sold to the Brooklyn Museum in the 1930s.

The impetus for Heslin's interest in the catalog and acquisitions policy was definitely the Wroth report. Indeed, in his article, Heslin reiterated many of Wroth's recommendations, particularly the need for an acquisitions policy that would establish chronological and geographical limitations on collecting. Like Wroth, Heslin believed that many libraries were now adequately collecting material relating to the present period and to particular localities and that many libraries in the city and state of New York had collections that were strong in material dating from 1850. "The greatest strength of the Society's collections," Wroth wrote (and Heslin reprinted), "rested in rare Americana and retrospective material."

After considering the Wroth report, the Society's board of trustees adopted a new acquisitions policy that identified twenty-one separate categories, assessed the strength of the collections in each category, and issued a guiding statement for future acquisitions. The categories enumerated in the policy cover a broad spectrum, including American fiction, poetry, and belles lettres; the California gold rush; the Civil War; New York City and State; slavery; sheet music and songsters; and professional literature.[1]

One reason that Heslin and the board were able to pay such close attention to cataloging and acquisitions was the Society's prosperous financial condition. By

1962, the Society had run its ninth consecutive surplus, and the board-restricted accumulated surplus stood at $217,000.[2] The 1961 annual report referred to the Society's quiet and steady growth, and the 1962 report pointed out the Society's "healthy financial situation."

It may have come as a surprise to some, then, when Frederick B. Adams, who took over as president in 1963, appealed for help in addressing serious needs the Society faced. In his first annual report, Adams showed courage and foresight in his summary of the Society's financial position. He pointed out that although the value of the Society's endowment had increased significantly since 1948, there had also been a large increase in payroll and benefits for the staff over the same time period, despite the fact that the total payroll had been reduced from seventy-two to sixty-four persons. He warned that a continuation of that trend without additional revenue was not sustainable.

Furthermore, Adams stressed that since the Society was housed in a structure built at the turn of the century, major capital investments were necessary. Not only did the Society need to invest in a general renovation of the building and a re-installation of its galleries, but it also very much needed to install an air-conditioning and ventilation system. Rather than being required merely for staff comfort, an air-conditioning system was essential to protect the Society's collections. Not only would the system provide temperature control, but it would also eliminate open windows that brought the city's damaging soot into the building. Adams estimated that $1 million would be required to complete these projects, an amount that could not be captured through operating surpluses. We have "begun to marshal our forces," he wrote, "to seek special grants and gifts from foundations and individuals"—in other words, to launch a capital campaign.

While the development drive was under way, Adams underscored the Society's need for assistance: "I used to hear it said, by the Society's members as well as by outsiders, that we were a rich institution with never a worry about budgets. I am glad that this is not true; such affluence would make us complacent." He noted that the response to the Society's campaign "had not been overwhelming" but that "the state of the Society is healthy in that we are aware of our shortcomings and are prepared to do something about them."

Adams also showed strong leadership in other ways. In an effort to expand and diversify the Society's sources of revenue, he encouraged the board of trustees to revise its by-laws to provide, "among other things, for new classes of membership, with higher rates of contribution over the regular annual dues of $10." Although such steps did not necessarily bring in significant income, they sent a signal to the Society's supporters that more revenue was needed. In addition, he moved to simplify the administrative structure of the board by reducing the number of committees from eleven to eight by dissolving two committees and merging two others. Adams pointed out that the committees, though there were fewer of them, had become considerably more active. Under Adams's guidance, the Society's board was more active than it had been since the days of George Zabriskie.

The Society began the renovation in 1966, closing most of the galleries and parts of the library for much of the year. Although a substantial sum had been raised during the capital campaign—approximately $574,000 by the end of 1966—the money did not cover all construction expenses. Fortunately, aware of the scale of the project, Adams and the board had anticipated this possibility and had redesignated the accumulated surplus fund as a "reserve for equipment, building replacement, and major repair." Approximately $316,000 of the money used to fund the improvements came from these reserves.

In early 1967, Frank Streeter, the Society's treasurer, reminded the board of the more than $300,000 that had been drawn from reserves to fund the capital renovations. He encouraged the Society to mount a campaign to replace those funds.[3] Such a campaign was never initiated. In March 1967, however, the board of trustees did create a new class of supporters called the Pintard Fellows to aid in furthering the purposes of the Society. To become a Pintard Fellow, one had to contribute $100 or more to the Pintard Fund. Specifically, the objectives of the Pintard Fellows were (1) "to promote a better understanding of the Society's purpose and significance, and a closer knowledge of its collections" and (2) "to promote the interests of the Society by contributing funds for its benefit, especially for acquisitions, installations, and publications." Although establishing the Pintard Fellows was a commendable step, the amount of funds raised was quite small ($12,368 in 1967) and hence were used for smaller projects or to purchase particular items for the Society's collections. The Pintard Fund did not, and could not, begin to replace the reserves drawn down during the 1966 renovations.

Instead, with its reserves mostly depleted and struggling to balance revenues and expenditures, the Society's board of trustees took a step to increase the income that could be spent from its endowment: it adopted a "total return" investment policy. Prior to this action, the Society spent only the dividend and interest income generated by its endowment. It did not spend any portion of realized gains generated through capital appreciation of the portfolio. Such a policy encouraged the Society to forgo growth investments (such as small company stocks) for investments that generated the most current return (such as bonds).

The new total return policy allowed the Society to spend up to 5 percent of the endowment's market value annually (based on a three-year moving average of the endowment), irrespective of whether the endowment actually generated that amount of dividends and interest. In the annual report for 1967, Adams, referring to the remarkable growth in the market value of the endowment, explained it this way: "This [1967 investment] performance would not have been possible if the funds had been entirely invested in bonds to secure maximum re-turn. Yet the portion of our money invested in 'growth' stocks produces initially a very low rate of income because of the retention of earnings by rapidly expanding companies. With rising costs of operation, the Society needs to increase income, yet prudent investment for the future in an inflationary economy dictates the pur-chase of substantial percentages of securities whose present yield is low." Adopt-ing a total return philosophy allowed the Society to pursue a goal of maximizing the growth of its endowment without sacrificing current income.[4]

The impact of the new strategy on the Society's operating budget was sub-stantial. In 1967, for example, proceeds from transferred realized gains (to bring spending up to the 5 percent limit) amounted to $244,204, increasing investment income by 48 percent over the 1966 investment income total of $509,000. This in-crease is represented by the discontinuity, or jump, in the Society's total revenues as depicted in Figure 4.1. It should be pointed out, however, that the newly avail-able realized gains relieved the pressure on Society leadership both to develop new revenue sources and to limit the growth of expenditures. Between 1966 and 1970, total operating expenses increased at a rate of 9.5 percent per year, while revenues were flat, increasing at an average rate of literally 0 percent per year.[5] The growth in expenditures coupled with the lack of growth in revenue created a financial vise that would begin to close on the Society as the 1970s neared.

Nevertheless, the tremendous jump in revenue put Society leadership in an expansive mood. A major building renovation had been completed, the galleries were reinstalled and redecorated, and in the library, the lighting was redesigned and a new carpet was installed. With the renovations complete and the increase in spendable investment income, the Society's focus shifted toward becoming a more popular institution, increasing the emphasis given to the museum, educa-tion, and special programs.

In 1967, Heslin reported "that the Sunday afternoon concerts were the most successful in the fifteen-year history of these events, and it is obvious that they have become an institution." Heslin also suggested that "the need for more school pro-grams is clearly a pressing one." Late in 1967, the Society received a three-year grant ($26,700 annually) from the New York State Council on the Arts to expand its education program. A four-person education department was established in 1968 and was responsible for the Society's program for schools as well as for over-seeing the growing number of films, music recitals, and children's programs offered by the Society. Within eight years, attendance at these programs increased more than 50 percent, from 21,937 in 1964 to 33,063 in 1970. Moreover, general attendance at the Society reached an all-time high of nearly 109,000 in 1968, a year that Society leadership referred to as "one of the best in the Society's long history." At this point, attendance at all Society events was free, and as Adams

FIGURE 4.1.   TRENDS IN OPERATING REVENUES
AND EXPENDITURES, 1960–1970.

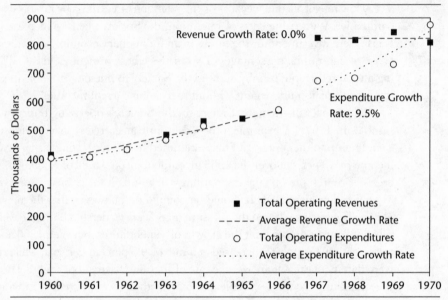

Source: New-York Historical Society annual reports; see also Table C.4–1 in Appendix C.

pointed out, the Society "fulfills an increasingly useful function in the city's educational and cultural life, at no charge to the municipal budget."

As the Society shifted its focus outward toward serving a growing constituency, the emphasis in its collections management shifted as well. The primary focus following the Wroth report had been on cataloging the collections; as the 1960s passed, the emphasis shifted to acquisitions. In the 1967 annual report, Adams wrote: "While we are conscious of the fact that our source material must be catalogued and made available, we are always aware that the first objective is to strengthen our collections." In the Report of the Library in 1969, James Gregory, the librarian, wrote that "the making of thoughtful and knowledgeable additions to the collections of the library is the most permanent and therefore the most important work of 1969, or any other year." Further evidence that cataloging was diminishing in importance is reflected by administrative decisions; between 1966 and 1970, the cataloging staff was reduced from five full-time catalogers to just three. By 1975, the cataloging staff had been reduced to one.

In addition to diverting resources from cataloging, management's renewed emphasis on acquisitions and growth of the collections conflicted with the recommendations of the Wroth report. The report's second major emphasis, narrowing the Society's acquisitions policy both chronologically and geographically, also faded in importance through the 1960s. In 1970, Gregory issued an appeal for *contemporary* books: "Friends of the Society who have useful—they need not be rare—books are urged to offer them to the Library. A fairly common book in 1970 may be quite scarce by 2070. But the need for these current books is much more immediate. . . . A growing number of young historians are studying the recent past from sources in nearly contemporary publications. It appears that interest in current history will continue." Similarly, the Society continued to acquire, by purchase and gift, items not related to New York or the surrounding region or colonial America, including a collection of lithographs purchased in 1969 depicting the California gold rush. In the acquisitions policy adopted by the trustees in 1959, it had been recommended that primary materials on the California gold rush not be acquired.

As the 1960s drew to a close, so did the presidency of Frederick B. Adams Jr. Under his leadership, the Society completed a successful campaign that helped finance major capital renovations; the Society's board was restructured and the Society's first female trustee was elected; the Society adopted a total return approach to the spending of investment proceeds from endowment; and the Pintard Fellows were established. In addition, the Society's renovated exhibition spaces and expanded emphasis on public programs positioned it to serve a larger constituency than it ever had before.

Not all the news had been good, however; the latter part of Adams's tenure exhibited a shift away from the careful stewardship that characterized his early years. Whereas Adams had shown great caution in 1963, warning the Society of impending budget problems and urging a capital campaign even as the Society was running surpluses, he and the board did not anticipate or respond to the financial difficulties of the late 1960s. There is no mention of financial concern in the remaining reports of the period; in fact, it was not until 1970, after the Society suffered its first operating deficit in many years, that Adams sounded the alarm. That was the first year that the Society's total return investment policy and 5 percent spending rule did not provide sufficient income to cover expenditures. As he turned over the presidency to Robert G. Goelet, Adams warned that "the prospect for 1971 and beyond is not cheerful; we shall have to draw heavily on our carefully husbanded Reserve Fund balance to make up operating deficits."

Formula for Disaster: Dramatic Change Outside, Status Quo Inside, 1971–1982

The 1970s proved to be an extraordinarily difficult decade for all cultural institutions, especially those that depended on endowment for much of their income.

The "stagflation" of that period affected these institutions negatively in terms of both revenues and expenses. On the revenue side, the recessionary economy that prevailed during the early 1970s reduced the return on these institutions' investments, driving down total income. In 1973 and 1974, for example, the annual total return for domestic common stocks was –14.8 percent and –26.4 percent, respectively.[6] As for expenses, inflationary pressure from the oil crisis, among other things, drove up the cost of operations during the same period.

The Society's ability to meet the challenges was constrained. First, the capital improvements and renovations had reduced the Society's unrestricted reserves, inhibiting its financial flexibility. Second, and equally important, the Society continued to move aggressively to expand its services to a rapidly growing public constituency just as the financial noose was tightening. As had happened at other times in the Society's history, the expansion of services (and the concomitant growth in expenditures) was not matched by a comparable growth in existing revenue or by the identification of new sources of revenue.

On January 27, 1971, Robert G. Goelet was elected president of the N-YHS, thereby earning the unenviable task of leading the Society through this challenging period. Goelet was a direct descendent of Francis Goelet, a Huguenot who had immigrated to North America in 1676. Over the years, the Goelet family rose to the highest levels of real estate, banking, and the arts in New York. In the early 1900s, Goelet's father, Robert Walton Goelet, built on the family's already sizable fortune, amassing real estate parcels that even at Depression era prices were estimated to be worth well over $15 million in 1932.[7] At about that time, the Goelet real estate holdings were estimated to be the most valuable owned by any single New York family other than the Astors. Upon graduating from Harvard in 1945, Goelet worked in the family's various business and real estate concerns, eventually serving as chairman of R.I. Corporation and president of Goelet Realty.

Like many of his peers, Goelet took great interest in a variety of cultural and philanthropic institutions. At the time of his election to the Society's board of trustees in 1961, he was on the board of the American Museum of Natural History (of which he later became chairman), the New York Zoological Society, the Phipps Houses, and the National Audubon Society. During his nearly ten years on the N-YHS board, his primary focus was the Society's museum; in fact, he had chaired the board's museum committee for much of his tenure. His election to president marked the first time that the Society's top-ranking board officer had not served on either the library committee or the finance committee.

Under Goelet, the Society continued down the path on which it had embarked in the late 1960s, focusing on improving the galleries, increasing general attendance, broadening the Society's acquisitions and collections management policies, and expanding public programs. In the 1971 annual report, Richard Koke, the director of the museum, expressed the Society's renewed commitment to the museum: "For several years the course for the museum, chosen by the Trustees, has been directed toward strengthening its program and collections to bring it to the high position that it enjoyed in public favor in the 19th century." To help it achieve that lofty goal, the Society hired Mary Black to fill a new position, curator of painting, sculpture, and decorative arts.

For his part, Goelet gave the museum top billing in his first annual report, introducing the report of the president by expressing his satisfaction with the improvements of the museum, noting "the Society's . . . continued progress in the modernization and reinstallation of our museum galleries." Although no one would question the basic desire to improve the museum, returning it to its nineteenth-century stature was simply not possible. The museum had achieved its earlier status without competition from the many museums that had established themselves in New York City in the intervening hundred years, including the Metropolitan Museum of Art, located directly across Central Park.

Still, by most standards, the Society's initiatives were successful. In 1972, the Society's museum was awarded a certificate of formal accreditation by the American Association of Museums. More important, the Society's efforts were well received by the public. For the first time ever, the Society exhibited its entire collection of 433 Audubon watercolors, and tens of thousands of visitors came to see the exhibition. The Society also created the Library Gallery to exhibit selected items from the library collections. The popularity of those exhibits exceeded even the Society's expectations. Because of these and other initiatives, general attendance at the Society increased dramatically. Between 1971 and 1973, the Society's attendance figures increased by 172 percent, from 136,324 to 351,727. As the United States prepared to celebrate its Bicentennial, the extraordinary collections of the Society would be much in demand.

The Society's desire to expand was not limited to its programs and services; it extended to its collections management policy as well. As previously mentioned, the Society's accessions in the late 1960s did not conform strictly to the guidelines set forth in the 1959 acquisitions policy enacted following the Wroth report. On April 28, 1971, the board of trustees moved to formalize the broadening of that policy, approving a set of modifications to provide "a broader base" for the maintenance and strengthening of the Society's collections. The modifications significantly expanded the Society's reach. For example, the 1959 policy suggested that "no primary material relating to the California Gold Rush be acquired in the future. It is suggested that secondary material be purchased only selectively." As amended, the new policy stated that "printed primary and secondary material [on the California Gold Rush] will be purchased which relates to the collection we now have."[8] Similar changes, relaxing either thematic or geographical restrictions, were made to recommendations for five collections: slavery, military history, biographies, travels in the United States, and political caricatures and posters.

In the years following this change in official policy, the Society's officers and staff also widened the scope of its collecting chronologically. In his 1973 Report of the Library, James Gregory wrote that "as always, the majority of the books added to the library are recent ones that we believe to have lasting research value." To justify this growing emphasis on recent works, in the 1974 annual report Heslin wrote: "History could be as long ago as 1775, or it can be as recent as last week. To collect items of importance relating to both periods is our function." Gregory elaborated further in the same annual report: "We acquire recently published books as well as old ones. New books and current periodicals are vital to the collection, for some contain the findings of recent historical scholarship and others are the firsthand records of our own time and the primary sources for tomorrow's historians. . . . A commonplace book today may be a rarity of the future." It is true that there is a need for libraries that will collect these materials; one wonders, however, if the policies are appropriate for an institution of limited resources with a mission and demonstrated strengths firmly planted in the history of America prior to 1900.

The increasing emphasis on acquisitions was reflected in changes in the levels of the board-restricted funds. Year-end balances of these funds, originated under then-president LeRoy Kimball in 1954 to help the board manage the Society's accumulated surpluses, are depicted in Figure 4.2.

Prior to Frederick Adams's tenure as board president, the three board-restricted funds were the accumulated surplus, the pension reserve, and the fund for special accessions. As mentioned previously, Adams had established a development fund and renamed the accumulated surplus (calling it, instead, the reserve for equipment, building replacement, and major repair) as part of the capital campaign to improve the Society's facilities. To pay for the renovation in 1966, the building reserve was totally depleted and the development fund was substantially reduced. After the renovation, Adams rebuilt the development fund with surpluses generated in the late 1960s. When Adams stepped down in 1970, the development fund stood at $302,000.

Under Goelet, the board spent down this reserve quickly, depleting it entirely in just three years. Rather surprisingly, however, the development fund was not spent down to finance deficits. Expenditures were cut in 1971 and 1972, and the Society posted relatively small deficits (approximately 3 percent of total expenditures) in 1971 and 1973.[9] Although the financial statements do not explicitly state where the development fund reserves were transferred, it is apparent from Figure 4.2 that the special accessions fund was the beneficiary of a good portion

FIGURE 4.2. BOARD-DESIGNATED FUND BALANCES UNDER THREE SOCIETY BOARD PRESIDENTS, 1960–1974.

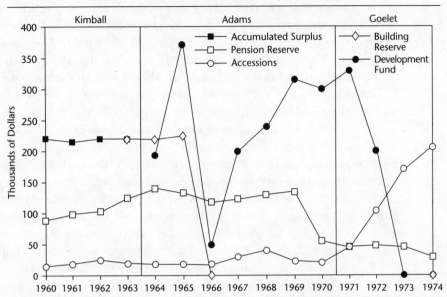

Source: New-York Historical Society annual reports; see also Table C.4–1 in Appendix C.

of those transfers. As the development fund fell from $302,000 to zero, the accessions fund rose from $42,000 to $250,000.

Pressure to ensure that funds would be available to make important accessions can be seen in other ways as well. The Society began to entertain the possibility of selling some of its collections, particularly its European paintings. Originally received by the Society in 1867, many of these pictures were amassed by Thomas J. Bryan, one of America's first serious collectors of European art. Although some considered the collection important as a unique representation of early American tastes in European art, the Society maintained that the paintings did not fall within its mission. By selling the paintings, some of which were quite valuable, the Society hoped to further its capacity to purchase collections that were relevant to its mission and purposes.[10] The proposal was to sell the majority of the paintings and use the proceeds to finance future acquisitions of American paintings. The Society would retain a small varied group of the Bryan paintings to continue to serve as an example of early American collecting tastes.

The Society originally petitioned the Supreme Court of New York for *cy pres* relief in the mid 1960s.[11] It was not until May 1970 that the Society received permission from the court to sell 210 pictures. In May 1971, the Society sold at auction 13 paintings for $109,200. The first $80,000 was used to pay legal expenses, and the balance was used to establish the Bryan Fund, which was to be used only for the purchase of paintings. On December 2, 1971, the Society sold 179 more paintings from the collection for $299,220. The Society did not attempt to sell any more of the paintings for the rest of the 1970s (although ten paintings were loaned to the Metropolitan Museum of Art during that period). In October 1980, the Society sold another large group of the paintings, for which it again had to get approval from the courts, for $1,330,650.

The sale of the Bryan paintings and the establishment of the Bryan restricted fund illustrates another way in which the Society was becoming a more complex institution to manage. Determining what costs can be allocated to restricted funds and what cannot is a complicated process that can burden an institution's unrestricted resources if not properly controlled. The Society experienced tremendous growth in the amount of restricted financial assets under its care during this period. In 1959, the Society's total balances in restricted funds (other than endowment) was $78,000. By 1974, the balance had grown to over $1.5 million.

Programmatically, the museum and library were not the only departments in the Society that were growing and expanding; public programs, specifically the education department, were expanding as well. In 1974, a new section was added to the annual report, titled "Education Department Activities." Initiatives undertaken in the mid 1970s included a program of repeated visits by neighborhood schools; participation in Growth Through Art and Museum Experience (GAME), a workshop program to join the city's schools and cultural institutions; and an alternative education program called City-as-School that offered credit to student interns who helped the department with its activities. Through the 1970s, a whole series of similar programs, some of them funded by restricted grants from the city, the New York Community Trust, and the National Endowment for the Humanities were started and managed by the education department.

Holding other things equal, the expansion of the Society during the 1970s would hardly be considered as a negative; quite the contrary, the Society was serving a broader clientele than it had at any time in its long history. However, at the same time the Society was expanding, its financial situation was deteriorating. Because the Society did not charge an admission fee, the explosive growth in visitors strained the budget, placing an additional burden not only on the Society's staff but also on its physical plant. In addition, by relaxing the acquisitions policy, effort was being expended on accessioning, cataloging, and preserving contemporary materials, leaving fewer resources to care for and catalog the older and most valuable collections. Finally, the expansion of the education department placed additional burdens on the Society's core administrative staff. While some of the programs were presumably financed with restricted grants, some of the overhead costs of salaries, building, and infrastructure were paid for with general operating resources.

The combination of financial strain and programmatic expansion yielded predictable results, but the speed with which the Society's fortunes changed is amazing. The first major drop in the market value of the Society's endowment occurred at this time. In the days before the adoption of the total return policy, the Society, like most nonprofit institutions, tended to purchase a higher proportion of low-growth, high-yield investments of moderate to low risk. Once freed of this constraint, the Society began carrying a much higher percentage of stocks. It is important to remember, however, that the allocation of investments in equities should be limited by an investor's tolerance for risk. Apparently, the desire to maximize the growth of the endowment took precedence over risk concerns. In 1967, the Society had 73 percent of its endowment invested in stocks; by November 1972, equity investments had grown to comprise 90 percent of the Society's portfolio. At that time, the market value of the Society's endowment was $17.5 million.

As has been mentioned, the onset of several economic crises in 1973 and 1974 dealt a painful blow to the stock markets. The average total return in equities in 1973 was −14.8 percent.[12] The Society's total return, also −14.8 percent, reflected its commitment to equities.[13] In 1974, the average total return in the stock market fell further, to −26.4 percent.[14] Even though the Society had reduced its allocation in equities to 55 percent, the damage had been done. By the end of 1974, the market value of the endowment had fallen to $10.5 million, a loss of 40 percent of the corpus.

The Society's operating performance reflected the changes in the market. In 1968, the Society ran an operating surplus of $122,000, a figure 18 percent more than its total expenditures of $696,000. Investment income alone exceeded total expenditures by $40,000. The total balance of the various board-restricted reserves stood at $397,000. Just five years later, at the end of 1973, the Society ran a deficit of $31,000 on a budget of $981,000, and its board-designated reserves had fallen to $209,000.[15]

The Society's 1967 decision to move to a total return endowment management policy was sound and is consistent with the way well-endowed and professionally managed institutions operate today, but only as long as the Society remained within the 5 percent spending limit. In 1974, under pressure to balance its operating budget, the Society exceeded that limit for the first time. In that year, the Society received $590,000 in interest and dividends and sold stock to realize gains of $358,000. The total investment income recorded on the Society's financial statements was $948,000, or 7 percent of the three-year moving average of the market value of its endowment. This figure exceeded the 5 percent spending limit by $250,000. Because the transfer of realized gains in excess of the spending limit does not represent true operating activity, it is inappropriate to show these gains as regular operating revenue. Because of this fact, this analysis uses a calculation to determine an estimate of the Society's true operating income (and thus its deficits) by limiting the Society's investment income to a maximum of 5 percent of the endowment in a given year. Figure 4.3 shows the Society's operating revenues, expenditures, and deficits for the latter part of Heslin's tenure using the full amount recorded in the Society's financial statements. Figure 4.4 depicts the Society's operating activity with the 5 percent limit on investment income.

It is difficult to understand how the Society could have continued to pursue its bold and aggressive expansion without articulating a plan for how such a program would be financed. In the reports of the president in the 1970s, Goelet expressed the Society's need for money, but without a strong sense of urgency. In 1971, in his first annual report, Goelet wrote that "expenses have gone up appreciably, despite careful management and stringent economies. Endowment income hasn't kept up. . . . We must find additional support." In the early 1970s, steps were taken to try to address the growing financial problem, but they were small ones: for example, raising the dues for members by $5 and adding new classes to the membership structure. Such initiatives were of symbolic importance in the 1960s, when the Society was running surpluses; in the 1970s, however, the Society was in need of substantial sums of money, and these actions had little chance of providing them.

As the 1970s progressed and the Society's financial situation continued to deteriorate, it seems clear in retrospect that the Society's move to a total return spending policy came to be regarded by the board more as a way of increasing spendable income than as a way of maximizing the growth of its investment portfolio. It is almost as if spending realized capital gains was seen as the solution to the Society's budget woes. In 1973, Goelet wrote: "Despite having gone to a 'total return on capital' approach to income from endowment, we end the year with a substantial deficit and it is clear that we must generate additional financial support in the years ahead."

The following year, as budgets were being prepared that projected a $300,000 deficit, one trustee, in a letter of protest accompanying his contribution for the year, wrote: "Having voted with misgivings for the increase in the budget recommended by the finance committee, I feel an obligation to contribute toward it, particularly as the percentage of capital formula for expenditure has become inadequate to the point of being unrealistic."

Meanwhile, Goelet, in his understated fashion, described the fiscal dilemma in the 1974 annual report: "Economic factors, including inflation, necessitated a further large operating deficit. We must now appeal for financial help to our friends, [to] the community at large, and to whatever sources may be helpful. I

FIGURE 4.3.   OPERATING PERFORMANCE, 1971–1981.

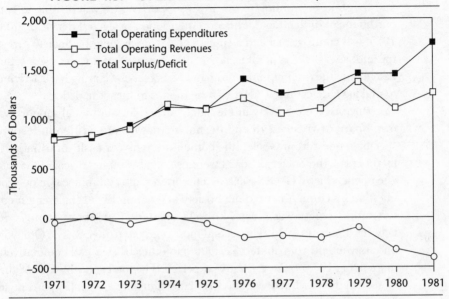

Source: New-York Historical Society annual reports; see also Table C.4–3 in Appendix C.

FIGURE 4.4.   OPERATING PERFORMANCE WITH 5 PERCENT SPENDING LIMIT IMPOSED, 1971–1981.

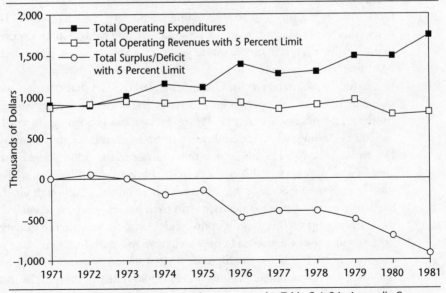

Source: New-York Historical Society annual reports; see also Table C.4–3 in Appendix C.

feel confident, however, that with the strong continuing support of the Trustees and the staff, in addition to our loyal supporters, we will be able to cope with our financial difficulties." The aforementioned projected deficit, $300,000 for 1975, was controversial and a subject of debate among the Society's trustees. In the end, it was "the general feeling of [the board] that it would be most unfortunate to lose the present momentum of the Society by cutting back activities prior to making a determined effort to raise money to meet the deficit."

One place the Society immediately turned for additional support was to its own board of trustees. In an internal memorandum written in response to a specific request from Goelet, the cumulative ten-year cash contributions of the members of the Society's board were listed. This report revealed that although one might criticize Goelet's skills as a fundraiser and communicator, one could not question his commitment to the Society as a donor. By far the greatest contributor to the Society was Goelet himself. He had given approximately $95,000 between 1965 and 1975. The second most generous trustee was C. Otto von Kienbusch, who had contributed $23,500. No other trustee had cumulatively given more than $10,000 over the ten-year period. The total contributions of the group of sixteen trustees listed was $173,400, meaning that Goelet (55 percent) and von Kienbusch (14 percent) accounted for 69 percent of the total. For the ten-year period, the average cumulative contribution of the other fourteen trustees was approximately $3,900, or $390 per trustee, per year. The prospects for closing a $300,000 gap from annual gifts by the trustees seemed slim; however, the drive for gifts during 1975 was highly successful. Gifts, grants, and contributions received during the year amounted to $319,479, compared to just $99,000 in 1974. These funds went a long way toward eliminating the Society's deficit for 1975. Unfortunately, that level of giving could not be sustained, and contributions dropped back to their historic levels in the following years. The Society's struggles to balance its operating budget worsened in the late 1970s.

In the 1977 annual report, Goelet lamented the fact that "despite every possible care to cope with operating expenses of the Society, the economic situation continued its inflationary trend." The budget gap was widening, and still Goelet was just beginning to lose the confidence he had shown in his statements of 1974. He wrote: "The N-YHS fulfills an important role in the cultural and educational life of New York City and New York State. I hope that with continued support from friends of the Society, this situation will continue." Although Goelet must have been growing more concerned with each passing year—and each deficit—these statements further highlight his tendency to understate the gravity of the Society's financial situation. He may well have restrained himself in an attempt to walk the fine line between emphasizing that the organization was needy without going so far that potential contributors would refuse to support the institution for fear that it was destined to fail.[16] In any event, the result was that the Society was unable to generate the level of contributed income it needed to sustain its operations. In 1978, after suffering through several years of steadily increasing deficits, Goelet wrote that "it is tedious to harp on rising costs and lessening income, but such factors can determine to a great degree the present and future course of the Society."

As if pressures to balance the operating budget weren't enough, during the 1970s the Society was forced to undertake a series of major capital projects. First, while investigating the possibility of renovating its auditorium, the Society discovered that it did not have a certificate of occupancy on file with the city. It seems that the Society's building on Central Park West predated those city ordinances. It took more than three years and well over $100,000 in construction and legal fees for the Society to receive the certificate it required. In addition, the Society did not have adequate fire detection and extinguishing systems for the library stacks. In case of a fire, the Society's antiquated sprinkler system could destroy the priceless collections. This was an area that concerned Goelet greatly, and he took a leadership role in contributing funds to help finance installation of the latest available fire detection technologies and an extinguishing system that used halon gas. The total cost of the system was $300,000, a good portion of which came from Goelet, but some of which came from its unrestricted accounts. No sooner had that project been completed than the Society found it had to rebuild its main passenger elevator. These capital expenditures erased the Society's already diminished margin for error.

An unfortunate result of the combination of inflationary pressures and unforeseen major capital expenditures was neglect of regular maintenance of the facility. After 1967, when the Society installed the air-conditioning system, an increasing portion of its budget was spent on utilities. Of course, the energy crisis of the early 1970s exacerbated the problem. By 1974, a year when only $39,000 was spent on regular maintenance, utilities comprised 81 percent of the amount spent on building and maintenance. The deferral of maintenance expenditures continued through the rest of Heslin's tenure as Society expenditures on utilities grew at an average rate of 8.7 percent per year. Between 1974 and 1981, expenditures on regular maintenance, like supplies and repairs, averaged just $62,000 per year, a very small amount for a 150,000-square-foot building that was close to eighty years old.

Other pressures mounted. Beleaguered as it was by its difficult circumstances, the Society had held the line for some time on pay increases for its staff. For example, its librarians' salaries lagged behind those of librarians at comparable research institutions by 25 percent.[17] In the summer of 1979, the Society's clerical, technical, and professional workers (including most of the library staff) joined

District 65 of the United Auto Workers, which began negotiating with management for union representation, wage increases, and job security. When negotiations broke down in December, the workers went on strike. The strike lasted nearly six months, closed the library (although the museum remained open), and required an enormous amount of institutional attention and generated negative publicity when the Society could ill afford it. Illustrative of the frustrations of the times, Goelet was accosted by a wealthy woman (whom he recognized) as he was crossing the picket line to enter the Society. She yelled to him, "Why don't you give these people what they want?" He shouted back, "Because we don't have it. Why don't you give us the money to give them what they want?" She declined.[18]

In the end, the workers received a slight wage increase, a grievance procedure was established, and a seniority provision was added to the process for awarding promotions. As part of the negotiations, the union agreed to allow management to eliminate the education and editorial departments. One result of that part of the agreement was cessation of the publication of *New-York Historical Society Quarterly* after more than seventy years. Clearly, the negative side effects of the strike were substantial. The impact on staff morale and public perception of the Society would prove to be long-lasting.

Although the strike was resolved, the various financial difficulties the Society faced were not. In October 1980, Goelet established an ad hoc board committee to take a broad overview of the Society. The committee was to advise the president and the board of trustees on future steps the Society should take to improve the organization and make the best use of its human and other resources. In April 1981, the committee reported that the "overall financial prospects for the Society were very gloomy." It outlined several options for improving the situation, all of which were short-term and dealt with generating revenue: increase membership dues, hold a fundraising benefit, hire a professional fundraiser, and expand the Society's gift shop. After hearing the committee's discouraging report, Goelet called a special meeting of the board for April 7, 1981, apparently to discuss the potential development of the Society's real estate and air rights over the building. On April 22, at the Society's general board meeting, Goelet formally requested authority to hire a consultant to "continue negotiations on behalf of the Society with representatives of Harry B. Helmsley." At the following board meeting on May 27, Goelet requested authorization to sign a letter of intent on behalf of the Society that "outlined plans for development of the Society's unimproved property and the adjacent brownstone and air space presently used partially for storage. . . . The proposal would utilize unused F.A.R. [floor area ratio] over the Society's existing building. Any development must be compatible with the Landmark status of the building, its character, and the character of the Historic District." Negotiations with Helmsley continued, but ten days before a formal contract was to be signed, the deal was called off due to zoning problems.

As Goelet continued to study the possibility for real estate development, James Heslin announced his plan to retire as of June 1982. A committee was formed to conduct a search for his replacement. The work of the board during this time was split between two tasks of extraordinary importance: deciding on a way to monetize the Society's real estate assets and hiring a new chief executive.

In May, the Society's board issued a resolution authorizing and approving an agreement between the Society and a real estate developer named Robert Quinlan. Quinlan agreed to purchase the right to develop a high-rise residential building using available Society property and air rights for not less than $4 million. The agreement was subject to Quinlan's being able to secure certain city and local approvals but still required that Quinlan make periodic payments to the Society prior to actual construction. The term of the agreement was thirty-six months.

The agreement to develop its real estate holdings was the Society's last significant action during the tenure of James Heslin. In June, shortly after the completion of the contract with Quinlan, the Society decided on a candidate to take over the reins. During Heslin's twenty-two years, the Society's presidents, first Frederick Adams Jr. and then Robert Goelet, took an increasingly active role in setting the course for the Society. As Heslin prepared to step down, he seemed to have lost his enthusiasm for his position and for his accomplishments. In his final director's report, when he had a chance to place his tenure in perspective and establish a tone for the next leader, he wrote the following, which is quoted in its entirety:

> One of the chief objectives of The New-York Historical Society is the collection of material relating to New York City, in particular, and New York State in general. In pursuit of this goal, the Society attempts to acquire by gift and purchase, the latter chiefly from special funds restricted for this purpose, material for the Library and Museum that illustrates the history of this city and state. We have set guidelines that are observed in this process. As I write this last annual report ending my term as Director, I am struck by the constant accession of items as described in the reports of the Library and Museum. The growth of the collections continues in a planned and practical manner. Such a growth attests to the vitality of the institution and further reflects the commitment of the trustees, staff, members, and friends of the Society. All of this indicates a healthy and strong future.

It would be left to Goelet to set the tone for the Society during the transition to new leadership. Apparently secure in his sense that the Society could expect a windfall from the development of its real estate, he encouraged the new director to revitalize the Society and its programs.

Notes

1. The 1959 Library Acquisitions Policy is reprinted in its entirety in Appendix D.
2. See Table C.4–1 in Appendix C.
3. This and all other unattributed assertions in the text are based on the minutes of New-York Historical Society board meetings.
4. For a detailed explanation of total return and other principles of endowment management, see Chapter Ten.
5. See Table C.4–1 in Appendix C.
6. Kennedy and Schneider (1994, p. 19).
7. "Robert Walton Goelet, 61, Dies" (1941).
8. New-York Historical Society (1971, p. 2).
9. See Table C.4–1 in Appendix C.
10. Personal communication, Dec. 13, 1994.
11. Simply stated, the doctrine of *cy pres* provides that where property is given in trust for a particular charitable purpose, the trust ordinarily will not fail even if that particular purpose cannot be carried out. The rationale is that the grantor had a more general intent to have the property used for something similar to the specific purpose specified in the gift or grant. To apply for relief from *cy pres* is to ask the courts to rule that a recipient's circumstances are such that the doctrine of *cy pres* does not apply and that the restrictions on the grant or gift can be lifted.
12. Kennedy and Schneider (1994, p. 19).
13. An approximation of the Society's total return is calculated in the following manner. The beginning-of-year market value of the endowment is subtracted from the end-of-year endowment value. Adjustments are made for funds withdrawn (such as investment income) and funds added (such as operating surpluses or capital gifts). The change in the endowment value is then divided by the beginning-of-year market value to estimate the total return.
14. Kennedy and Schneider (1994, p. 19).
15. See Table C.4–1 in Appendix C.
16. Personal communication, Dec. 13, 1994.
17. Richards (1984, p. 115).
18. Personal communication, Dec. 8, 1994.

CHAPTER FIVE

NEW INITIATIVES AND ECONOMIC SHOCKS, 1982–1987

Expansion and the Pursuit of a Real Estate Windfall, 1982–1984

On June 10, 1982, a special meeting of the board was held to name James B. Bell director of The New-York Historical Society. A graduate of the University of Minnesota with a doctorate in history from Balliol College at Oxford, Bell had taught at Ohio State and Princeton. Immediately before coming to the Society, he had been the director of the New England Historic Genealogical Society for more than nine years. Introducing Bell in the annual report of 1982, Society President Robert Goelet expressed his enthusiasm for the new director: "Although he has been with us for only a short period, Dr. Bell has already begun to place his mark on the Society. In the report that follows, he details new programs that he and his staff have introduced. Judging from what he has undertaken, the years to come promise to be productive and exciting ones."

Still, Goelet closed the 1982 annual report with these words of caution addressed to the membership: "Your society needs to broaden its membership base and enlarge the number of its corporate and foundation contributors. The level of annual deficits incurred in recent years simply cannot be allowed to continue. We will need your help in implementing what I trust will be a most successful era in the history of your society."

From the very start, Bell's emphasis was on new programs, new initiatives, and the development of a new attitude at the Society. Perhaps in response to the beleaguered and more or less moribund last years of his predecessor, Bell sought to reestablish the Society as an active institution. In his first annual report, Bell wrote of the progress that had been made by the Society in a variety of areas. He pointed to the publication of the *New-York Historical Society Gazette,* a newsletter to keep members informed of the goings-on at the Society. A comprehensive evaluation was under way of the collecting, lending, and exhibition policies of the museum as well as a plan to renovate the Society's museum storage areas. On the library side, Bell wrote of two grants that brought the Society into the computer age. Awarded by the National Endowment for the Humanities, the grants funded two new programs: one provided resources to enable the Society to enter its holdings in an on-line catalog called the Research Libraries Information Network (RLIN), and the other helped the Society to develop a computerized catalog of its extensive newspaper holdings. In terms of public service, the Society continued its long-running lecture series and began to sponsor conferences for scholars on topics of general interest and significance.

Bell was out to remake the Society, and he was going to do it with gusto. Looking back on his first months in office, Bell wrote: "These are only some of the programs that the Society will provide in the years to come. The challenge that the staff and I have undertaken is to build on the Society's record of 178 years of distinguished service to the city, state, and nation. We accept that challenge with enthusiasm."

Bell moved to take advantage of the positive glow that surrounds new leadership. In an article in the *New York Times* headed "How a Small Museum Puts on Its Big Shows," Bell called his institution "the best-kept secret in New York." The article pointed out that "few people" visit The New-York Historical Society. "A lot of people don't know what's in it. Some people have never even heard of it."[1] The article then attempted to augment the Society's reputation by discussing its valuable collections and its many different exhibits. In addition to describing how a small museum differs from a large museum, the article also gave Bell an opportunity to discuss his future plans for the N-YHS. He said the Society was going to "take off in new directions," mounting more theme exhibitions and paying more attention to what he termed "neglected collections" such as the extraordinary cache of architectural drawings.

Bell aggressively enlarged and expanded the Society's services and programs, but he did so with little apparent regard for how these initiatives would be financed. Perhaps he and the trustees believed that development of the Society's real estate was the answer to the fiscal predicament. Without sufficient current revenues available to support the new initiatives, the Society continued the policy that had been established in the late 1970s, spending realized gains in excess of the established limit of 5 percent of the market value of the endowment. In fact, the expansion undertaken by Bell required the Society to withdraw more from its endowment than it ever had before. After six months with Bell as director, the Society's total unrestricted operating expenses for the year had increased 11 percent, while operating revenues decreased 4 percent. To pay for this expansion, the Society spent $1.9 million in proceeds from the endowment, a staggering 16.9 percent of the endowment's total value.[2]

　　Society leadership was aware that it had to generate more funds. As 1982 drew to a close, the Society issued its first "annual appeal," a mailing sent out to the membership encouraging end-of-year contributions. It was the first time the membership had been systematically canvassed for funds beyond the standard dues. Response to the appeal was positive but did not have a significant impact on the Society's financial situation. During 1983, and on a nearly monthly basis, the Society's treasurer, Margaret Platten, repeatedly warned her fellow trustees of the growing gap between revenues and expenditures.[3] In January 1983, she urged the trustees to consider hiring a professional to help with fundraising. She repeated her plea in trustee meetings in February and March; finally, in April, George Trescher, a fundraising consultant, was retained. In May, Platten reiterated her concern about the budget gap and spoke of the Society's urgent need for revenues. In July, she was critical of the steps being taken, saying that "fundraising efforts are, at best, modest." As members of the board grew increasingly worried about the financial situation, Bell, too, became concerned: the burgeoning deficit limited his ability to offer the programs he regarded as important. The library had urgent needs, Bell contended. He explained to the trustees that the library "needs space, has personnel problems, and is in need of defining again its collecting and acquisition interests." Bell also reminded the trustees that the recommendations of the 1956 Wroth report had never been pursued. Bell also pointed out that the Society's problems were not limited to the library. He asserted that "the museum department was not properly funded to carry out its work, although more than 98 percent of the visitors to the Society come to see the various exhibitions." Within the Society, responsibility for the budget seemed to remain, at least at this point, a board matter. There is no evidence that Bell was criticized or was even held accountable for the growing budget deficit. Bell's monthly reports to the board consisted of discussions of the progress of programs, not the progress toward financial stability.

　　Bell's administrative honeymoon was brief. Less than six months after he took office, public controversy developed around his dismissal of Mary Black, the Society's curator of painting and sculpture. Black, who had been at the Society since 1970 and was sixty years old, was dismissed on December 29, 1982, without, she said, "prior notice or explanation." She also said that Bell refused to give her a letter outlining the reasons for her dismissal. She filed a complaint against the Society in early 1983 claiming that the Society had violated sex and age discrimination laws.[4]

In February, the Society's board of trustees formed a special committee to deal with the matter. Shortly thereafter, sixteen prominent New Yorkers sent a letter to the Society protesting Black's termination and released it to the press. The letter, parts of which were excerpted in an article in the *New York Times,* asserted that "Mary Black had been fired—dismissed with no explanation, on short notice, with meager allowance for financial hardship, and given three hours for the removal of personal belongings with the threat of eviction for trespass after that." It added that the dismissal was "very difficult for anyone acquainted with Mary Black's age, career and accomplishments to comprehend."[5] Both Bell and Goelet declined to comment, citing Black's civil complaint. Trustee discussions on this issue continued for more than a year, until in April 1984, the Society and Black reached a settlement.

Although it is not uncommon for a new leader to struggle through difficult personnel issues during a transition period, the negative publicity helped neither Bell nor the Society. For example, among the signers of the letter of protest was Kent L. Barwick, chairman of New York City's Landmarks Preservation Commission. The leader of that agency was not a person the Society wanted to offend as it was quietly preparing plans to develop a residential tower adjacent to and over its landmark building.

Another controversy developed, this time within the Society's walls, around Bell's pledge to "pay more attention" to the Society's architectural drawings. The new emphasis created tensions between Society staff and the board. Although a survey of the drawings was completed quickly and presented to the trustees on January 26, 1983, changing the way drawings were used proved to be more difficult. Battle lines were drawn within the Society over whether the drawings, along with other prints and photographs, ought to reside under the jurisdiction of the museum or the library. Apparently, Bell's idea to do more with these neglected collections involved moving them from the library into the museum, a move proposed in a museum committee report issued in February 1983. In that report, the committee criticized the underutilization of the prints and indicated that the Society should be more aggressive in pursuing twentieth-century items. It presented a "wish list" of print makers and photographers whose works the Society ought to pursue.

Larry Sullivan, the librarian, was vehemently opposed to shifting responsibility for the prints, photos, and drawings to the museum. In April 1983, he presented to the trustees a document titled "Report on the Print Room as a Library

Division." The report attacked the proposal from the museum committee and outlined the many and varied reasons for his opposition.

Sullivan wrote that "the Print Room is most heavily used as a research facility and its traditional designation as a Library division acknowledges its primary role as a visual and architectural archive." Sullivan also emphasized that the collections of the Print Room had been built with knowledge of the holdings of its sister institutions. Sullivan pointed out that the museum committee report ignored the collections of other institutions in assembling its wish list, including artists whose works were already well represented at institutions like the New York Public Library and the Whitney Museum of American Art. Furthermore, although Sullivan did not directly question the appropriateness of pursuing twentieth-century work given the Society's mission and strengths, he did write that "pursuit of 20th century prints and photographs should not detract from a longstanding commitment to the N-YHS's strength in 18th and 19th century material." In addition, Sullivan argued that applying the more detailed museum accessioning and cataloging processes to the 10,000 prints, 500,000 photographs, 140,000 architectural drawings, and over a million Landauer items would be impossible. Conversely, the Society's library cataloging procedures and participation in RLIN would make it possible for the collections to become accessible through library database networks. Finally, Sullivan pointed out that a recent exhibition from the Landauer collection illustrated the proper relationship between the library and the museum. The museum staff selected the material and designed the show, while the library staff kept the collection open to researchers, assisted in locating items for the exhibit, and provided background information as needed. In essence, important functions were fulfilled without interrupting normal service to scholars. Sullivan implied that no such interaction would be possible if the prints, photos, and drawings were exclusively under the aegis of the museum.

To emphasize further his opposition to the proposal, Sullivan quoted extensively from a memo written by Richard Koke, the museum director, which showed that he, too, opposed the transfer. Koke wrote that he considered the suggestion to move the print collections out of the library "pointless and reflecting very little knowledge of the function of the Print Department and its relation to the Society. . . . The fact that the museum, at times, draws upon the print collections for exhibitions provides *no valid reason* to transfer custody of this material. . . . The collection serves as a valuable adjunct (apart from preservation) for the use of scholars, researchers, and the public, which has nothing to do with exhibits." Koke concluded by saying that "the print department is not, as the [proposal] would intimate, a 'grab bag' for the benefit of the museum, and I certainly fail to see anything in the suggestion that it be transferred to the museum. It certainly is [in] nobody's interest to do this."

When Sullivan's report was presented to the board, it provoked spirited discussion. Goelet noted that "the issue in question is one of longstanding interest to the board of trustees as it has been raised on many previous occasions but never addressed in a serious and systematic manner." Goelet urged a joint meeting of the museum and library committees to resolve the matter. After analysis, no action was taken. The prints, photos, and architectural drawings remained under the management of the librarian, but the definition of the collections remains to this day a matter of continuing debate at the Society.

Less than two weeks after the *New York Times* article on Mary Black's dismissal was published, Society officials and the developer Robert Quinlan appeared before one hundred neighborhood residents to discuss the possibilities for real estate development on the site. The reaction from West Side residents was hostile. Although no formal plans were presented, Quinlan said the Society could add 292,000 square feet of space in a twenty-story structure and remain within existing zoning limitations. When asked why such a development was necessary, Goelet said, "Frankly, [the Society] is badly in need of income." He then referred to the Society's annual operating losses of between $500,000 and $700,000 and added that "you can't keep that up indefinitely. The trustees decided that the one asset they had that was nonproducing was the land . . . and the development rights that ran with it. It seemed to us that this could provide an important source of capital and would also possibly solve our space problems."[6]

Neighborhood residents were not convinced by the argument. After Goelet said that most of the Society's operating expenses were paid for by endowment income, many in the audience questioned the seriousness of the Society's other fundraising efforts. Goelet's long-standing inability to articulate clearly the acute nature of the Society's financial situation was coming back to haunt him. The Society was unable to engender any sympathy for its economic difficulties. Most people felt that the Society wanted to develop its real estate to enlarge its galleries and offices and to expand its programs.

The plans for the twenty-one-story peak-roofed tower were presented to the Landmarks Preservation Commission in early 1984, and the response was overwhelmingly negative. The animosity was not directed at the design of the tower so much as at the precedent it would set and the institution seeking to set it. George Lewis, executive director of the New York chapter of the American Institute of Architects, said, "Surely most people will agree that the architect's design has many strong attractions. Would that apartment houses all over town were done half so well. . . . [But] to certify this proposal as appropriate would open the doors for developers to begin imagining the possibilities in major alterations of landmarks all over town." Councilwoman Ruth Messinger said, "For the Society to seek this luxury residential structure violates its stated commitment to history and preservation and would allow it to engage in speculative real-estate development."[7] The Landmarks Preservation Commission rejected the Society's application.

The possibility that real estate development would solve the Society's financial problems was dead, even though Goelet attempted to work with Quinlan and others to revive it. After three years, the agreement with Quinlan was allowed to expire and Quinlan gave the Society his plans and architectural drawings in lieu of the payments that had been scheduled into the contract.

Growing Deficits and a Preoccupation with Consultants and Self-Study, 1984–1986

With the prospects for a windfall from real estate development gone, the Society was forced to reexamine its revenue opportunities. It had no contingency plan. After a nine-month study, George Trescher, the Society's fundraising consultant, presented his findings to the board in January 1984. Trescher's report identified several initiatives that he thought the Society ought to pursue:

1. *Direct mail.* The Society must continue to send out mass appeals in an effort to increase its membership.
2. *Fundraising benefits.* The Society should consider sponsoring a major fundraising benefit.
3. *Board leadership.* The Society must have leadership from the board in terms of donations. It was also suggested that a development committee be established.
4. *Corporate membership.* The Society should aggressively pursue corporate membership and sponsorship opportunities.

In response to Trescher's recommendations, the Society initiated plans for a celebration to be held in October in honor of its 180th birthday. In addition, more aggressive efforts were undertaken to have Bell work with key members of the board of trustees to encourage friends and associates to contribute funds, especially from corporations. Finally, the board changed its committee structure. A new committee on development was established, as was a committee on planning and policy. Together, these committees were to address all aspects of the Society's difficult financial circumstances, including "the possibility of disposing of a portion of the library's or museum's collections or to explore finding a new home for the entire collection." Because of the seriousness of the task these committees faced and the extra effort that they would require, Goelet recommended that the museum committee and the library committee be abolished, and they were.

The adverse publicity surrounding the failed real estate proposal, combined with the Society's gloomy financial prospects, seemed to create discord among members of the board. During deliberations on negotiations with developers, there is evidence that the Society's trustees were not kept fully informed on all matters. After Hugh Hardy, the architect of the proposed residential tower, presented detailed and finished plans to the board, Harmon Goldstone noted that it was "the first time he had heard in a systematic manner the details of the proposed project." He added that he had many questions about the project but that the board should proceed with the various administrative steps required for the building. Margaret Platten also voiced reservations, noting for the record that "financial details regarding the project have not been discussed and those matters must be explored carefully."

Board dissension was reflected in other ways as well. Rather surprisingly, given the bad financial situation, the vote on whether to stage the fundraising benefit was not unanimous. Of the fourteen members present, the vote was eleven for, two against, and one abstention. Perhaps the most telling example of board dissension was the fact that just one month after abolishing the library and museum committees, the board overrode its previous action (which had been taken at Goelet's urging) and reestablished them both.

The financial picture also remained bleak. Year-end figures for 1983, Bell's first full year as director, painted a distressing picture. During the year, the Society's total unrestricted operating expenditures grew 53 percent, from $1.9 million to $2.9 million, while revenues grew only 15 percent, from $806,000 to $929,000, thereby creating a 1983 deficit of approximately $2 million—a staggering 66 percent of total expenditures (see Figures 5.1 and 5.2 for a depiction of the Society's operating results).[8] To finance the deficit, the Society withdrew $1.7 million from the endowment, 14.3 percent of its three-year average market value.[9]

Platten, the treasurer, who had been warning her fellow trustees about the deficit continuously since she assumed the position in late 1982, continued to do so and suggested that the Society consider pursuing additional revenues by investing an increased portion of the endowment in high-yielding fixed-income securities. Conditions did not improve appreciably, and by November 1984, the Society was running a monthly deficit of approximately $100,000. Goelet urged trustees to take the matter into their own hands. He proposed that the board raise $200,000 in the last two months of the year so that the annual deficit would at least not grow further. He then pledged $100,000 toward that goal and challenged the rest of the board to meet it. Goelet's gift and appeal to the board helped address the current year's situation but had no impact on the fundamental structural imbalance in the Society's activities. Despite Goelet's efforts, the Society's operating deficit in 1984 was $1.3 million, 48 percent of its total operating budget.

FIGURE 5.1. OPERATING PERFORMANCE, 1982–1988.

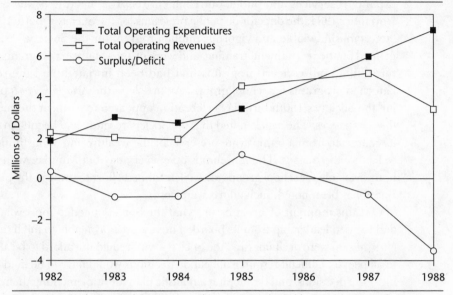

Source: New-York Historical Society annual reports; see also Table C.5–1 in Appendix C.

FIGURE 5.2. OPERATING PERFORMANCE WITH 5 PERCENT LIMIT IMPOSED, 1982–1988.

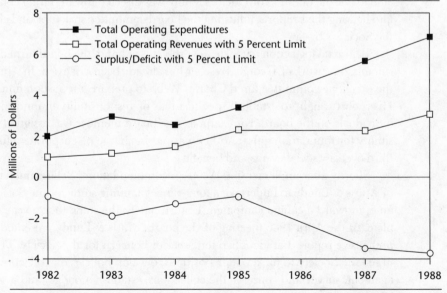

Source: New-York Historical Society annual reports; see also Table C.5–1 in Appendix C.

Even as the budget situation worsened, the Society continued to work to expand its services and public outreach efforts. At a meeting of the board in November 1984, the director of public programs for the Society reported on steps "to establish a viable and vigorous public program for the Society." She commented on the recruitment, training, and work of the volunteers program; the lectures, film, and concert programs that had been initiated; and the recently launched programs for school groups. An article in the *New York Times* promoting the Society's 180th birthday celebration appeared to confirm the success of these initiatives. The article noted that the Society recently had begun "to change its character, from a semiprivate preserve for the wealthy into an institution that welcomes the masses. The museum is open every day but Monday, with special tours available for school groups and a determined effort to draw in the public."[10] But as has been noted, such efforts were costly.

At this moment of great crisis, what the Society needed most was strong and focused leadership from its board. The resources available to fulfill the Society's mission were declining, and the Society simply could not afford to be all things to all people. Difficult resource allocation decisions would have to be made. Making those decisions, and developing a realistic plan for implementing them, would require the determination and hard work of a board working together.

Unfortunately, just when the Society needed board leadership the most, circumstances made getting that leadership less likely. Instead of action, members of the board focused on trying to determine exactly how bad the situation was and on how the Society had gotten into difficulty. A significant portion of board activity for the duration of Goelet's tenure was directed toward hiring consultants and hearing their reports, adjusting the board committee structure, and changing the Society's by-laws.

Before taking action to tackle the problems at hand, the board turned to consultants. The work of George Trescher has already been discussed. In April 1985, the executive committee hired Charles Webb to prepare a report on fundraising. His report sought to establish specific areas of responsibility in fundraising for individuals on the board. For example, one board member was assigned responsibility for foundation gifts, another was put in charge of corporate gifts, and a third oversaw social events and benefits.

Shortly after implementing Webb's recommendations, Bell retained the firm of Marts & Lundy to undertake a long-range planning study for the Society with an eye toward a capital campaign. Unfortunately, the study took a year to complete. At the April 1986 meeting of the board, Marts & Lundy presented a comprehensive report that identified ten areas of concern for the Society. The study urged the Society to fill key staff positions, develop policies on collections management, survey and conserve the collections, establish a budget and a schedule for reducing the cataloging backlog, improve the physical facilities, and establish exhibition priorities. These were just the initiatives that required immediate and urgent attention. The report concluded that The New-York Historical Society was not well known and recommended that it consider a capital campaign in the $3 million to $5 million range. The report also identified a series of steps that would have to be taken before launching the campaign: the budget would have to be balanced, experienced fundraisers would have to be recruited, a case statement would have to be prepared, and a nucleus fund would have to be solicited. It was unclear how an organization with the Society's deficit history could have even begun to address the recommendations of the report.

Not long after hiring Marts & Lundy, the board heard a report from a consulting group from Arthur Andersen & Co., who conducted an investigation of the Society's business operations. Their charge was "to identify the administrative functions carried out by the various departments . . . and [determine] the effectiveness of the organization." The report's primary recommendation was that the Society appoint a business manager to oversee financial operations. It also recommended that the Society adopt a new organization structure and hire a deputy director. The board ultimately chose not to change the structure or establish the deputy director position, but it did hire an associate director for administration and a comptroller. The Marts & Lundy study also determined, through interviews with staff members, that the Society did little long-range planning or annual goal setting, had a serious cataloging backlog in both the museum and the library, and was not maximizing its potential to generate income from its museum store, rental of its facilities for events, and sales of photographic reproductions. It is likely that the board was already aware of these shortcomings. Clearly, the list of problems was growing at the very time that the financial resources to deal with them were dwindling.

While the consultants were doing their work, the trustees took steps to resolve organizational problems by revising the board committee structure. First, on Goelet's urging, the board established an executive committee, which was to concern itself with all aspects of the Society's operations. But the committee neither covered new ground nor focused on the top-priority issues. At the February 1985 trustees meeting, the executive committee reported that the Society needed "to strengthen [its] financial resources." The committee also recommended that the Society further expand its public programs, reestablish its publications program, and revive the *New-York Historical Society Quarterly*. It also spearheaded a new public program that was to provide a summer workshop for New York high school history teachers. To pay for this expansion, the committee urged the Society to retain professional counsel to help it pursue a multifaceted fundraising program that would include "not only the Society's present annual appeal campaign, membership recruitment efforts and proposals for various projects to corporations and foundations, but also a capital fund drive and a benefit program." In a response that was typical of this period, the board deliberated over the recommendations of the executive committee but could not reach a consensus, and "it was agreed to refer the matter again to the executive committee for further consideration."

The board was becoming ever more preoccupied with its own structure. A new committee on publications was established, as was a committee on by-laws and organization. In addition to the executive, publications, and by-laws committees, there were also committees on membership and development, on education, and on law. The executive committee recommended that Goelet appoint an additional committee to study the organization and work of the board. In all, there were twelve committees for a board that consisted of twenty-one sitting members (although the nominations committee had recently recommended that the number of board members be increased to twenty-nine).

Against the backdrop of seemingly chaotic procedural machinations of the board, personal tensions were growing between certain board members. Apparently, one group of trustees thought Goelet should be replaced as board president, and another remained loyal to him. One outcome of this brewing conflict was the creation of a new position, chairman of the board. At a special meeting of the trustees, held in January 1986, Goelet was elected to that office. In the interest of diluting Goelet's power, however, the office of board president was not eliminated, and Albert Key, a successful investment banker, was named to that post.

In many cases, the work of the various committees awaited the results and recommendations of the consultants. An example will help demonstrate how difficult it had become for the Society's board to take action. In a major study on revenue sources conducted by the membership and development committee, recommendations in four of the seven areas hinged on studies that had not yet been completed. The seven areas were as follows:

1. *The museum shop.* Consultants had recommended enlarging the floor area of the store to increase revenues. Work on the shop had not yet been completed.
2. *Capital campaign.* Trustees and members of the staff of Marts & Lundy went over lists of people to determine who should be interviewed for the feasibility study. It was expected that the study would be completed by January 1985 (as mentioned, it was not finished until April).
3. *Planned giving.* A trustee had paid the fees for the Society's director of development and her assistant to attend a seminar conducted by John Brown, a consultant with expertise on planned giving programs that had been successfully used at colleges and universities. No planned giving program had been implemented.

4. *Benefits and entertainment.* Two events were scheduled for 1986.
5. *Corporate giving.* The society was awaiting the results of the Marts & Lundy study.
6. *Membership.* The director of development was conducting a study of the Society's membership goals for the next six, twelve, and eighteen months.
7. *Public relations.* Five public relations firms had been interviewed to determine what they might do to bring the Society's collections before the public eye. The committee warned the Society that it should move slowly on this front, as retaining these firms would cost between $30,000 and $100,000 annually.

The relevance and likely value of the various consultants' reports, board restructurings, and staff studies were debatable, especially in light of their cost. Fees paid to consultants amounted to approximately $1.6 million during this period, and that figure does not include the opportunity costs of staff time spent on studies and board time spent on by-laws changes. Still, one consultant's study did prove to have a material impact on the Society.

In the summer of 1985, Dr. Bryant C. Tolles, director of museum studies at the University of Delaware, was hired to "make a comprehensive analysis of and report on the society's museum, library, publications, public programming, and education functions." Because of his background, Tolles directed his study toward the care, development, and use of the Society's collections, including their management, conservation, storage, exhibition, and interpretation.

Tolles's report, completed in April 1986, was highly critical of the Society, especially regarding off-site storage of the art collections. In the report, Tolles wrote, "Some particularly fine works of art and historical artifacts are being exposed to an injurious storage environment, and in fact appear to be beyond hope of restoration. . . . I can emphatically and succinctly state that the conditions at the rented warehouse in Paterson [New Jersey] are the most blatantly shocking that I have observed during my entire museum career."

In addition to its criticism of the Society's art storage facilities, the Tolles report also outlined numerous other areas in need of attention. In fact, although Tolles clearly recognized the serious implications of invading the endowment and the alarming deficits, his report seemed to separate the Society's extensive physical, personnel, and programmatic shortcomings from their financial implications. In the end, Tolles recommended more than twenty additional positions, ranging from new curators for decorative arts, paper, photos, and prints to new librarians for architecture and maps, along with numerous support staff positions. Program expansions proposed by Tolles included reviving undergraduate and graduate internship programs, expanded publications, extensive public relations campaigns, and the introduction of "hands-on" interactive devices in exhibits, among many others. The costs to fund these new initiatives would be above and beyond the extensive and urgent costs of improved facilities, storage, and security.

When the Tolles report was presented to the board, it provoked extensive and serious discussion on the Society's financial operations, the care and preservation of the collections, and the strengths and weaknesses of the Society's personnel. It was agreed that Tolles's recommendations should be followed. In particular, the board was unanimous in the opinion that removing the collections from the Paterson facility was a matter of the highest priority. In more general terms, Goelet called the report "informative, constructive and comprehensive." As the Society's board considered how to act on Tolles's recommendations, Goelet noted "that it is necessary for each trustee to respect the confidentiality of the Tolles report."

With the Tolles report and the Marts & Lundy feasibility study complete, it was up to Bell to implement the recommendations. He explained to the board that the work of the consultants had identified the Society's people problems, financial problems, and program problems, and it was now time to determine when and how to solve them. To succeed, Bell said, any plan must address four major areas:

1. It must establish development programs that will lead to a strong financial position and a capital campaign.
2. It must establish acquisition policies for the museum and the library.
3. It must provide for more adequate care for and preservation of the museum and library collections.
4. It must resolve the Society's crisis of storage space.

Bell indicated that he had begun work on a master strategic plan for the Society's next five years, a preliminary version of which he hoped to present for the board's consideration in sixty to ninety days. And despite successful new initiatives undertaken in the areas of public programs and conservation, the underlying problems concerning board governance and fiscal responsibility remained.

As the administrative staff worked on the strategic plan, conflict among members of the board remained a continuing distraction that was consuming an inordinate amount of the board's time. The committee on by-laws presented a major study for the board that recommended that the Society establish term limits of five years for trustees, with a consecutive limit of two terms. After a second term, board members would have to step down from their positions on the board for a year before they could stand for reelection. The committee also recommended that board members not be permitted to stand for reelection after their 75th birthday. These recommendations, generated by a committee chaired by one of the Society's newest board members, Barbara Knowles Debs, was an effort to transform the leadership of the board. After lengthy discussion regarding the proposed changes, the five-year terms and age limit passed, but the one-year interim period did not. So controversial were these changes, however, that after the new by-laws had been approved, a trustee proposed an amendment that would govern changes to the by-laws. This amendment, which was subsequently passed, required that written notice of proposed by-law amendments or alterations be distributed to the entire board at least three weeks prior to the meeting in which the changes would be addressed.

The board was changing, but not quickly. The Society was, and had been for some time, under pressure to become a more inclusive institution. This pressure affected not only the Society's programmatic efforts but also the composition of its board. Throughout its history, the board had been made up of collectors and amateur historians. These individuals were not selected for their demonstrated skills in leading complex institutions; rather, they were chosen because of the people they knew and their enthusiasm for collecting Americana. Some members of the board recognized that this policy had to change. The report of the special committee on future planning, presented to the board in February 1981, suggested that "additional persons should be selected for membership on the board of trustees. . . . These persons should be carefully chosen so that their particular specialties would complement each other and be helpful in the operations of the Society." A year later, in March 1982, there was "extended discussion concerning suggestions for new members and it was the opinion of the board that younger members be added . . . as soon as possible."

In September 1985, the board elected a new class of trustees that included Barbara Debs, Miner Warner, and Rachel Robinson (the widow of baseball player Jackie Robinson). These new trustees became active members of the board and pushed aggressively for change (for example, some played a role in getting the by-laws amendments passed). Still, because of the inertia generated by 180 years of a particular mode of governance, change occurred slowly.

The Peck Bequest and Programmatic Accomplishments, 1986–1987

In the meantime, the Society's financial distress was hidden temporarily by a major bequest received from Clara Peck. The bequest, the proceeds of which were spread over 1985 and 1986, was unrestricted and amounted to more than $2 million. It is important to note that a board has some control over how it designates certain types of financial receipts. In the early 1960s, for example, Frederick Adams used the Society's surpluses to build a board-restricted development fund. This board could have taken a similar step and designated the Peck bequest as endowment, since it was clearly a one-time inflow. It did not. When presented on the financial statements, the bequest was included as regular operating income, making it appear that the Society had registered its first surplus in many years. Once those funds were spent, however, the Society found itself in familiar territory, facing expenditures that far exceeded its revenues.

The Peck bequest was both a blessing and a curse. On the one hand, it provided the Society with some breathing room, allowing it to pursue aggressively its programs and plans for community outreach. On the other hand, it postponed the inevitable, allowing the Society to continue to operate without making significant cuts in its expenditures—expenditures that were at a level far in excess of the Society's capacity to generate revenue. Operating expenses jumped from $2.6 million in 1984 to $3.2 million in 1985, an increase of 26 percent. In 1986, a six-month "year" in which the Society converted to a June fiscal year-end, operating expenses were $2.0 million ($4.2 million annualized).

With all of the money that was being spent, what were the programmatic accomplishments of Bell's staff? In addition to the research assistance and services provided by the library staff, the Society offered a wide variety of exhibits and programs, ranging from an exhibit on Niagara Falls cosponsored with the Corcoran Gallery of Art in Washington, D.C., to a celebration of the 200th anniversary of the U.S. Constitution to a summer program in U.S. history for New York City high school teachers. It is impossible to summarize the full range of services and programs offered, but three examples will illustrate the priorities of the staff during this period.

One initiative toward which the Society committed a great deal of resources was an effort to catalog its collections, a labor-intensive and extremely expensive undertaking. As has been noted repeatedly in this book, the Society displayed very little discipline in its acquisition policies over its 180-year history and had developed a huge cataloging backlog. This backlog not only inhibited the Society's ability to fulfill one of its most important goals (to make rare research resources available to scholars) but also prevented the Society from realizing any income from sales of duplicate or out-of-scope materials. It was not possible for the Society to sell what it did not know it had. Consequently, a bold and aggressive plan was mounted to catalog the Society's holdings.

On the library side, this plan relied heavily on grants from The Andrew W. Mellon Foundation. A one-to-one challenge grant of $100,000 in 1983 brought in $200,000 that was used to catalog collections and make them accessible through the RLIN on-line database. A second grant, this time a two-to-one challenge grant of $350,000 awarded in 1986, helped the Society hire a total of eight full-time catalogers to continue the program. A final report on the two grants illustrates the costly nature of cataloging. After $1,013,919 had been spent, 22,006 titles had been cataloged, at an average cost of $46.08 per title. A similar cataloging initiative was undertaken in the museum.

Another major initiative was the painting conservation program. Launched in 1985 with grants from Paul Newman and the Institute of Museum Services and later supported with grants from the Mellon Foundation, the program sought to restore the many works of art that were in need of attention. In a report to the board in May 1985, Holly Hotchner, the chief conservator, discussed the fact that very little conservation work had been done on the collection in recent years and that nearly all of the works in the collection were in need of professional attention. She reported to the board that the task at hand would take many years and much money to complete. The board enthusiastically endorsed the furthering of the conservation work.

In October 1986, Hotchner appeared before the board to report on the program's progress. She outlined the many positive developments of the previous year, remarking on the expansion of the department to seven full- and part-time staff members, the awarding of several major grants to the department (from Newman, $165,000 over two years; from the Mellon Foundation, $135,000 over three years; from the Getty National Trust, $30,000; and from the National Endowment for the Humanities, $40,000), and the restoration and repair of 465 objects. The conservation staff also played an important role in the relocation of art works from the terrible conditions in the Paterson warehouse into safer surroundings in a warehouse in Manhattan. Hotchner pointed out that although much had been accomplished, much still remained to be done. According to her, several million objects on exhibition and in storage were in urgent need of conservation attention. In addition, Hotchner appealed to the board for further support to complete installation of a varnish spray room and the establishment of a paper conservation studio. The board was most impressed with Hotchner's presentation and congratulated her on her important work safeguarding the collections.

A third programmatic initiative of this time illustrates the Society's efforts to improve relations with its surrounding community. It was noted earlier that there was pressure on the Society to become more inclusive and that changes were made in the composition of the board in response. In terms of programs, the attempt to broaden the Society's appeal was best exemplified by a multimedia exhibit mounted by the Society in April 1987 celebrating the fortieth anniversary of Jackie Robinson's career with the Brooklyn Dodgers. One might argue that an exhibit about the life of a baseball player of the mid twentieth century fell outside even the broadest definition of the Society's mission, but it was a clear effort on the part of the Society to reach out to a community it had been criticized for ignoring for many years.

Society management worked hard to ensure that the exhibit would be a success. A festive opening was attended by Mayor Ed Koch, Major League Baseball Commissioner Peter Ueberroth, members of the Robinson Foundation's board of trustees Franklin Williams and Howard Cosell, and many others. An advertising campaign promoted the exhibition on radio and in the sports pages of New York newspapers, and a promotional deal was struck with WLIB, a New York radio station with a predominantly minority listenership, to maximize the exposure of the event in that community. The Society's efforts were quite successful; on Saturdays and Sundays, lines spilled out onto the sidewalk outside the Society's doors. Over the exhibit's three-month run, it averaged more than a thousand visitors per week.

Despite the programmatic successes of the Jackie Robinson exhibit and the conservation lab, the Society continued to face financial difficulties. Platten reiterated her warnings to the trustees about the operating deficits. With no new revenue opportunities in sight, the board called on the newly established collections committee, of which Debs was also chair, to look into raising money by disposing of works of art or library materials that were outside the scope of the Society's purposes.

While the collections committee did its work, the board rejoined its ongoing battle over by-laws, this time moving to undo structures that had been put in place previously. Prior to formal action being taken on the by-law changes, extensive correspondence traveled back and forth between Goelet and the officers on the board. At the May 1987 meeting, a vote was taken both on by-laws amendments and on a series of resolutions brought to the board by Goelet. After extensive discussion, a carefully worded board resolution to eliminate the position of chairman of the board, replacing it with president, effective with the September 1987 meeting, was adopted. The resolution also reduced the number of standing committees to just four (nominating committee, finance committee, examining and audit committee, and executive committee) and outlined the duties of the secretary and the director. Two additional resolutions were adopted that day. The first charged the collections committee with formulating a collections policy and deaccessions statement. The second formed a special search committee for the purpose of recommending one or more candidates to serve as the new president of the Society following the September 1987 meeting. The committee was encouraged to consider both present trustees and nontrustees.

The actions taken at the May trustee meeting were an overwhelming defeat for Goelet. It was clear that Goelet no longer had the support of his fellow trustees. As it turned out, the May meeting was the last meeting Goelet would attend. He did not appear at either the July or the September meeting, and at the November meeting he submitted his resignation. Albert Key was elected to replace him.

Barbara Debs also submitted her resignation at this time, but for reasons unrelated to Goelet's decision. Debs resigned to protest what she viewed as irresponsible oversight and care of the collections by the Society's board. It was Debs's opinion that the trustees were going to attempt to raise money through deaccessioning without following proper procedures and without careful consideration from the Society's curatorial staff.[11]

Stock Market Crash and a Desperate Search for Funds, 1987–1988

In replacing Robert Goelet, Albert Key took the reins of an institution at the financial precipice. As it reviewed the fiscal year 1987–1988 budget, the board once again engaged in extensive discussion about how to deal with the continuing operating deficits. Key emphasized the need to put the fiscal house in order but moved to end discussion by recommending that the board approve the budget with the understanding that "vigorous efforts would continue . . . to keep expenses under control and to increase revenues." The budget was approved on that basis.

In the fall of 1987, representatives of Fiduciary Trust International, the investment management firm responsible for the Society's endowment portfolio, reported to the board. In the presentation, Jeremy Biggs noted that the performance of the portfolio since 1978 had been good but warned that "a substantial portion of realized capital gains had been distributed from the portfolio to the Society's operating accounts rather than reinvested." Platten noted that present economic conditions indicate that the Society should "make every effort to hold further distributions from the portfolio to a minimum."

If it hadn't been clear before, the stock market crash in October 1987 finally made it undeniable that the Society could not indefinitely hide its operating deficits behind transfers of realized gains from the endowment. Responding to the crisis, President Key established an ad hoc committee on the budget. The committee recommended that the Society "undertake an austerity program for the current fiscal year which will incorporate *inter alia* a freeze on hiring and capital expenditures, the elimination of overtime, the reduction of travel and entertainment expense, together with . . . a reduction of seven staff personnel" engaged in the registrar program. In addition, the Society's board retained the consulting firm Cambridge Associates to conduct a "financial equilibrium assessment."

With the Society facing an uncertain future, it once again looked at its collections, and specifically its European paintings, as a potential savior. Just prior to the stock market crash, the committee had recommended that the Society pursue an active program to dispose of items "in cases where other institutions or collectors would be more suitable owners." It was reported that the board was "keenly interested in how this project develops." After the crash, the collections committee recommended "the sale of all the remaining European paintings in the Bryan Collection" and later retained Christie's, the international auction broker, to represent the Society in such a sale. The collections committee also recommended a "*small change* in that section of Collections Management Policy relating to funds realized from sales" (emphasis added). The changed paragraph was to read as follows: "Unless there is a restriction on the use of proceeds realized from the sale of an object, such net proceeds and the income thereon may be used for any lawful purpose as the board of trustees may determine. Acquisitions made by use of such proceeds, and objects received in exchange, will be recorded in the name of the original donor, if any."

This paragraph, which was unanimously adopted by the board, directly contradicted a generally accepted museum practice that required that proceeds from deaccessions be used only for new acquisitions.

Obviously, the Society was desperate for funds. The ad hoc budget committee reported that the Society's staff had submitted a plan to reduce expenses by $1.2 million. But much more needed to be done. Even if all expense reductions were actually to materialize, without additional revenue the Society's deficit would still exceed $1.6 million. Although the Society had given up on developing the real estate adjacent to its building, one opportunity for cash that the Society continued to pursue was the possible sale of a property it owned on Forty-Second Street. It was thought that the Society might realize approximately $1.5 million from such a sale. In addition, the development committee, which had just elected Norman Pearlstine as its co-chair, reported that it had high hopes for what it was calling the annual History Makers' Gala. The first of these events was scheduled for October 31, 1988, and Paul Volcker, former chairman of the Federal Reserve Board, had accepted the Society's invitation to be the guest of honor.

Another source of funds the Society began to consider was city appropriations. As mentioned, the last time the Society had petitioned the city for support was in the 1860s, when the Society was looking to move out of cramped quarters on Second Avenue at Eleventh Street. For more than one hundred years, the Society had made no effort to attract city support.

It took quite some time for even the recent crises to motivate the Society to overcome its bias against petitioning the city. The first evidence in the official record that the Society was rethinking this principle was in November 1984, when one of the trustees, Dr. Robert S. Beekman, "stated that he had indicated on earlier occasions that he felt that the Society should explore the possibility of obtaining financial assistance from the City's Department of Cultural Affairs. President Goelet pointed out that the Society needed to position itself prior to making an approach, but the prospect would be explored." Nothing happened. In late 1987, the prospect was revisited, albeit briefly, when the board of trustees minutes reported that "it was the sense of the meeting that plans to bring the budget in balance should include . . . increased annual giving, planned giving, a capital fund drive and possible support from the City of New York." In February 1988, the

Society finally took action when Miner Warner, a Society trustee since September 1985, helped arrange a meeting between Robert Wagner, representing the city, and Albert Key and Theodore Gamble, trustees of the Society. It was reported that although there were no concrete outcomes of the meeting, both Key and Gamble were encouraged by its tone. It was a first step—admittedly a small one—in what would later become a serious appeal to the city and state governments for assistance.

By April 1988, Cambridge Associates had completed its study and had developed, in collaboration with Bell and his staff, a restructuring plan for the Society, which was presented at the April 27, 1988 board meeting. In a memo to the board, Cambridge Associates pointed out that the Society's fiscal 1988 deficit was projected to be $2.5 million:

> The deficit, quite simply, is a result of expenses that are far out of proportion to reasonable expectations for revenues. . . . Of greater significance, however, is the structural nature of this deficit. This fiscal year's deficit is not an aberration but will continue, since recurring, unrestricted expenses are projected to exceed recurring, unrestricted revenues. Annual operating deficits of $3.8 million to $4.5 million are forecasted. . . . To compensate for these shortfalls in the past, the . . . Society has relied heavily upon spending from the endowment. . . . When the unrestricted endowment is exhausted, the . . . Society loses its ability to fund these deficits. Thus, under present levels of activity, the Society may anticipate only about 18 more months of solvent operations.

The report went on to outline the steps to correct this problem. It described a series of drastic cuts in staffing and programmatic activity that would have to be enacted to begin to address the Society's financial predicament. It then explained that the purpose of the cuts was "to 'buy time' for the Historical Society to recapitalize itself." It identified five potential sources of near-term capital available to the Society:

1. Transfer of approximately $2.4 million from the Bryan Fund to the unrestricted endowment to pay for past conservation support
2. Sale of the Forty-Second Street property for $1.5 million
3. Sale of the Catlin paintings for $5 million
4. Sale of the real estate adjacent to the Society's building for $7.8 million
5. Sale of other items from the collections for $10 million.

Owing to the drastic nature of the recommendations, no decision was reached on how they ought to be implemented. At the May 11, 1988, board meeting, there was extensive discussion about how the Society should carry out the plan. At that meeting, the board unanimously resolved that "in the light of the Society's continuing severe financial deficits the board as soon as possible adopt a budget for fiscal year 1988–1989 which will produce an operating deficit not to exceed $750,000." But the board could not hold to that resolution. At the June meeting, the resolution was amended to read that the operating deficit would not exceed $1.2 million.

During June, the board's decision on the restructuring plan for the Society became known. The plan called for the Society to cut 21 of its 133 employees, close two of its four floors of galleries, and sell parts of its collections, including duplicate rare books, most of what remained of the Bryan Collection of European paintings, and other objects. It was hoped that such sales would yield between $15 and $20 million. Key stated that proceeds from the sales would be used primarily for the purchase of other works but that interest income could be used for some operating costs. In addition, the plan called for the board to raise $10 million for endowment over ten years and to mount a campaign to raise funds to pay for capital needs such as roof repair and building modernization.

Before the Society actually took action, an article appeared in the *New York Times* that described the Society's plans. The article quoted an internal memorandum from Bell that was to be distributed to the Society's staff that explained the reasons for the restructuring and the cutbacks. The memo stated: "We have a looming budget gap that threatens the integrity and very survival of the institution. We must act today to put our house in financial order—or there will be no house and no tomorrow worthy of our shared legacy, commitment and aspirations."[12] The article also quoted Frank Streeter, a member of the Society's board of trustees since 1964, who admitted that the Society's "reach [had] exceeded its grasp."

In other articles following the Society's announcement, the Society's trustees expressed regret, and some measure of responsibility, for the institution's predicament. Streeter was again quoted, this time saying, "We went along with the deficit because we felt this was the way the Society had gone for 150-odd years. Things had always worked out, but this time they didn't. You could say perhaps we were foolish."[13]

The Society's restructuring plan was controversial, especially the decision to deaccession the European pictures. In an article that appeared the day the layoffs actually took effect, several staff members, all of whom refused to be identified, objected strongly to the fact that the Society planned to sell collections "without first having mounted a public fund-raising campaign."[14] Needless to say, there was a great deal of discontent on the staff, and apparently someone broke the veil of secrecy that had surrounded the Tolles report since 1986, making it available to the *Times*. In a front-page article that appeared in the Sunday edition, the abominable conditions that had existed at the Paterson warehouse were reported publicly for the first time. Although the works had been transferred to a Manhattan warehouse nearly two years before, there had been no money available to restore them. The deteriorated condition of approximately one hundred paintings and more than three thousand works of early American decorative art was described in graphic detail. Christopher Forbes, a Society trustee, commented on the Society's predicament, saying, "It's tragic that the situation was allowed to deteriorate to the point that it was. The nadir has been reached."[15]

But the nadir had not been reached. It was soon discovered that some of the damaged paintings were not even owned by the Society but were on permanent loan from the New York Public Library. This fact escalated the controversy beyond the internal troubles of a single institution and made it a city and state cultural crisis. Robert Abrams, the New York State attorney general, launched an investigation of the Society to "look into the questions raised by *The New York Times*, whether the art collection is being properly cared for and what legal consequences that may have." In addition, the attorney general planned to investigate "whether the financial affairs of the Society are being properly handled by the board of trustees."[16] Obviously, none of this boded well for the Society's plans to deaccession the European pictures—such sales would require approval from the attorney general before they could take place.

In a July 14 letter to the Society's membership, Bell attempted to contain the damage. He wrote that the Society's $11.5 million endowment was "patently inadequate" to meet its needs. Further, Bell noted that other historical societies with less complete collections, smaller facilities, and narrower missions had larger endowments. He did not, however, take responsibility for the diminished endowment; in fact, he blamed the October 1987 crash for erosion of the Society's capital base: "Although the October stock market crash diminished our endowment and hurt our efforts to increase gifts and contributions, we will vigorously pursue additional sources of revenue through various fund raising campaigns and activities. We cannot—and will not—pursue a real estate solution involving the construction of a condominium tower such as was rejected by the city in 1984."

But it was too little too late. The Society was fully embroiled in public controversy. Museum directors around the country voiced their objections to the Society's deaccessioning plans. A highly critical article headed "Museum's Downfall: Raiding Endowment to Pay for Growth," appeared in the *New York Times*,[17] followed by an equally scathing article titled "Plundering the Past" in *New York* magazine.[18] It also came to light that the Society's deficit for the fiscal year 1987–1988 was approximately $3.5 million. And on July 26, an editorial appeared in the *New York Times* criticizing Society management and questioning the Society's plan to sell art works to pay for operations.

The next day, James Bell resigned his position as director of the Society, and the associate director, Joel Sollender, was dismissed. It was agreed that the trustees should hire an interim director to oversee day-to-day operations until a proper search for a permanent replacement could be conducted. The trustees also adopted a series of resolutions in response to the public criticism. First, on the recommendation of Helene Kaplan, who had recently been retained as the Society's principal legal adviser, they decided to postpone indefinitely sales of any works from the collection and appointed a special trustee committee "to review the advisability of revising the Society's collection management policy with respect to the use of proceeds from deaccessioning." The special committee was to solicit the opinions not only of Society staff but also of others in the museum world. The board also authorized a group of the Society's officers (Albert Key, Frank Streeter, Wendell Garrett, James Griffin, and Norman Pearlstine) "to form a committee of persons unaffiliated with the Society and knowledgeable in financial, curatorial, operational, and administrative matters to advise the board on a strategic, financial, and curatorial plan for the Society."

With the July 27 board meeting, James Bell's tenure was over. It was soon learned that Bell and Sollender had received substantial overtime pay during their tenure. That news erased from everyone's memory any favorable impressions resulting from programmatic progress that had been made by the Society through its collections conservation efforts, its educational programming, and its exhibits. As had been the case during the crises of the 1820s and the 1920s, the Society was enmeshed in a public controversy that threatened its very existence. Would it survive? Who would be its savior? These were the questions before the board as Bell departed.

Notes

1. Robertson (1983).
2. The Society's 1982 audited financial statements show an operating surplus of $268,000. If one imposes a 5 percent limit on investment income, the year actually ended with an operating deficit of just over $1 million. As was stated in Chapter Four, this analysis will use the 5 percent investment income limit when presenting the Society's operating results. See Table C.5–1 in Appendix C.
3. This and all other unattributed assertions in the text are based on the minutes of New-York Historical Society board meetings or other internal documents.
4. "Curator's Dismissal Draws Protest" (1983).
5. "Curator's Dismissal Draws Protest" (1983). The sixteen signers of the letter were Kent L. Barwick, Robert Bishop, Edmund Carpenter, Joan K. Davidson, Adelaide de Menil, John Dobkin, Ralph Esmarian, Linda Ferber, Hugh Hardy, T. George Harris, John K. Howat, Alice M. Kaplan, Barbara Millhouse, Diane Pilgrim, Ann Roberts, and Joan Rosenbaum.
6. Dunlap (1983).

7. Dunlap (1984).
8. In 1986, the Society converted from a calendar year-end to a June 30 year-end. Because they depict only six months of activity, 1986 operating results are omitted from Figures 5.1 and 5.2. See also Table C.5–1 in Appendix C.
9. For a thorough discussion of the implications of the Society's withdrawals from the endowment during this time period, see Chapter Ten.
10. Carroll (1984).
11. Personal communication, July 27, 1994.
12. McGill (1988d).
13. McGill (1988h).
14. McGill (1988c).
15. McGill (1988f).
16. McGill (1988g).
17. McGill (1988h).
18. Larson (1988).

CHAPTER SIX

ATTEMPTING A TURNAROUND, 1988–1992

The Macomber Advisory Report and the Development of the Bridge Plan, 1988–1989

As publicity and turmoil swirled around the Society, the immediate challenge for the board of trustees was to introduce some measure of stability to the institution. The trustees' first step was to assemble a blue-ribbon advisory committee. This committee, chaired by John Macomber, the former chairman and CEO of Celanese Corporation, was officially created on August 10, 1988, and was composed of a stellar group of professionals representing a wide spectrum of backgrounds and experiences.[1] The second step was convincing Barbara Debs to come back to the Society and serve as its interim director. Debs had established a reputation for financial acumen[2] during her tenure as president of Manhattanville College from 1975 through 1985 and had served on the Society's board from September 1985 until November 1987, chairing several committees. With a proven track record leading a nonprofit institution, a Ph.D. in art history, and a familiarity with the difficulties the Society had to confront, Debs was a strong candidate to guide the Society through its difficult transition.

Barbara Debs accepted the board's invitation to serve as the Society's interim director, although she specifically requested that she not be considered for the permanent position. She was happy in retirement and had no desire to resume the full-time responsibilities of a permanent chief executive.[3] Because the Society had been operating in a state of crisis for quite some time, her first task was to provide the leadership necessary to hold the staff together and repair an administrative structure that had broken down during the Society's period of crisis. In a report presented to the board in September 1988, Debs outlined the immediate goals the Society faced and the progress that had been made. Within the institution, Debs and her staff had worked to establish staff reporting processes, had hired a chief financial officer to develop a fiscally sound operating budget, and had begun to assess the Society's organizational structure. Externally, Debs worked to restore public faith in the institution, meeting with important potential donors, government officials, neighborhood residents, and local community groups. In addition, Debs oversaw the Society's communications with the New York State attorney general's office, which was proceeding with its investigation into nearly all aspects of the Society's operations.

What made these tasks more difficult was the uncertainty that prevailed regarding the Society's long-term future. The advisory committee's charge was to address all options including reorganization, merger, and even dissolution if necessary. Debs and her staff had to coordinate their efforts with the evolving opinions of the committee so that steps taken would not conflict with the committee's final recommendations.

As Debs worked to establish administrative stability, the board also acted, once again taking steps to improve its governance structure and to increase its capacity to provide financial support. In November 1988, at the prompting of the advisory committee, the board approved several changes to its by-laws, some of which reversed changes that had been made during the latter part of the Bell administration. The board increased its maximum allowable membership from twenty-nine to fifty. The director's position was renamed president and was invested with all the powers of a chief executive officer, including ex officio status on the board of trustees. The title of president was changed to chairman of the board. A process of systematic rotation and evaluation of trustee performance was established and was to be administered by a new committee on trustees. Other new committees established were a development committee; a finance committee; a joint subcommittee on development, planning, and finance; and a collections committee with three subcommittees: exhibitions and interpretation, conservation and preservation, and collections management.[4]

By the latter part of 1988, circumstances had improved. The board had approved the sale of real estate that the Society owned on Forty-Second Street for $1.7 million. Unlike the Peck bequest, the Society's board treated this one-time inflow as capital, adding it to the unrestricted endowment.

An article in the *New York Times* discussed some of the "small but surely meaningful" changes occurring at the Society. It said, "Most remarkably, the Society, which for its 184-year history has been run largely like a private institution, shunning contact with city and neighborhood groups, is now eagerly soliciting advice, help and friendship from those groups."[5] In October, the inaugural History Makers' Gala, which honored Paul Volcker, netted the Society nearly $400,000. In addition, public attention on the Society's financial difficulties during the summer had helped increase private contributions, especially from trustees. By November, the trustees had contributed nearly $1 million, with six trustees giving $100,000 or more. Although only time would tell whether such levels of giving were sustainable, the increases reduced the projected operating deficit and seemed to indicate that the Society was moving in the right direction.

By the end of November, public opinion had shifted in the Society's favor. An article in the *New York Times* trumpeted the improving situation. Discussing the Society's $2 million deficit, John Macomber said, "There would be no credibility for this institution if the trustees didn't raise the $2 million, which we think is a lead-pipe cinch. . . . The trustees have responded very well."[6] Staff members spoke of the positive impact that Debs was having on the institution. Holly Hotchner, the director of the Society's painting conservation department, said, "All these years can't be turned around in a few months. But every correct step that can be taken, at this point, is being taken. Every hard question is being asked." Comparing staff morale under Debs with the situation under Bell, Karen Buck, the Society's assistant director of development, said that "it's the difference between night and day."

Programmatically speaking, Debs had galvanized her staff behind the goal of protecting the collections, which was not surprising given the nature of the publicity that led to the resignation of the Society's previous administration. In January, the Society announced the opening of two separate conservation laboratories, one for books and one for paper and manuscripts. In an article announcing the opening of the two new labs, Debs spoke about the importance of preserving the collections: "Conservation is our top priority. . . . Our collections have to be restored so that they can be accessible to the public."[7]

Working with the advisory committee during this period, Debs and her staff developed a long-term financial and programmatic plan for the Society, which was first brought to the trustees for discussion in January 1989. It should be pointed out that the first steps in this planning process had been carried out by the advisory committee. Options that had been rejected by the committee included the possibility of selling or otherwise divesting either the library or the museum, merging with another institution, liquidation, and relocation to less expensive facilities. The committee had determined that saving the Society in something close to its present form was important. In addition, the committee was working on a new mission statement for the Society that would be "re-directed in emphasis, somewhat restricted in content, but not essentially different in kind" and had determined that the Society should remain in New York City in its present building. Having determined these initial variables, the Society constructed what came to be known as the "bridge plan." It detailed the steps along a three-year path that would lead to institutional stability for the Society.

The bridge plan was, in a word, ambitious. The Society's stated goal was to be "a premier resource for the study and teaching of all aspects of the history of New York City, New York State and the early United States represented in our collections." Emanating from the revised mission statement and opinions expressed by the advisory committee, "the basic premise of the plan [was] that every aspect of the Society [was] considered a part of the whole, that the approach to planning and programs must be comprehensive, and that every activity will be both multipurpose and multifaceted." To be successful, both the staff and the board agreed that the Society had to address three major priorities in its plan: "(1) to gain better control of its collections through comprehensive programs of conservation, preservation, collections maintenance and management; (2) to more than double its public programming, which entails a reduced schedule of exhibitions but renovation of permanent galleries with installations that would demonstrate the Society's new mission; and (3) to raise $10 million in bridge financing to stabilize the Society's financial structure, support the foregoing goals, and enable the implementation of a critical $25 million endowment campaign." The basic elements of the plan were commendable; however, a closer look at the details reveals the enormous challenge that lay ahead if the bridge plan was to succeed.

A descriptive example of part of the plan best illustrates the point. Work on the collections, one of the three elements of the plan, included a listing of twenty-three separate action items. Each of these items represented substantial investments in staff time, capital improvements, or both. The twenty-three items were broken down into three sections: conservation, cataloging, and collections refinement. Listed here are the nine items associated with conservation of the collections:

1. Complete a conservation survey of major object collections.
2. Proceed with the priority conservation program of paintings and works on paper (include rehousing).
3. Complete funding and construction of a painting study/storage area.
4. Develop a plan for a study/storage center for works on paper.
5. Devise a conservation housing access plan for architectural materials, prints, photographs, and maps.
6. Review off-site storage needs for all collections.
7. Develop an overall preservation plan for library collections.

8. Proceed with conservation, rehousing, and reproduction of library materials.
9. Expand the paper and book conservation capability to accommodate the needs of the material.

The ambitious nature of the goals was not limited to conservation; listings showed similar objectives for cataloging and collections management. For example, in cataloging, it was deemed important to "develop a *single* data base for all collections; data base to be able to receive *visual information*." Other objectives included completing an inventory of object collections, cataloging the library collections, restructuring and strengthening the museum department, and reviewing and adopting a space plan for new study/storage locations. Goals for refining the collections included a review of "*all* collections in light of mission statement" and development of a plan for reshaping the collections through deaccessioning and selective acquisitions.

These goals represented only one-third of the plan. The objectives for improving the Society's programs and financial reporting systems were similarly exhaustive and comprehensive. The point of recounting this plan in such detail is not to debate the merits of specific items but rather to show the magnitude of the task the Society was setting for itself. Any one of the components of the plan would have been challenging; to pursue them all simultaneously was a monumental undertaking.

Of course, the important question was, how was the Society going to pay for these initiatives? Table 6.1 shows the projected operating expenses and revenues for 1989–1992, the period of the bridge plan. The total operating budget was to begin at $6.5 million and increase at a rate of 5 percent per year. Given the challenging and comprehensive nature of the Society's operating plan, there is some question whether it would be possible to limit expenditures to that level and growth rate; however, even if operating outlays were held to $6.5 million, the Society would require very high levels of contributed income in order to balance the budget. Such a significant undertaking would require complete commitment of the Society's board of trustees.

Revenues to pay for this expenditure base were to come from four sources: fundraising, investment income, earned income, and public support. Because the Society's unrestricted endowment was small, investment income would cover a small part of the total ($900,000, or 14 percent, in 1990). With attendance averaging just 45,000 between 1986 and 1989, earned income could not play a dominant role either ($1 million, or 15 percent). Public funding, which would include government grants as well as direct operating support from the city and state, was budgeted at $800,000 in 1990, $900,000 in 1991, and $1,250,000 in 1992. Of course, this income was not at all assured and represented a key element of the plan. Regular public appropriations, even if they were relatively small, would

TABLE 6.1. BRIDGE PLAN PROJECTIONS, 1989–1992 (THOUSANDS OF DOLLARS, FISCAL YEAR ENDING JUNE 30).

		Bridge Phase		
	1989	1990	1991	1992
Operating Expenditures				
Operating expenditures	6,500	6,500	6,825	7,166
One-time capital expenditures	800			
Inflation (compounded at 5%)		325	341	358
Operating expenditures	6,500	6,825	7,166	7,525
Operating Revenues				
Fundraising	4,700	6,133	6,433	7,083
Bridge support (foundations)		3,333	3,333	3,333
Trustee giving		1,100	1,200	1,500
Individual giving		700	700	700
Foundations		600	700	800
Corporations		400	500	750
Public funds: grants and appropriations		800	900	1,250
Earned income	900	1,000	1,400	1,400
Investment income	900	900	1,100	1,250
Projected operating revenues	5,600	8,033	8,933	9,733
Surplus to unrestricted endowment	(900)	1,208	1,767	2,208
Capital campaign to endowment		5,000	5,000	5,000
Deaccessioning to restricted endowment		3,333	3,333	3,333
	6/30/89			6/30/92
Unrestricted endowment (approximate)	9,500			28,000
Restricted endowment (approximate)	4,000			14,000

Source: New-York Historical Society records.

send an important signal to private contributors about the Society's future. The rest of the operating budget was to be covered by fundraising of various kinds, all of which was subject to significant risk. The bridge funding, to be raised from a consortium of private foundations, was projected to amount to a total of $10 million, or $3.3 million per year (51 percent of all private fundraising in 1990). Trustee giving was budgeted at $1.1 million, $1.2 million, and $1.5 million for the three years. Individual, other foundation, and corporate giving was budgeted at a total of $1.7 million, $1.9 million, and $2.25 million.

On top of this operating support, the Society also intended to launch a capital campaign to raise $5 million per year during the bridge period. If all of the pieces were to fall into place, by June 1992, the Society would have an unrestricted endowment of approximately $28 million and a restricted endowment of $14 million, a sound base from which to begin a second phase of its long-term plan.[8]

The Society and its staff continued to take major steps forward, even before the advisory committee had issued its report. During early 1989, Debs and her staff successfully negotiated two contracts with unions representing Society workers, reorganized the administration into four departments (museum, library, external affairs, and finance and administration), restructured the public programming and installation planning to ensure that the programs and galleries reflected the new mission in a unified way, and secured the support of Community Board 7 of the Upper West Side, the community group that had been most vocal in opposing the Society in its effort to develop its real estate in the mid 1980s.

One aspect of Debs's reorganization that would have a lasting impact concerned how responsibility for management of the collections would be divided between the museum and the library. Specifically, responsibility for management of the prints, photographs, and architectural drawings was shifted from the library to the museum. Unlike the extensive discussion on the topic that had taken place at the trustee level during the early 1970s, when this step was discussed and rejected, this time the action was an administrative decision. In the opinion of many members of the Society's professional staff, the prints, photos, and architectural drawings had been neglected by the library. Debs believed that the leadership in the museum was better qualified to make use of these collections. She did not regard her decision to move the collections to the museum as a permanent step; in fact, she thought the prints, photos, and drawings would eventually be relocated to their own department, under leadership with proper experience in the special care of these types of materials.[9] Nevertheless, in the long-standing rivalry and competition for resources between the museum and the library, the change in organizational responsibility for these collections was a victory for the museum and was seen as an early signal to staff about which part of the organization would be emphasized in the Debs administration.

In April 1989, the advisory committee issued its report and presented it to the Society's board of trustees. The report could not have been more positive about the importance of the Society, its collections, and the progress that had been made during Debs's tenure as interim director. In its introduction, the report commented on the Society's improved prospects. "Morale is higher, there is a clear sense of direction, and a small but important improvement has been made in the Society's financial situation. There is no substitute for leadership and Dr. Debs has been providing that in a very effective way. . . . Our experience with the Society leads us to believe that the Society is capable of thriving and fulfilling its important mission."

The advisory committee's report identified three overriding issues the Society had to face: What is the Society's mission? Can that mission be financed, and if so, how? And what are the organizational implications of these decisions on operations? As part of its report, the committee proposed a new revised mission statement; identified short, intermediate, and long-term financial goals; recommended that the Society develop a multiyear capital budget for renovating its building; and take steps to develop its real estate assets only after the other recommendations had been implemented.

The advisory committee recommended that the Society adopt the following new mission statement:

The mission of The New-York Historical Society is to promote research and provide education concerning the social, political, economic, and cultural history of New York City, its environs, and the State of New York from earliest times to the present; and of the American experience from the early years of the nation, with a primary focus on the strengths of its 17th, 18th, and 19th century collections on through the Civil War period. To attain this mission the Society shall collect, preserve, and make available materials that document that history. This mission will be carried out through programs including research services, publications, exhibitions, and other education programs. In the pursuit of its programs, the Society should cooperate and coordinate its activities with appropriate institutions. Achieving this mission will contribute to a broader understanding of the history of the region and nation.

The recommended mission statement did not represent a radical departure from the statement that had been in effect, but committee members thought it achieved four objectives. First, because it was more precise, committee members believed that it related the Society's programs to its resources more effectively. Second, they thought that the new mission statement required the Society to recognize that it was not just a museum or a library but that its appeal lay in the integration of its varied collections, through which it could make history meaningful. Third, the new mission statement emphasized the educational responsibility of the Society. Fourth, the mission statement was to guide the Society in refining its collections, in terms of both acquisitions and selective and careful deaccessions. The committee was quite specific that deaccessioning should not be thought of as a solution to the Society's financial problems. It stated that "great care should be taken to insure that proceeds from deaccessioning are not used for operating purposes except for specific instances related to the collections."

The advisory committee recommended a series of short-, intermediate-, and long-term financial goals. Because the committee had been working in concert with Debs and her staff, these goals paralleled those that had been outlined in Debs's bridge plan. For the short term, the committee emphasized not only the absolute necessity that the Society balance its fiscal 1989 budget but also that it "raise adequate funds annually so that operating deficits are eliminated." The intermediate step called for the Society to raise $10 million from a consortium of private foundations and public sources to pay for care of the collections, to maintain public programs, and to begin to carry out deferred maintenance on the Society's landmark building, all within a balanced budget. The long-term goal of the plan was to launch a campaign to raise $25 million in endowment by 1995.

The committee's report discussed the first and most immediate goal—the Society's fiscal 1989 budget deficit—at length. The progress that the Society had made toward closing that deficit was perhaps the most significant reason for the committee's optimism about the Society's long-term future. The committee noted that seven months into the 1989 fiscal year, the Society's board of trustees had reduced the projected deficit by 41.5 percent, from $1,190,000 to $700,000. The report also highlighted the fact that the $700,000 year-to-date deficit from July through March was a significant improvement over the previous year's deficit of over $2 million. The committee was most congratulatory regarding the commitment shown by the trustees, reporting that deficit reduction came almost exclusively on the revenue side and almost totally through increased trustee contributions. "More money has been raised since September for operating purposes than ever before, with the trustees themselves having contributed over $1.3 million in funds and gifts-in-kind during the present fiscal year."

Concluding its report, the advisory committee emphasized several programmatic improvements at the Society: the planning of major new public outreach programs and exhibitions, the exploration of affiliations with other cultural institutions, the opening of a state-of-the-art paper conservation lab, and the improvement in private and public fundraising efforts. "The Society appears to have put aside the distractions caused by its financial crisis and its problems of last summer. . . . Its public image and reputation have markedly improved as the Society moves vigorously ahead." The Macomber report stressed that "the future success of the Society depends on the quality of its leadership, including the staff and the trustees." With the presentation of the report, the Society took steps to solidify that leadership.

Pursuing a Bold Agenda, 1989–1991

During the Macomber committee evaluation, the Society had been overseen by a transition chairman and an interim chief executive. Permanent leadership was now needed, and Albert Key, who had served as president (now called chairman) of the board during the transition period, stepped down, and Norman Pearlstine (at the time managing editor of the *Wall Street Journal*) was elected to replace him. At that same meeting, Barbara Debs was named permanent president of the Society.

In an article in the *New York Times* announcing her appointment, Debs discussed her efforts to revitalize the Society: "Apart from assuring financial stability and getting our collections in order, the next step is to make our collections completely available to people so that we can be an active institution in the teaching of history. We want to create more and different public programs, and give the Society a new look with more creative installations."[10]

Though her public comments at the time were optimistic, her consultations with the Society's board made it strikingly clear that she had few illusions about the difficulty of the task that lay ahead. As was previously mentioned, she had specifically stated upon being named interim director that she did not want to be considered for the permanent post; however, the Society needed permanent leadership, and since the board had not even begun a search, she decided to accept the post.

As part of her employment contract, Debs required that the board express its commitment to a set of principles. These principles, which were recorded in the minutes, were as follows:

- Recognition of the complexity and difficulty of the Society's situation and that it cannot be "business as usual"
- Recognition of the need for substantial fundraising for the Society over the longer term and a commitment to work with Debs to give or get the necessary funds
- Acknowledgment that deaccessioning alone will not solve the problems of the Society
- Full support of the "Bridge Plan" as set forth in the draft of January 23, 1989 presented to the board and the chart presented at the recent meeting of the executive committee
- Agreement to the need for strong staff and administrative support to enable Dr. Debs to achieve her objectives
- Agreement to work with Debs to elect more trustees to the board who will support the foregoing

With the advisory committee's work finished, the commitment of the board on record, and the staff reorganization accomplished, Debs and her staff pressed ahead with the bridge plan. In May, a new vice president for finance and administration was hired to oversee the personnel, security, and maintenance departments as well as to coordinate financial reporting systems and overall adherence to budgets. Work progressed on a ten-year museum conservation, rehousing, and storage plan; a building master plan; and the beginnings of a library preservation plan. On the fundraising side, the Society's staff submitted a major proposal to the National Endowment for the Humanities for a $1 million challenge grant (to be matched on a four-to-one basis), began aggressively to pursue public support from both the city and the state in the form of line-item funding and a bond act, and received the first significant contribution toward the bridge plan by securing a $1 million three-year grant from The Andrew W. Mellon Foundation (to be matched two to one).

As has been mentioned, the Society had established the preservation and conservation of its collections as its highest priority. The second priority was to more than double the number of public programs. With these two areas of initiative emphasized, management was aware that it could not continue to mount a regular program of rotating exhibitions. In fact, it was decided that aside from a small number of permanent exhibitions designed to feature the Society's new integrated approach to displaying its varied collections, the exhibition program would be postponed for three years.

Given that postponement, it seemed a stroke of great fortune when the Society discovered that the Jewish Museum was looking for exhibition space to maintain a public presence while it expanded and renovated its building. For the Society, such a novel arrangement represented an opportunity to increase its attendance, introduce a new clientele to its collections, and take a symbolic step toward greater inclusiveness. The Society's administrative offices and permanent exhibitions were going to be open anyway, so the Society's leadership did not anticipate incurring significant additional expenses as a result of the arrangement. Furthermore, the Society assumed that the Jewish Museum collaboration would attract thousands of additional visitors, making it possible to cover any additional marginal costs with voluntary admissions contributions and visitor-related earned income. In June 1989, the Society entered into an agreement to provide space for the Jewish Museum for two years, from January 1991 until December 1992.

Maintaining its positive momentum, the Society's leadership took steps to strengthen its board. In September 1989, a new class of trustees was elected that included some very highly regarded members. The new trustees were Marian Castell, founder of the Bank of Darien, in Connecticut; Joe Flom, a partner in the law firm Skadden, Arps, Slate, Meagher & Flom; Richard Jenrette, chairman of the Equitable Life Assurance Society; Pat Klingenstein, a member of the New York State Museum in Albany; John Macomber, former chairman and CEO of the Celanese Corporation and chairman of the advisory committee; Ronald Perelman, chairman and CEO of Revlon, Inc.; John Reed, chairman and CEO of Citicorp and Citibank; Linda Gosden Robinson, president of the communications firm Robinson, Lake, Lerer & Montgomery; Jack Sheinkman, president of the Amalgamated Clothing and Textile Workers Union; and Michael von Clemm, chairman of Merrill Lynch Capital Markets.

Just as this illustrious new class of trustees was ushered in to oversee the Society's new era, bad news came from Allen Greenberg, the architect hired to implement certain aspects of the Society's new master space plan. At the September meeting, Greenberg discussed "the status of the building" and "the consequences of delayed maintenance" and stressed that "after the building has been renovated, constant maintenance would always be necessary." Evidently, the condition of the building was so severe that the safety of the collections was in doubt. The roof was in particularly bad shape and would require emergency repair independent of other long-term work that needed to be done. The Society allocated $125,000 for that work while it hired building consultants to assess the total amount of work that was needed.

The bill for the Society's deferred maintenance had come due. After extensive study over several months, it was determined the Society's eighty-five-year-old building was badly in need of $10 to $12 million worth of repairs. These were not capital improvements, as had been budgeted in the bridge plan; they were repairs required to make the building safe to house the Society's valuable collections. Concern for the collections being paramount, the Society decided to move more of its collections into off-site storage, this time with the requirement that the storage facilities be absolutely first-rate. Neither the capital repairs nor the cost of first-class off-site storage had been factored into the Society's operations budget, although some of these costs were later funded with restricted grants.

To make matters worse, the investigation by the New York State attorney general had still not been resolved. Nearly a year after launching the official inquiry, the attorney general's office continued to probe deeply into all aspects of the Society's operations. In a report to the board of trustees, Barbara Debs described the effect of the investigation in this way: "The long delay in closure of this matter has had serious consequences . . . on nearly every front (for example, more aggressive fund-raising would have been possible if this matter had been settled in a timely fashion). This though is not offered as an excuse. . . . This has been a crisis year, so one can accept, while protesting, the continuing presence of the AG as part of that crisis. . . . [But] it will be ironic and tragic if the AG's continuing interest in us prevents us from building on our success."

In a letter to the attorney general written in June 1990, Norman Pearlstine described in detail the impact of the continuing investigation on fundraising, board building, press relations, and staff time. Pearlstine wrote that major donors had indicated their reluctance to assist the Society as long as the investigation remained active. Pearlstine indicated that attracting new board members and generating positive press were similarly inhibited by the shadow of the investigation.

But perhaps the most damaging aspect of the continuing investigation were the costs—both direct and indirect—to an institution whose resources were already depleted. Pearlstine wrote of the "enormous amount of staff time and energy (hence salaries) consumed by the investigation. All senior staff, in a very thinly staffed institution, have been heavily involved in providing information and professional expertise. Our new president estimates that she has spent fully a quarter of her time on this matter in the ten months she has been at the Society." There were direct costs as well. Pearlstine reported that as of July 17, 1989, the Society had spent "in excess of $600,000—nearly 10 percent of our total operating budget—on legal fees connected with the investigation." By the time the investigation was concluded, the Society would spend approximately $1 million on legal fees.

In March 1990, twenty months after the investigation was launched, the attorney general and the Society finally reached an agreement that closed the investigation. The attorney general *required* that the Society "prepare an annual balanced budget and report periodically to the Attorney General on the status of its budget for the balance of this fiscal year and for the following four years." The settlement also addressed the Society's endowment management practices of the 1980s, saying that "for many years, the New-York Historical Society expended portions of its endowment to pay for its operating expenses. The Society will now curtail that practice and focus more of its attention towards aggressive fundraising in the future."[11] Finally, the attorney general would monitor the management of the Society's collections, requiring the Society to notify the attorney general in advance of selling items from its collections.

Just eight months after accepting the permanent post as president and a little over a year after coming back to the Society to serve as interim director, Debs faced a critical situation, and she knew it. In an annual report written in December 1989, Debs outlined the severity of the situation: "On the one hand, unparalleled opportunity exists to realize at last the full potential of the Society and its great collections. . . . On the other, the long-ignored financial needs of the Society's collections, endowment and building, . . . coming together and requiring immediate and simultaneous solution, threaten the very existence of the institution." She articulated the challenge presented by the Society's new mission statement, which, she wrote, required nothing less than "institutional transformation." Although the new statement does not appear upon first reading to be radically different from the original, Debs noted that "in reality, . . . it requires a profound change in emphasis. By stressing our role as an educational institution, it requires us to take an active, outreaching stance toward our public rather than merely accumulating material. . . . It redefines the essence of the Society's being, and offers us the challenge and the opportunity of demonstrating that an institution founded by a small group of white gentlemen, long viewed as a bastion of privilege, . . .

can remake itself into an open, expansive and inclusive actor of value and vitality in a heterogenous society."

To pursue such laudable goals is one thing; to pay for them is another. Debs continued:

> There is simply not enough endowment to support the necessary staff and programs. In addition, the opportunity to earn income through attendance and membership is severely limited. . . . Nor . . . does [the Society] receive public funding on an ongoing basis. . . . Other sources must be found to cover the operating shortfall, [and] the endowment must be restored and greatly increased. And in addition, the recently identified imperative and immediate needs of our landmark building must be met. We are, that is to say, required to raise large amounts of money annually simply to operate. We must raise even larger amounts for endowment to protect the institution for the future. And we must raise large amounts immediately to ensure that our building . . . can adequately house and protect our collections. . . . Because basic needs have so long been neglected, nothing can wait.

Debs pointed out that the Society owned tremendously valuable assets and that they should not escape scrutiny: "We must examine our asset base, which is enormous and inert (our collections worth at least a billion dollars, our land and building about 45 million) to see whether there are ways it can be made to work for us." Concluding her report, Debs posed a series of rhetorical questions: "Can a private . . . underfunded institution with enormous value to the public continue to serve that public if entirely privately funded? Can the Society continue to exist in its present form and in its present location? It is time for the Board and staff to seriously examine the alternatives available to us with courage and imagination and in deadly earnest."

The most distressing aspect of the problems Debs described is that they were not long-range issues that could be put off or addressed over a long period of time. The capital repairs on the roof, the legal fees, and the expansion of the Society's programs had to be paid for, exerting added pressure on the Society's already depleted cash reserves. The Society was facing a cash flow shortage. At the time of Debs's annual report, the board took its first step to alleviate the cash problem; it passed a resolution canceling all board-imposed restrictions on funds, thereby freeing money to be used for unrestricted purposes.

Almost before it was even begun, then, the bridge plan in its original form was no longer viable. Not only did the Society's plan not include the unforeseen expenditures, but it also underestimated the cost of carrying out the basic programmatic objectives. An internal Society memo prepared in February 1990 presented a revised version of the plan, outlining three-year financial needs for operations, building, and endowment (see Table 6.2). The most notable changes were an increase in the initial operating budget, which went from $6.5 million to $7.8 million, and increases in expected government funding. In concluding a progress report on the bridge plan to the board, Debs indicated that "in order to accommodate current levels of operations in balance and the immediate needs of the building, we will require close to $40 million. In order to achieve the longer term goals of financial soundness, balanced operating budgets and growth, we will require either continuing massive fund-raising for operations annually or significant additions to endowment, or a combination thereof for the foreseeable future."

As the second half of the 1990 fiscal year progressed, it became clear that the Society was going to have difficulty balancing its budget. Revenues were running far behind projections. Efforts to convince the state and city to provide regular ongoing support took on added urgency. In January, the board unanimously resolved that "the chairman of the board and the president undertake discussions with the City and file such papers as may be necessary to qualify the Society for membership in the Cultural Institutions Group (CIG)."[12] The Society had waited 112 years after the Metropolitan Museum of Art first received operating funds from New York City to apply officially for unrestricted city funding. To emphasize the importance of this support, the board again formally ratified the resolution at its March meeting.

Knowing that getting onto the city's budget was a long-term project, management focused on raising unrestricted funds through private contributions. In March, Debs formally presented the bridge plan and associated budgets to the board and asked the board "to recognize the scale of the undertaking and the need for full board commitment to the required fundraising effort."

The Society's board and staff were unable to produce the necessary revenue to balance the 1990 budget, and the Society incurred a deficit of $1.9 million. To reassure constituencies that might have been concerned about the deficit, management pointed to the fact that the deficit had been reduced in each of the previous three years and that the Society would have a balanced budget for 1991. Debs noted that intense lobbying was under way with city officials to try to get the city to pay for the Society's energy costs and to get programmatic support, steps that could lead to formal inclusion in the CIG.

By the fall of 1990, both the board and Debs knew that the Society had reached a pivotal point. One of the trustees, Gordon Pattee, called fiscal 1991 "a critical year," and Debs called it a "make-or-break" year. The four major areas of emphasis were the building repairs, the massive collections work, expanding the public programming, and, underlying it all, the major fundraising effort. Particularly important was the need to raise unrestricted operating funds to ease the

TABLE 6.2.   MODIFIED BRIDGE PLAN PROJECTIONS, 1990–1992 (THOUSANDS OF DOLLARS, FISCAL YEAR ENDING JUNE 30).

	Bridge Phase		
	1990	1991	1992
Operating Expenditures			
Operating expenditures	7,800	8,200	8,600
Operating Revenues			
Fundraising	5,625	5,150	4,500
Bridge support (foundations)	4,500	4,500	4,500
Additional trustee giving	1,125	650	0
Government grants	0	700	700
CIG funds from New York City	0	2,000	2,000
Earned income	1,400	2,200	2,500
Investment income[a]	775	850	1,825
Operating revenues	7,800	8,200	8,825
Surplus to unrestricted endowment	0	0	225
Additional capital fundraising	500	4,000	8,000
Capital campaign to endowment	0	5,000	10,000

[a] Part of investment income is dependent on successful endowment fundraising in 1991 and 1992.

Source: New-York Historical Society records.

Society's impending cash flow crisis. "The extraordinary challenge of the year ahead," Debs said, "will be dealing with the cash situation."

The Society was late preparing its 1991 budget and did not present it to the board until September, three months into the fiscal year. James Griffin, the Society's treasurer, pointed out that the fiscal 1991 budget represented the first time the budget process had been properly managed to include the preparation of a business plan and adequate internal reviews. Griffin also stated that it was the first time the Society had ever generated a cash flow forecast. Still, although processes had been improved and the Society was projecting a balanced budget, meeting that budget would require incredibly high levels of private fundraising. In fiscal 1990, the Society had generated gifts and pledges of approximately $9.2 million. Though this was an impressive figure, much of it was in the form of multi-year restricted grants. In terms of operating funds, the Society had raised $3.7 million, $2.6 million short of its goal of $6.4 million. For fiscal 1991, the Society established a total operations fundraising goal of $7.8 million, more than twice the amount it had been able to raise in the previous year. Because of the rapidly diminishing cash reserves, Griffin reemphasized that meeting the unrestricted contributions component of the goal was absolutely critical. The goal in the fiscal 1991 budget for unrestricted contributions was $3.9 million, $1.5 million (43 percent) more than had been raised in 1990.

Were these fundraising goals reasonable? Perhaps not, but the primary body that committed to them, the Society's board of trustees, was the same entity responsible for attaining them. It is not difficult to understand how the Society found itself in such a predicament. First, society leadership had worked with the advisory committee to establish an extremely ambitious set of goals for the level of services it should and would provide. Second, it had sold its primary stakeholders, including government officials, the general public, and its own programmatic staff, on the importance of those goals, various elements of which were crucial for gaining the support of a wide range of constituencies. And third, it had those goals further validated by the settlement of the attorney general's investigation, but with the added *requirement* that the Society submit balanced budgets for the next four years. With all of the programmatic elements in place and despite a great deal of positive momentum for its renewed public service role, the Society found itself with neither the cash nor the types of assets needed to generate the cash flow to fulfill its promise. This combination of developments left Society leadership with essentially two choices: (1) publicly give up on the plan that had so recently been launched and restructure or possibly dismantle the Society or (2) take a leap of faith, hoping that by becoming a more inclusive and public-service-minded institution, it could enlarge its base of potential funders, both private and public. It chose the latter.

Seeking Affiliations, 1991–1992

The Society's leadership had to be initially encouraged by its improving public reputation. An article in the *New York Times* reviewing the Society's new exhibition "Paris 1889: American Artists at the Universal Exposition" was positively glowing: "Visitors will immediately sense a place different in spirit from the dour institution that was there before."[13] The article also identified and discussed various new initiatives at the Society, stating that "for an institution that for decades had shown scant interest in the public it ostensibly served, all of this comes as nothing less than an extraordinary change of affairs." These developments underscore "the impression that the Society is finally in capable hands" and are "the most immediate demonstration of the society's new mission to transform itself from a kind of private club into an institution that truly serves the public. . . . There is now the promise, at least, that it will become one of the city's most engaging cultural centers."

The positive public response to its programs, however, did not translate into increases in the Society's unrestricted cash balances. The Society's cash flow problems grew even more acute in late 1990 and early 1991, and management feared at one point that it would not be able to make payroll. The Society was able to avert a crisis when it secured a $1 million one-year loan from the Golden Family Foundation, which was collateralized with the Society's neighboring townhouse on Seventy-Sixth Street.

Although the loan solved the Society's immediate cash problem, it did not begin to address the long-term structural financial problems Debs had first discussed in her 1989 year-end report. Debs was further handicapped in her efforts to correct the Society's financial situation by the fact that she had been unable to replace her financial vice president, who resigned in September 1990. The Society was unable to find a qualified candidate willing to take the position at a salary level the Society could afford to pay.[14]

By March 1991, the treasurer reported that the Society had incurred an operating deficit of nearly $2.5 million over the first eight months of the fiscal year and "that the forecast for the final three months . . . was still bleak." To make matters worse, the Society learned that the National Endowment for the Humanities had declined its application for a major challenge grant. The Society had been optimistic about its chances of being awarded the grant, and the news was an enormous disappointment to Society leadership. In addition, there was no reason to be optimistic about receiving operating support from the city. With the passage of time, fewer and fewer options remained for the Society to dig its way out of its financial predicament. The combination of continuing operating deficits and the addition of $1 million of debt forced the board to question the Society's long-term viability as an independent institution. Under the cover of strict confidentiality, the focus of the Society's leadership shifted from overseeing the implementation of the bridge plan to investigating whether a more radical solution might be feasible. Some ideas under consideration included merging with another cultural entity, affiliating with an educational institution, moving the Society to a less expensive location, and closing the Society.

As the board focused on assessing long-term options, the Society's staff continued to implement the programmatic initiatives laid out in the bridge plan. Major work continued on the comprehensive collections management plan, especially for the Society's museum collections. The Society's collections of paintings and drawings, sculptures, decorative arts, and silver had been surveyed, cataloged, and had undergone conservation treatment. Work continued on the architectural drawings, especially the Cass Gilbert collection, and on the monumental task of surveying, cataloging, and storing hundreds of thousands of prints and photographs. Library staff was in the process of preparing a five-year conservation plan based on the results of a general library collections survey conducted by Hendrik Edelman of Rutgers University.

By gaining control of its collections, the Society hoped to be better positioned to offer exhibitions and educational programs. An example of this strategy was the Luman Reed Gallery. Five years in the making, this gallery was "the first in a planned series of interpretive re-installations of the permanent collections, integrating Museum and Library materials according to carefully conceptualized, humanistic themes." Using period furniture and other objects from the decorative arts collection, along with books and manuscripts from the library, and of course, the paintings from Luman Reed's collection, the gallery was a re-creation of the private gallery that Reed maintained in his home on Greenwich Street in 1832.

In addition to the efforts to gain control of the collections and to increase public access to them, the second priority of the Society's plan was to double public programming. It was hoped that improving the Society's public reputation for community outreach might lead to increased contributions. As Debs put it, "The more we work on presenting our collections and programs to the public, the closer we get to becoming an indispensable institution." The Society's public programming efforts were centered in two areas: a public panel, film, and music series titled "Why History?" which attracted three thousand visitors in its first fall season, and several programs addressed more directly to teachers and schools. The spring 1991 "Why History?" series focused on race and class in New York City. The keynote lecture in the series was by Cornel West and was titled "The Role of Visionary Leadership." Six other panel discussions followed, titled "Historical Perspectives," "Contemporary Issues," "Bridging the Gap," "Responsibility, Change, and Power," "Life and Survival in the City," and "Prejudice and the 'Other' New Yorker." Five of the thirteen "Why History?" programs were sellouts, and the total series averaged more than two hundred attendees per event and were warmly received by their audiences. Detailed surveys were given to audiences that allowed the Society to track audience demographics and to get feedback to determine how it could improve the programs.

The Society also offered public programming that fulfilled more directly the educational component of its mission. One such program was the curricula development project at the William J. O'Shea Junior High School (Intermediate School 44), the Society's neighboring intermediate school. A short-range goal of the project was to enable teachers "to utilize the Society's collections in ways that allow for new approaches to the teaching of American history and art." The longer-term goal was to familiarize students at a young age with the Society's collections and to help develop within them the knowledge and skills that would allow them to become regular users of museums and research libraries. The work at O'Shea was extremely well received by school administrators.[15] In addition, in recognition of the program's model application, Fordham University offered credit to interns in its history program for participation in the project. Although the Society limited participation to this single school while the curricula were being tested, it was hoped that the program would be replicable at schools throughout the city.

The success of the various Society programs notwithstanding, it was clear to the board that without significant and regular government funding or a huge private gift, the Society simply could not sustain its current level of activity and remain independent. The 1991 fiscal year, the "make-or-break" year, ended with a $2.4 million deficit. Even though the board was evaluating long-term options, it had continued to operate the Society at nearly full capacity, with a large staff and a fairly complete set of programs. The total budget for fiscal 1991 was the Society's largest ever, with expenses at $8.2 million. However, no long-term solution had been found.

Norman Pearlstine, the Society's chairman, discussed the fact that the Society could no longer afford to continue in a "business as usual" mode. He emphasized to the board that "it is crucial to seek some kind of partnership or other arrangement which will preserve the Society's collections and continue to make them available to scholars and the public." He then discussed a series of possible long-term options for the Society, including a possible merger with the Museum of the City of New York (MCNY).[16]

A merger between the Society and the MCNY offered a variety of potential benefits. For one, the MCNY is a member of the CIG and therefore receives annual appropriations from New York City. In 1991, it received over 30 percent of its operating budget from the city's Department of Cultural Affairs. Presumably, a merged institution could expect to receive continuing operating support at a comparable level. Second, the MCNY's building and real estate are owned by the city, and a capital appropriation of $11 million had already been made to refurbish the physical plant. If the merged institution were to move to the Society's location, it presented the possibility for the MCNY building to be sold, for the $11 million capital appropriation to be transferred to the new entity to be used for work on the Society's building, and for additional capital to be raised through a sale-leaseback arrangement with the city. In addition, from an operating standpoint, both institutions estimated that there would be 25 percent savings in operating costs as compared with the costs of the two independent entities. The final and, from a curatorial standpoint, most compelling reason for a merger was the complementarity between the two collections. The MCNY's strength in portraits, toys, and theatrical memorabilia would fit well with the Society's strengths, giving a combined institution a truly incomparable collection documenting the history of New York City and State.

Over the summer, Debs and her counterpart at the MCNY, Robert Mac-Donald, exchanged comprehensive and detailed information about all aspects of their institutions. Each agreed that nothing short of a complete merger would make sense and that such a merger would require significant financial support from both the city and the state. A special task force of the Society's board was established to evaluate the possible merger. The difficult job of addressing the Society's financial problems continued. For the third consecutive year, the Society's budget had to be approved by the executive committee and was not presented to the full board until September, even though the fiscal year began July 1. Once again, the budget relied heavily on grants and contributions for revenue, but significant cuts in expenditures were proposed for the first time since 1989. The 1992 budget was trimmed by approximately $1.5 million. The reductions were to be accomplished through layoffs and attrition; by closing the Society for an additional day each week (that is, operating only five days per week); by closing the museum shop, which had lost money on direct costs as long as it had been in operation; and by general belt-tightening across the board. Debs indicated that the 1992 budget was very thin and that it did not represent a healthy level of institutional operation on an ongoing basis.

On the revenue side, Debs reemphasized the importance of unrestricted contributions to the Society's cash position. She pointed out "that it is the board's obligation to assure that there is sufficient time to work through the alternatives and options . . . in order to realize a new model for the Society." Debs's comments further illustrated the fact that the Society's emphasis was no longer on trying to operate the Society for long-term independent financial success; rather, it was focused on finding a solution through "a new model." At the same September board meeting, Debs announced that she had decided not to renew her contract to serve as president beyond her initial three-year term, which was to end on December 31, 1991. Debs did offer, however, to continue on without a contract beyond that date to lobby the state government in Albany for major support and to oversee continuing negotiations with other institutions about possible mergers and affiliations.[17]

The Society's fundraising efforts were falling far short of expectations. By December, the development committee chairman reported that the Society had been able to raise only $500,000 of a $4 million goal in unrestricted contributions; trustee contributions were lagging far behind the performance of the three previous years. In restricted contributions, the Society was faring better, with $1.5

million of a $2 million goal in hand; however, these grants did nothing to help the Society's depleted unrestricted reserves.

Meanwhile, the discussions between the MCNY and the Society yielded no agreement. In March 1992, the institutions decided to discontinue discussions. It was determined that "the costs of combining the two collections at a single institution proved to be unexpectedly high." A joint statement issued upon the announcement that the two institutions would remain independent said, "Both institutions hold the vision that uniting their unparalleled holdings would be a lasting benefit to New York and the nation. However, current financial and organizational realities indicate that merger would not result in a viable institution at this time."[18]

The published reasons given for the failure of the merger only begin to convey several important factors that prevented the two entities from reaching agreement. First, merging two independent nonprofit institutions is an incredibly difficult task because there is no external market mechanism to force consensus. How does one decide, for example, who will lead the combined entity? If getting a single board to reach a consensus is difficult, getting two separate boards to forge an agreement in a timely way is next to impossible. In this case, it took six months even to get committees of the N-YHS and MCNY boards together for a meeting.[19] Second, the two institutions had problems reaching an agreement because the strengths and weaknesses of their negotiating positions did not make a good match. Because of its cash flow problems, the Society was perceived by the Museum of the City of New York to be the weaker institution, yet the Society wanted the MCNY to give up a tremendous amount, including moving to Central Park West and transferring its capital appropriation to the combined entity. Finally, the mayor did not want to move a major city cultural institution from East One Hundred Third Street, located in an economically and racially mixed neighborhood, to Central Park West, an exclusive neighborhood. Without substantial financial contribution from the city, the deal had absolutely no chance for success.

Given the board leadership's emphasis on finding a creative solution to the Society's troubles, the failure to reach an agreement with the MCNY closed yet another of the few remaining doors open to the Society. With the near-term prospects for a merger gone, the Society set its sights back on the tough job of governing. The board of trustees reinitiated its recruiting process for new trustees, which had been put on hold during the MCNY talks. Debs negotiated a contract with the labor union, giving the Society's workers a 4 percent pay raise, retroactive to the beginning of the year. Having been without a chief financial officer since September 1991, Debs received authorization from the board to retain KPMG/Peat Marwick to assist her in developing financial plans for the 1993 fiscal year. Finally, of greatest importance, the Society's loan from the Golden

Foundation came due in March. The foundation was willing to extend the loan for a month but not to roll the loan over. The Society tried, without success, to retire the loan with contributions from the trustees. Only part of the money was raised when three trustees stepped forward to assume the remainder of the loan, approximately $840,000.

In June 1992, Debs announced her intention to resign her post as president effective September 30, 1992. Debs reminded the board that her contract had expired the previous December. She had stayed on beyond that date to try to convince New York State legislators and the governor that the Society was worthy of major support. Unfortunately, the Society had been unsuccessful in its attempt to win appropriations in the 1993 budgets of either the city or the state of New York. With prospects for city and state help deferred for another year, Debs decided it was time to step down as chief executive officer.[20] She assured her colleagues that she would continue to serve on the board and as chairman of the collections committee. In reviewing her tenure, Debs discussed her bridge plan and its three institutional priorities: (1) emphasize care of the collections, (2) emphasize identity as a great educational resource, and (3) achieve financial stability.

Debs congratulated her staff on the successful attainment of the first two objectives and pointed out that while they had not been successful in reaching the third objective, there had been significant accomplishments. She alluded to the fact that the Society had raised nearly $20 million and that the deficit had been reduced from 54 percent to 20 percent of the operating budget. She listed the major institutional alternative options that had been pursued, the attempts to gain CIG status, the failed effort to merge with the MCNY, discussions with educational institutions regarding possible affiliations, and efforts to receive major assistance from the state of New York. She asserted that "the Society is dependent on either affiliation or merger with another institution or on the infusion of public money on a large scale."

But the Society had been unable to secure such a relationship, so at her final meeting as president, Debs presented a drastically reduced fiscal 1993 budget that she had prepared with the help of KPMG/Peat Marwick. It called for the Society's galleries to close at the end of the term of the Jewish Museum agreement on December 31, 1992. Instead of exhibitions, the museum staff was to concentrate on developing traveling exhibits and publications and to work on identifying works for possible deaccessioning. The library was to remain open to the public twenty-three hours per week, and the duplicate deaccessioning program was to be continued. Through cuts in staffing, principally in security and maintenance, the Society was able to reduce payroll by $600,000. In addition, every nonessential expenditure was eliminated, resulting in a total budget of approximately $5.7 million (approximately $1 million less than for fiscal 1992). Revenues were projected to increase by almost $1 million, to $5.65 million.

As Debs stepped down, the Society was once again careening toward institutional crisis. The 1992 fiscal year ended with a significant deficit, this time $2.5 million. Not only were cash reserves depleted, but the Society had added nearly $1 million of debt to its balance sheet. Though the Debs administration had accomplished a great deal, it had been unable to complete a year of operations without running a deficit. Responsibility for leading the Society along its rocky path passed to Norman Pearlstine, who assumed the role of acting president.

Notes

1. The committee was made up of eleven members: Chairman John Macomber, former chairman and CEO of Celanese Corporation; Ellen V. Futter, president of Barnard College; Vartan Gregorian, president of the New York Public Library; Bernard Harleston, president of City College; Eugene Keilin, general partner in Lazard Frères and director of the Municipal Assistance Corporation; Roger Kennedy, director of the National Museum of American History; Sherman Lee, former director of the Cleveland Museum; Richard Ravitch, chairman of the NYC Charter Revision Committee; John Sawyer, former president of The Andrew W. Mellon Foundation; Richard Shinn, former chairman and CEO of the Metropolitan Life Insurance Company; and Lisa Taylor, former curator at the Cooper-Hewitt Museum.
2. McGill (1988b).
3. Personal communication, Jan. 18, 1995.
4. This and all other unattributed information and quotations are taken from board meeting minutes or other internal documents and records.
5. McGill (1988i).
6. McGill (1988e).
7. Yarrow (1989b).
8. See Chapter Ten for a detailed discussion regarding the distinctions between restricted and unrestricted funds and their uses.
9. Personal communication, Jan. 18, 1995.
10. Yarrow (1989a).
11. Press release, Office of the Attorney General of the State of New York, Mar. 13, 1990.
12. The Cultural Institutions Group is a collection of cultural institutions that receive core operating support from the New York City Department of Cultural Affairs (DCA). Thirty-two CIG organizations were slated to receive funds in the 1995 budget, which totaled $76.2 million. CIG institutions are located in all five boroughs of the city of New York, provide a wide range of programs and services, and receive varying levels of support. Among the institutions in the CIG are the Metropolitan Museum of Art (1995 allocation: $16 million), the American Museum of Natural History ($8 million), the Staten Island Botanic Garden ($167,000), and the Bronx County Historical Society ($222,000).
13. Kimmelman (1990).
14. Personal communication, July 27, 1994.

15. When the Society's financial difficulties again became a matter of public controversy in 1993 and there were accusations that the Society continued to ignore the community, Roger Spry, the vice principal of O'Shea Junior High School, came to the Society's defense. At a meeting of the local community board, Spry explained what a fantastic resource the Society had been for his school and his students and expressed his enthusiastic support for the institution.

16. There is some irony in the possibility of merging the N-YHS and the MCNY. The MCNY was originally established by a group headed by May Van Rensselaer, a disaffected member of the N-YHS who created a crisis for the Society in 1917.

17. Personal communication, Jan. 18, 1995.

18. Honan (1992a).

19. Personal communication, Mar. 23, 1995.

20. Personal communication, Jan. 18, 1995.

CHAPTER SEVEN

RETRENCHMENT AND THE STRUGGLE FOR SURVIVAL, 1992–1994

Closing the Doors

The resignation of Barbara Debs marked the beginning of a period that defies direct comparison to any previous time in the Society's history. The combination of enormous—intransigent—financial problems and a lack of full-time administrative leadership made it impossible for the Society to maintain an organized program of operations. As had been the case for some time, the board's focus could not be on supporting the Society's staff and overseeing their efforts to pursue its programmatic mission; the financial situation was simply too dire for that. At his first board meeting as interim chief executive, in November 1992, Norman Pearlstine reported that the "cash flow situation is much worse than anticipated and unless we receive a cash infusion in the near term, [there is] no other alternative but to close the door at year-end."

At the senior staff level, Debs's departure created a power vacuum that fed a natural and growing rivalry among her three chief deputies: the vice president of external affairs, Juliana Sciolla; the director of the library, Jean Ashton; and the director of the museum, Holly Hotchner. Even in more stable financial times, with a strong full-time administrator at its helm, the Society's multidimensional structure was difficult to manage. Allocating scarce resources between the museum and the library, for example, had always been contentious and difficult.

It was even more so now. Pearlstine recognized that he could not manage the day-to-day operations of an institution in such turmoil on a part-time basis.

In late October, Pearlstine named Sciolla to be his interim chief financial officer. In her role as vice president for external affairs, Sciolla had been responsible for overseeing the development, membership, and public relations offices. She had also been the primary liaison between the Society and state representatives in Albany. Prior to joining the Society, Sciolla had been an administrator at the New York State Council on the Arts. For someone with no experience in financial management, hers was truly going to be a tremendous challenge.

With Sciolla responsible for management of the day-to-day finances, Pearlstine concentrated on pursuing affiliations with other cultural institutions. Of the many contacts Pearlstine initiated, his conversations with the New York Public Library (NYPL) were the most serious and led to the possibility for a major collaboration. On November 19, the NYPL board of trustees approved a plan to consider loaning the Society up to $1.5 million. In an article that appeared in the *New York Times,* Pearlstine explained that even though the Society had "made considerable progress over the past few years in preserving our collections and making them more available to the public, . . . the plain fact is that we have run out of cash and we have run out of time. . . . The library's assistance will give us time to consider appropriate options, including possible affiliations with the library or some other institution."[1] Although Pearlstine did not rule out the possibility of working with other institutions, he indicated that he thought the library provided the best hope for preserving the collections and keeping them in New York City. He added that "the Society's collections are uniquely complementary with" those of the NYPL.

For its part, the NYPL agreed that the Society's library collections were complementary to its own. In fact, because of the strength of the N-YHS library collections, the NYPL had shaped its acquisition policy so as not to duplicate the Society's holdings. Loss of local scholarly access to the N-YHS's collections was viewed by the NYPL as an intolerable prospect. The NYPL's chief interest in helping the Society, then, was to ensure that those collections remained publicly accessible and in New York City.

Closing the loan proved to be far more difficult than announcing an agreement in principle. In conducting its due diligence, five members of the NYPL's financial staff spent three weeks working full time at the Society with Sciolla, learning all they could about the Society's financial situation and evaluating the Society's capacity to repay the loan.

The Society's precarious financial condition mandated that collateral for the loan was going to have to come from the Society's collections. Because of that necessity, the Society had to prove that it was acting within its rights to sell any works it was offering as collateral. In other words, the works had to be legally deaccessioned. Aside from being controversial, this fact meant that the attorney general would once again have to become involved to ensure that proper procedures were being followed.

The process of identifying collections for deaccessioning proved to be complicated, time-consuming, and expensive. Even after Hotchner and the museum staff and Ashton and the library staff had identified valuable items that were peripheral to the Society's core mission, it was difficult to determine whether the Society held clear legal title to the items to be deaccessioned. For many of the Society's early acquisitions, record keeping had been poor, and the provenances of items were not clear. Not only was this identification process painstaking and slow, but because of the sensitivity of the issue, the advice of outside counsel was required to help staff members make these determinations.

With Ashton and Hotchner focused on deaccessioning, Sciolla, whose title was changed from chief financial officer to chief operating officer at the December board meeting, concentrated on trying to manage the Society's cash flow. Sciolla canvassed donors of various restricted appropriations to urge them to remove restrictions on their grants so that the funds could be used to meet general operating expenditures during the transition period. In addition, Sciolla was holding payment on nearly $300,000 in invoices, telling creditors that they would be paid when the NYPL loan became available. Finally, she continued to pursue the cash payments on contributions that had been promised but had not yet been received. Even with these steps, there was some question whether the Society would be able to make its Christmas Eve payroll. In early December, the Society had only $55,000 left in its unrestricted account; its projected December payroll was nearly $140,000.

Negotiations between the library and the Society bogged down. As a nonprofit institution with a fiduciary responsibility to protect assets held in public trust, the New York Public Library had to approach the loan with extreme caution. Discussions were at an impasse on several points, including the total amount of collateral required (NYPL wanted 300 percent, or $4.5 million), how much of the collateral would have to be formally deaccessioned at the closing (NYPL wanted 50 percent), and whether the loan would be provided as a line of credit (NYPL's preference) or cash up front. At this point, Wendell Garrett, a member of the Society's board and a senior vice president of Sotheby's, suggested that perhaps Sotheby's would be willing to loan the Society the money under more flexible terms. Negotiations that the Society and the NYPL had been unable to complete in nearly a month were completed in two-and-a-half days. Sotheby's agreed to loan the Society $1.5 million for a period of one year. It required 200 percent ($3 million) of the loan amount in collateral and was willing to provide the Society with the full amount in cash at the closing. Although the Sotheby's deal was agreed to by all parties in mid December, it was decided that it would not be announced publicly until after the Society's January board meeting.

Everyone was aware that this unusual liaison between an auction house and a museum would be controversial. The Society explained that the Sotheby's loan was "an extraordinary goodwill gesture to a troubled institution that has been getting very little support from the traditional sources."[2] It also pointed out that the approximately 150 items identified as collateral had been previously selected by Society curators for sale and that they had been approved both by the Society's board of trustees and by the New York State attorney general. A spokesman for Sotheby's said his company's motive was strictly that of "being a very good corporate citizen. . . . It would have been a commercial arrangement if we stood to make a profit. However, in the worst-case scenario, we would not make a profit. The collateral would be sold, and we would be reimbursed only for the amount of the loan and the interest on the loan." He added that "the library support wasn't coming fast enough for [the Society's] needs, whereas we acted on very short notice."[3] As part of the effort to diffuse criticism, for the second time in five years, the Society named an outside panel of experts to advise its board on possible future strategies.

Despite efforts to make the situation palatable, museum administrators were critical of both the loan and even the basic concept of putting collections up as collateral for a loan. Robert MacDonald, director of the Museum of the City of New York and a past president of the American Association of Museums, said, "The museum has jeopardized its soul. Losing a collection like this that relates to the city of New York would be a major tragedy." He added that use of a museum's collection to raise money would be "contrary to long-held ethical standards unless the money was used for new acquisitions." Steven Miller, director of the Western Reserve Historical Society in Cleveland, said: "The collection is a public trust. You don't turn it over to the development office."[4]

The closing of the Sotheby's loan and its associated public controversy marked the beginning of yet another chapter in the Society's saga. The special advisory committee, like its predecessor five years before, was charged with recommending a course for the Society, which ranged from pursuing mergers and affiliations to the possibility of total dissolution. The committee was chaired by Wilbur Ross, senior managing director at Rothschild, Inc., an investment bank, and chairman of the National Museum of American Art in Washington, D.C.[5] Ross's professional specialty, restructuring troubled and bankrupt companies, seemed tailor-made for the Society's financial difficulties.

The Ross Advisory Committee

Under Ross, the advisory committee wasted no time taking bold and decisive action. At its first meeting, on February 3, 1993, it voted to close the Society, recommending that forty-one of the Society's seventy-six remaining employees be relieved of their duties. The action, which was scheduled to take effect on February 19, would end public access to the Society's library and would discontinue the society's lecture series and school programs. (Museum exhibitions had been closed since January 1.) Only a core group of employees would be retained to maintain the collections and participate in long-range planning. In a press release issued by the Society, Pearlstine said: "It is sad that we have reached this point, but without substantial public support or a radical restructuring, the Society simply cannot exist. The tremendous gains made by the staff over the past four years are outweighed by the formidable financial requirements to operate an institution of this size and stature. Until a long-term solution can be reached, we are forced to make hard decisions and prepare for the possible dissolution of the Society."

It had been determined that the Sotheby's loan for $1.5 million, which had become official only a week before, did not provide the amount of cash necessary to keep the Society open through June as originally expected. The committee decided it did not make sense to continue to fund the Society's persistent structural deficit. Closing the institution would allow the Society to conserve its limited remaining resources until an appropriate solution could be reached. Ross, the advisory committee's chairman, explained: "Our primary focus at this point must be the safety of the Society's magnificent collections. We will direct all our actions towards guaranteeing the best possible outcome for the library and museum holdings."

Remaining members of the Society's staff moved quickly to make their concerns known to the advisory committee. In a memo written on February 3, fifteen members of the Society's senior curatorial staff expressed in strong terms their desire not only to be kept informed about the progress of the advisory committee's deliberations but to be involved in them as well. The memo implored the committee to make every effort to maintain an independent organization that "honors the intellectual integrity and unity of the collections." The memo also stated that further deaccessioning under the circumstances was "both imprudent and inappropriate" and that the staff expected to contribute directly to the deliberations that affect the future of the collections.

The advisory committee's first steps centered on finding partners for the institution. A planning document written for the committee's first meeting outlined its objectives. "Longer term, the Society must affiliate with one or more institutions, and likely will divest of some of its assets. . . . Affiliation should result in more assured revenues and lower operating costs. It is conceivable that three or more affiliations might be needed, one for the Library, one or more for the collection and one for the real estate." Attached to the document was a list of eighty-five nonprofit institutions, corporations, and wealthy individuals and families who were to be approached about participating in possible affiliations.

Outside of the Society, reaction to the announced closing was swift and dramatic. Particularly vocal in its response was the scholarly community, who considered access to the Society's library collections irreplaceable. In less than a week, a petition had been signed by six hundred scholars at forty campuses across the country urging state and city officials "to fashion a solution that will keep the collections intact and available to all New Yorkers."[6] Stanley Katz, the president of the American Council of Learned Societies, expressed his opinion of the situation quite succinctly: "It's the institution of continuity in the city. This could never happen in the South or in a city like Chicago because of the civic pride there. . . . If we can't keep all this in New York, the city will be committing cultural suicide."[7] Letters to the editor at the *New York Times* illustrated the diversity of the Society's collections. One lamented the possible loss of access to the Society's Audubon collection. Another called attention to the Society's rare and priceless collections of African-American documents from New York's early history, including one-of-a-kind papers from the city's first black school and first black church and the city's (and country's) first black newspaper.

Public pressure and concern continued to mount as the February 19 closing date approached. Responding to the attention, the advisory committee issued a statement reporting on the progress of its deliberations. It declared that the committee was "absolutely committed to preserving the Society's valuable collections intact, to maintaining public access to them, and to keeping them in New York where they so rightly belong. We believe just as firmly, however, that any solution will ultimately require significant aid from the public and private sectors." In addition, the committee reasserted its position regarding possible affiliation saying that the "Society can no longer remain viable independently and that any solution must involve a merger or affiliation with one or more institutions."

The outpouring of public support for the Society's collections and the increasing media scrutiny (several newspapers wrote editorials on the eve of the Society's closing) attracted the attention of local, city, and state politicians. Ruth Messinger, the Manhattan borough president, said that "the important work of the Society must be sustained." Mayor Dinkins voiced his support, saying that "the preservation of the important collections of The New-York Historical Society is a high priority."[8] New York State Attorney General Abrams issued a statement in which he indicated that his office was "committed to the goal of keeping the invaluable collections of The New-York Historical Society in the public domain."

And finally, Governor Mario Cuomo weighed in, praising the Society as "a vital part of the cultural heritage of New York State. If disbanded, the legacy of this venerable institution could never be reconstructed."[9]

The Society closed its doors, as scheduled, at the end of the day on Friday, February 19. More than a hundred scholars demonstrated on the front sidewalk, holding placards pleading for the rescue of the Society. Inside the library, 105 researchers—more than three times the usual number—used the Society's collections for what they feared might be the final time.[10]

Commentary on the Society's plight grew even more dramatic with the closing. Wilbur Ross said that he viewed the Society as "a metaphor for New York City. . . . If we let this go into dissolution, we're saying a lot about ourselves." Ruth Messinger echoed this sentiment: "You don't close collections unless you're opting out of civilization." She expressed her hope that a way could be found to keep the library open, even if on a part-time basis.

The efforts of the advisory committee, together with the huge outpouring of public concern for the collections, were successful in postponing a permanent closing of the Society. On February 23, the Society received an emergency grant in the amount of $66,000 to be used to reopen the library and keep it open for three days per week through April 2. The grant was pieced together from funds contributed by the city (through the Department of Cultural Affairs), the state (through the New York State Council on the Arts), the Manhattan borough president's office, and the city council.

The emergency grant, small as it was, marked the first time the Society had received financial support for general operations from the public sector in more than a century. It had taken the threat of total dissolution to make it happen. In discussing why the Society had been denied membership in the CIG in previous years, Luis Cancel, the commissioner of the Department of Cultural Affairs, pointed to the Society's narrow constituency. He noted that although he had received many calls from architects and historians bemoaning the loss of the Society, there had been little public outcry. He said, "We're not waiting for a groundswell of support before we try to rescue [the Society], but we recognize this lack of response as indicative of how thinly based this organization is and why it needs to take a hard look at itself, while we try to figure out how to keep it alive."[11]

Public attention and sentiment soon shifted away from the importance of the Society's collections toward a general questioning of how the institution itself could be in such bad financial shape. Articles more investigative in tone appeared in both the *New York Times* and the *New York Observer*. The *Observer* article was the first to take direct aim at the Society's most recent leadership. It criticized increases in administrative expenditures during Debs's tenure, questioned why the Society provided space to the Jewish Museum rent-free, and took the Debs administration to task for the continued erosion of the endowment. It was apparent that some of the information critical of the Society came from the advisory committee. The article quoted an unnamed member of the committee, who said: "How can it be that year in and year out they were dissipating the endowment without any sign of improvement? It makes you wonder what was going on?"[12] The *Observer* article was followed a week later by an editorial stating that the Society's "rehabilitation process will require an extended recovery from the stewardship of Norman Pearlstine."[13] The editorial specifically criticized the Society for its deficit spending, for what it called the continued raiding of the endowment, and for rising administrative expenses.

Meanwhile, the advisory committee was working feverishly to finish its report by mid March. One aspect of its work was preparing an operating budget that had a realistic chance of success. On the expense side, that involved contemplating a variety of serious cuts and/or structural changes to the Society's mode of operation. The question of whether the Society's museum and library could continue to be part of a single institution was raised, and the remaining staff were requested to prepare detailed operating budgets going forward for the library alone, for the museum alone, and for a single institution comprising both units. On the revenue side, committee deliberations involved a reopening of the various options for monetization of the Society's illiquid assets, including the sale or development of its real estate and deaccessioning of its collections. The possibility of deaccessioning once again raised the question of the relevance of the Society's mission. There had been calls for the Society to narrow its mission, and the advisory committee consulted with the staff in preparing a new mission statement.

On March 11, 1993, the advisory committee report was released to the public. In addressing the Society's financial difficulties, the report focused primarily on the Society's sources of revenue rather than on its level of expenditures. It emphasized that although the Society owned over $1 billion in assets, it was able to generate less than $1 million in recurring revenue. For the Society to survive, it said, it would simply have to find ways to generate more annual revenue. The recommendations of the committee centered on four primary components, all of which would have to be implemented simultaneously for the plan to succeed: (1) a new mission statement, (2) refinement of the collections, (3) development of real estate, and (4) major public sector support for both operating and capital expenditures. In addition, the committee called for major trustee giving and for increased emphasis on generating revenue from earned income opportunities. Although the committee's emphasis was definitely on revenue, the report also recommended major cuts in operations, presenting an annual operating budget of $4.95 million for the new institution.

The first component of the advisory committee's plan offered a more narrowly defined mission statement: "The primary mission of The New-York Historical Society shall be to develop, preserve and interpret to the broadest possible public material relevant to the rich history, cultural diversity and current evolution of New York City and State and the surrounding region." The committee viewed the new mission as the central component of its plan. Not only did other recommendations flow from it, but the mission also informed the committee as to how certain aspects of the Society ought to be organized and managed. For example, it was perceived as essential to the mission that the collections of the library, museum, and decorative arts collections be integrated into a seamless whole and that access to them be brought technologically up-to-date. The committee gave an example of how a visitor should be able to come into the Society, key in to a computer a request for information, and be able to retrieve and display all relevant information on that topic in the Society's possession. It was hoped that by using new technologies, the Society could provide one window of access into its various collections, be they paintings, manuscripts, or colonial carriages.

The committee also suggested that the Society do more to make its exhibits more contemporary and politically relevant. The report cited as an example how the Society could have mounted an exhibit of its collections pertaining to the lower Manhattan Negro Burial Ground while it was the subject of much attention in the city. It was thought that such approaches would make the Society a more inviting and more exciting place for visitors, resulting in significant improvement in the Society's revenue-generating capacity through increases in admissions, membership, gift shop, and restaurant revenues.

Another major component of the plan that flowed from the development of the new, more narrow mission involved deaccessioning. The Society's new focus would allow it to raise funds through the sale of a portion of its collections. Library deaccessioning of redundant items and materials of little or no usefulness would free storage space, helping reduce annual expenditures on outside storage, while museum deaccessioning of out-of-scope objects would help raise endowment capital. Proceeds from deaccessioning were projected to total approximately $20 million. Detailed explanations for why the deaccessioning was justified, along with steps for how proceeds were to be used and how the Society would attempt to ensure that deaccessioned collections would remain in the public domain, were also described.

Because deaccessioning is such a controversial topic, the committee lobbied the Association of Art Museum Directors (AAMD) to convince them that these steps were necessary. Rather surprisingly, the advisory committee was able to convince the association to issue a statement that did not challenge the committee's recommendations. It said, "In acknowledging the necessity of the actions being taken . . . , the AAMD recognizes that the N-YHS is not solely an art museum, but is an institution with a multiplicity of responsibilities. We strongly urge the Society . . . to avoid any permanent policy that earmarks proceeds from disposition of works of art for purposes other than the replenishment of the collection." Though the AAMD statement stopped short of endorsing the committee's recommendation, given the strong feelings in the museum community on the issue, the fact that it did not actively oppose the plan was truly a victory for the committee.

The third component of the committee's recommendation centered on how to generate both endowment capital and a recurring revenue stream from the Society's real estate holdings. Recognizing that real estate development had been rejected by the Society's neighbors and the Landmarks Preservation Commission in the mid 1980s, the committee wrote that it had "no desire to re-inflame old passions, but assumes that a pre-condition of governmental support will be that the Society monetize its real estate." The difference this time would be that the Society would be sensitive to community concerns concerning the scale of the project. It recommended that a community advisory board be established to communicate with the Society about neighborhood concerns. The committee recommended that the Society invite a variety of developer-architect teams to submit plans that could be discussed and approved by the various concerned constituencies at each step along the way. It was estimated that $15 million could be generated up front, along with $825,000 of annual income from real estate development.

Even with deaccessioning and real estate development bringing the Society's endowment up to $40 million, there was still a need to generate significant income through other methods. Using a spending rate of 5.5 percent, the committee determined that the new endowment could generate $2.2 million of the projected $4.95 million budget. The remaining $2.75 million was to be generated through trustee giving ($1 million), other annual private fundraising ($300,000), admissions and membership ($125,000), royalties and rights fees ($150,000), state library funding ($225,000), and annual operating support from the city ($950,000). The committee did not believe that requesting nearly $1 million in annual support from the city was unreasonable. For comparative purposes, the committee identified the annual appropriations of several other city cultural institutions that were members of the city's CIG. The contributions ranged from $2.5 million for the Brooklyn Botanic Garden to $13.7 million for the Metropolitan Museum of Art.

But $950,000 was just one part of what the committee's plan required of the public sector. In addition to the annual operating support, the committee also appealed to government for capital support. Serious building problems continued to exist, and it was estimated that approximately $10 million would be required to refurbish the building. Moreover, the committee's recommendations were not going to result in an immediate influx of cash to the Society's accounts. The committee estimated that it would take over a year to realize the various goals outlined in the report. The committee requested $2.6 million, again from government, to underwrite this transitionary period.

In summing up the Ross advisory committee's recommendations, several notable aspects should be highlighted. First, in making its recommendations, the advisory committee emphasized that *all* components of its report were absolutely interdependent. If even one of the major components could not be fulfilled, the plan would fail. It argued that the recommendations should be implemented only if it were clear that deaccessioning would take place, that real estate development would happen, and that significant public sector support was forthcoming. Second, the committee argued strongly that the N-YHS remain a single entity housing both a library and a museum. In a discussion reminiscent of the 1988 Macomber committee recommendations, the committee expressed the opinion that the Society's unique combination of collections was its distinct asset. It was suggested that the library and museum collections are sufficiently dependent on each other that splitting them would significantly reduce their total value. Third, the committee's recommendations were a departure from what had been the considered opinion of the Society's leadership for some time and had been reaffirmed in earlier statements by the committee—that is, that the Society could not survive without some kind of merger or affiliation. Instead of requiring or even recommending such a step, the committee chose to say that it did not rule one out. At some point in the latter part of the committee's deliberations, Ross and his colleagues decided that their plan, if all the parts fell in place, could save the Society and allow it to survive intact.

Implementing the Report's Recommendations: Securing Government Support

Initial reaction to the committee's report was quite positive. The committee presented its findings to the public in a series of meetings for government officials, for the press, and for the neighborhood, all held on March 11, 1993. Many prominent state and city officials attended the government meeting, including New York Attorney General Robert Abrams, State Senator Roy Goodman, State Representative Franz Leichter, retired State Senator Tarky Lombardi, Manhattan Borough President Ruth Messinger, Department of Cultural Affairs Commissioner Luis Cancel, and City Council member Ronnie Eldridge. Each and every public sector representative emphatically supported both the components of the plan and the concept of keeping the N-YHS as an independent entity with its combination of library and museum collections. Mayor Dinkins issued a statement endorsing "the newly defined mission statement of the Society" and pledged to have Deputy Mayor Barbara Fife and Cancel review the committee's recommendations and "define ways in which the public sector can assist the Society to fulfill its newly defined role." Roy Goodman offered "his unreserved pledge to work forthwith to make this plan work." He further expressed his belief that the government sector ought to come up with all of the money recommended in the plan.

Still, although each of the public officials offered general support for the plan, some concerns were also expressed. Senator Goodman, for example, voiced apprehension about the viability of real estate development. Another official questioned the ability of the Society to realize returns on the real estate within the one-year time frame given in the report. New York City's cultural affairs commissioner, Luis Cancel, worried whether the Society's deaccessioning plan was appropriate and whether it would set a bad precedent for the museum community. Regarding that topic, Attorney General Abrams issued a statement expressing his view that "any deaccessioning of objects from the collection be pursued only as a last resort, and only on a prudent, limited basis, consistent with the mission of the Society." He also committed to monitoring "this vital task to assure that the public interest is protected."

Those concerns notwithstanding, press reaction to the committee's plan was strongly positive, helping to generate pressure on public officials to act on the Society's behalf. An article in the *New York Times* detailed the implications of the committee's proposals and probed the difficult issues. The article discussed the controversial nature of the Society's deaccessioning plan and accepted the committee's argument that the narrowing of the mission justified it. It congratulated the committee for its sensitivity to the concerns of museum professionals regarding deaccessioning and for the steps outlined to ensure that the collections remain in the public domain. The article's most glowing praise was reserved for what it referred to as the "interconnectedness of the plan": "No one aspect of reorganization is to be undertaken until all others are in place. . . . Only when financial commitments from the city and state, and from what will almost certainly be a newly reconstituted board, are assured, and when a scheme for developing the real estate has been drawn up that meets with general approval, will the sale of works go forward. . . . What the advisory committee has devised, deftly and in short order, is clearly the best hope at this point for revitalizing one of the city's oldest and most troubled cultural institutions."[14]

Several days later, an editorial in the *New York Times* echoed the positive sentiments reflected in the article: "The advisory committee presents a plausible case for keeping a stripped down, better focused and more manageable New-York Historical Society. If its administrators can make the plan work, they fully deserve the kind of support from the city and state the committee envisions."[15] Similar editorials in *New York Newsday* and the *Daily News* urged the state and the city to provide the funds necessary to save the Society.

With the advisory committee's work complete, the board turned to the task of implementing its recommendations. It was agreed that the top-priority steps were to raise $110,000 to keep the library open from April 2 to June 30, to raise $2.6 million in transitional funding to support the Society during implementation, and to generate $10 million in capital funds for the much-needed building repairs and renovation. The Society focused on state and city government as the likely sources of these funds. Former State Senator Tarky Lombardi, who had recently been elected a Society trustee, spearheaded this effort. Wilbur Ross also lobbied state officials on the Society's behalf, as did Juliana Sciolla, the Society's chief operating officer.

To demonstrate its commitment to successful execution of the committee report, the Society's board contributed the $110,000 to keep the library open through the end of the fiscal year. The trustees' contributions sent a signal that Society leadership was committed to solving the institution's financial problems. The reaction from the public sector was unanimously supportive. In a press release, Mayor Dinkins applauded the board "for moving quickly . . . while those of us in government work together with the Trustees and the advisory committee to address the institution's long-term viability." At the state level, Senator Roy Goodman said, "The board of trustees has paved the way with its own exemplary generosity. It is now up to the State Legislature and the Governor to follow suit with emergency action to keep this gallant ship afloat." Finally, at the local level, in addition to the mayor's comments, New York City Council Member Ronnie Eldridge said that "there is much work to be done, and much of it requires the public sector. Now is our time to act to ensure that the Society flourishes."

Clearly, the proposals of the advisory committee were well received, and it appeared likely that government financial support would be forthcoming. It is important to point out, however, that the reach of the committee's report—its requirement that all sectors and constituencies make sacrifices—was more palatable on paper than in practice. When asked about the plan's likelihood of success, people were wary of the component of the plan that touched them most closely. For example, even if museum professionals accepted the necessity of the Society's deaccessioning plans (which many did not), they doubted the ability of the Society to raise the projected amount of money from deaccessioning in the time allotted. Real estate developers were similarly convinced that the Society could not possibly have cash in hand from a developer within the Society's projected one-year time period.

Most sobering, however, was the reaction of the Society's neighbors. In an effort to involve and inform the local community about the Society's progress and to alleviate concerns regarding deaccessioning and real estate development, the Society convened a special meeting of the local community board, which was attended by many neighborhood residents. It was immediately apparent that few people, if any, were prepared to subsume their own interests for the sake of saving the institution. Instead of recognizing that everyone must make sacrifices, the general tone of the questions and comments was highly critical and focused on past actions rather than on present and future opportunities for cooperation. "Why aren't there more signs outside?" "How can you choose to sell off materials that were donated to you? That's violating a public trust!" "Why haven't you tried harder to get money from the city?" "Why are your expenses four times higher than similar institutions in the city?" Wilbur Ross, who made the initial presentation of the advisory committee's recommendations, became the lightning rod for much of the criticism, which only demonstrated how little people truly understood the Society's history and situation (after all, Ross had been involved with the Society for all of two months). In any event, it was clear that there was little hope that local residents were going to play a constructive role in helping the Society resolve the real estate development question.

On another front, Luis Cancel continued to voice his objections to the deaccessioning plan, erecting a potential roadblock between the Society and government support. Eventually Cancel agreed to accept the views of the advisory committee, and a joint statement was released in late March in which the committee and Cancel agreed on detailed procedures for the deaccessioning process. Cancel was satisfied that "the procedures provide a proper framework so that this unique situation does not set a precedent for other institutions in financial difficulties to deaccession their collections in order to meet operating expenses." For his part, Ross said, in a press release, that the committee was "delighted that we have resolved Commissioner Cancel's initial concerns regarding the Report. We are now more confident than ever that the Society's financial requirements will be met."

Indeed, the first step toward meeting the Society's financial requirements was taken when, in early April, the state appropriated $6.3 million for the Society. The money was to be split between capital renovations ($5 million) and transitional financing ($1.3 million). The funding was contingent on an equal matching appropriation by the city of New York and required that the Society submit "an acceptable financial stabilization and development plan describing the steps it will take to achieve financial self-sufficiency, protection of its libraries and collections and expansion of its services to the public."[16] Speaking for the city, Barbara Fife, the deputy mayor for planning and development, said the match was "doable. It's a question of how we spend our money, but I would think the city will recognize this as a new need."[17] An editorial that appeared in the *Times* several days later encouraged the city to make the match, saying that "everyone who cares about what many call New York's 'attic,' or more poetically its 'memory,' will hope the city puts its money where Ms. Fife's mouth is."[18]

Not everyone at the city was as supportive of the Society and its request as Fife. An article in the *New York Times* quoted a highly placed city official as saying that Commissioner Cancel had given the Society's appropriation the lowest priority on a list of eight or nine items to be considered in the city's cultural budget. When questioned, Cancel stated that he wanted "to find a way for the Historical Society to survive," but that "the appearance of rewarding an organization for mismanagement is something we have to be very careful about. The public sector is in no position to rescue organizations that cannot manage themselves." The anonymous city official was quoted as saying that "the Mayor would prefer to have his team in cultural affairs all working together; however, . . . he understands the larger issue and will see to it that the Historical Society gets what it needs."[19]

During April, while Ross and others continued to lobby the city, Pearlstine reinitiated discussions with the New York Public Library. These conversations, which originated when the Society approached the library for a loan the previous December, had been on hiatus due to both the Society's problems and the sudden death of Timothy Healy, the NYPL's president. As it had been during loan negotiations, the NYPL was understandably cautious about the circumstances under which it would consider entering into a relationship with the Society. NYPL leaders felt that the relationship should evolve, progressing through a series of stages and being evaluated and endorsed by third parties at each stage. The leadership established a series of preconditions for signing an association agreement and another set to precede the signing of a final agreement between the two institutions. Although the NYPL was willing to make substantial investments in the Society in terms of both cash and in-kind services, it was not willing to do so without a measure of control. For example, the NYPL wanted assurance that the Society's board would be reconstituted, with the NYPL designating the chairman as well as a majority of the board's members. The library also proposed that a trust be established to fund in full a $35 million operating endowment for the Society until proceeds from deaccessions and real estate flowed in. Such a trust would remove the timing and other risks associated with those controversial elements of the Society's plan. Finally, the NYPL planned to move the Society's library collections to Forty-Second Street, an option that, given the advisory committee's commitment to keep the collections together, was not attractive to Society leadership.

In the end, the Society did receive the appropriation from the city. The mayor's proposed $31.4 billion fiscal 1994 budget provided a $3.6 million increase for the Department of Cultural Affairs and included the $6.3 million appropriation for the Society. Cancel said that "the Mayor has obviously taken to heart how the cultural community helps New York's economy. I'm ecstatic." When asked about his earlier objections regarding the Society, Cancel said, "This money will flow through the Department of Cultural Affairs, and you may rest assured that we will have vigorous oversight on how it is spent."[20]

But not all cultural institutions in New York were happy. Although the funds for the Society supposedly did not reduce potential grants available for other cultural institutions, some people clearly saw it that way. Norma Munn, chair of the New York City Arts Coalition, said that the twelve hundred arts organizations she represents "would not sit still while an organization which has had poor leadership on the board for a lot of years gets bailed out like this."[21] In addition, if the appropriation was indeed independent of other grants, it was an unfortunate coincidence that only thirteen of the CIG's thirty-one members were allotted increases in their 1994 appropriations. Gregory Long, president of the New York Botanical Garden and chairman of the CIG, said, "It used to be that the CIG would be funded together as a unit, but now they've politicized the process. The 18 groups that got no increase don't want to work together in the future. They're going to be forced to fight for themselves and lobby against each other."[22]

The politicization of the Society's situation was not limited to its dealings with the public sector. Political battles within the Society's walls were also intensifying. For one thing, outside members of the advisory committee were critical of the Debs administration in several areas and made little or no effort to correct misrepresentations and oversimplified explanations of the Society's difficulties that appeared in the press. Naturally, this did not endear outside members of the committee to members of the Society's previous administration. Second, the long-running territorial competition for resources between the museum and the library was heightened by the lack of full-time leadership. In such a volatile environment, it was no longer a struggle for a slightly higher budget; it was an intense struggle for the survival of jobs, departments, and collections.

The internal confusion moved toward some form of resolution at the April 15 meeting of the board, when Pearlstine noted that the advisory committee report called for a consolidation of responsibilities coupled with a downsizing of staff. Pearlstine announced that he had accepted the resignations of Juliana Sciolla, who had served as the Society's vice president for external affairs in the Debs administration and as chief operating officer during the transition, and Sheryl Jarvis, who had been the assistant to Barbara Debs and Pearlstine and had held the position of secretary of the board.

At the board level, the struggles reached their own climax at the May 5, 1993, meeting of the board of trustees. Upon hearing of the city's intention to match the state appropriation, Norman Pearlstine announced his immediate resignation as the Society's acting chief executive and chairman of the board. He nominated Wilbur Ross and Herbert Winokur Jr. to serve as co-chairmen of the Society. The board elected Ross to the board of trustees, named Ross and Winokur co-chairmen of the Society for a period of twelve to eighteen months, and appointed Winokur as the Society's acting chief executive officer. Barbara Debs resigned her position on the board.

Ross and Winokur at the Helm

The events of May 5 consolidated power in the hands of new leadership, but that did not mean that the Society was now prepared to return to anything remotely resembling normal operating activity. The Society did not have a full-time chief executive. The new arrangement was still very much an interim solution. The galleries remained closed, and the library was open just three days a week. The government appropriation, though an important endorsement of the Society's value, was just one of several interdependent elements of the advisory committee's recommendations. The Society still had to generate $35 million in endowment through deaccessioning and real estate development. It also had to decide how to make the best use of the $10 million capital appropriation. For example, in addition to repairs, the plan had suggested that the Society restructure space to allow it to eliminate costly outside storage. Determining the best plan for doing that was an extremely important and difficult process that would require input from museum curators, librarians, architects, and administrative staff. Finally, the Society's remaining interface with the public was through the library, which continued to provide services to scholars, historians, and the general public. Managing that library within tight budgets and with a thin staff was a continuing concern. To make matters even more difficult, Jean Ashton, the director of the library, announced that she was leaving to take a position in the manuscripts library at Columbia University. With Ashton's departure, only Holly Hotchner remained from Debs's leadership team, and in the absence of a full-time CEO, she took over many of the day-to-day responsibilities of managing the Society.

Clearly, a monumental challenge lay ahead, but Ross and the other Society leaders were optimistic that with the public funds secured, the Society could make it on its own, and negotiations regarding an affiliation with the NYPL were dropped. Instead, the Society entered into discussions with New York University (NYU) to determine if its library staff would be willing to help manage the Society's library on a contract basis as an alternative to hiring a new library director. Contracting the management of the library to an outside party would allow Society leadership to focus on building the endowment through deaccessioning and real estate development.

At the invitation of Society leaders, Carlton Rochell, dean of NYU's Bobst Library, and his staff began studying the collections, capabilities, and services of the Society's library. During that investigation, Rochell was made aware of struggles going on within the Society regarding the stewardship of the library collections and the administrative emphasis being accorded the library relative to the museum. At an Independent Research Libraries Association meeting, Jean Ashton spoke openly to her professional colleagues about her concern for the collections, saying that she had been ordered to clear six stack levels of library materials to make room for storage of museum materials, without plans for whether the library materials were to be sold, deaccessioned, or transferred to another institution. Rochell grew concerned about the prospects for the library and stepped up negotiations with the Society regarding a possible relationship.

Negotiations between NYU and the Society continued through July, and on August 1, 1993, the Society and NYU agreed to a one-year partnership for NYU to manage the Society's library. Under the agreement, the Society would pay NYU a monthly fee for consulting services to be provided by NYU's library staff. Savings attained by not hiring a librarian and through economies of scale would allow the Society's library to be open five days a week again beginning September 1. In addition, NYU agreed to load the Society's electronic catalog (forty thousand records) into the system at NYU, which was part of a more widely used network that would make this portion of the Society's collections accessible to scholars all over the world. NYU also agreed to oversee all acquisitions, processing, and cataloging for the Society and to begin work on the Society's cataloging backlog. In an article that appeared in the *New York Times*, Wilbur Ross said he believed the Society could "do all this at 14 percent less cost [for five days] than when we were operating three days a week."[23] Ross pointed out that there would be no changes in the library's staff and that the Society would retain ownership of the library collections. The reaction to the NYU/N-YHS agreement was favorable; NYU was perceived to be acting in the best interests of the collections as a concerned sister institution.

Both the Society and NYU were hopeful that their initial arrangement might evolve into a more permanent affiliation. There were obviously advantages for the Society in associating itself with a financially stable institution. In addition, the potential benefits to NYU were also significant. The opportunity to merge its American history collections, which are strong in late-nineteenth-century and twentieth-century materials, with one that is truly distinctive in the earlier period would strengthen NYU's research capacity in the humanities. Moreover, the linkage of the NYU and N-YHS libraries would help NYU's library qualify as a "collection of record," enhancing its prospects for grants from government funding agencies.

In September, little over a month into the arrangement, NYU's library staff was finding the job of managing the library far more difficult than expected. First, upon closer inspection, Rochell and his staff were surprised by the general condition of the Society library's holdings. Surveys of the shelves revealed that many items on the shelves were not only uncataloged but also not even property stamped. Furthermore, bibliographic information about volumes that had been duly recorded and cataloged was likely to be included in any of seven different catalogs. This made it impossible to provide services to scholars in an efficient manner.

In addition to the concerns regarding the collections, Rochell had also become embroiled in the long-running territorial battle between the library and the museum. In this battle, there were two primary matters of contention: (1) the determination of what were museum and what were library collections, the primary question being whether the prints, photographs, and architectural drawings ought to be considered part of the museum or the library, and (2) the relative allocation of space to the museum and to the library in the capital renovations. Rochell saw it as NYU's responsibility to defend the interests of the library collections, and he considered those interests to be threatened.

Rochell's frustrations with the situation grew with the passage of time. As a representative of an outside institution being paid consulting fees, his ability to fulfill what he regarded as his duty to protect the library collections was limited. In October 1993, Rochell, with encouragement from some Society board members, approached the Society with a proposal to forge a more permanent affiliation between the two institutions. At the same time, NYU formally requested a grant from The Andrew W. Mellon Foundation to perform essential work on the N-YHS collections. It was understood that NYU would be able to carry out these tasks only if clear understandings were reached with the Society concerning the definition of the library collection, the allocations of space, and financial and managerial responsibility. During November, a memorandum of understanding was negotiated by representatives of both the Society and NYU that outlined terms for an agreement between the two institutions on these issues.

On December 13, 1993, the Mellon Foundation's board of trustees voted to award a conditional grant of $1.25 million to NYU to inventory and catalog the collections at the N-YHS library and to prepare new bibliographic records. This appropriation was unprecedented for the Foundation, whose normal practice is to make substantial grants only in situations where the institutional setting is secure. To safeguard its grant, the Foundation attached a number of conditions:

1. The scope and integrity of the N-YHS library collections must be clearly defined and assured. Our assumption is that the library collections are now understood to encompass all materials of national as well as local and regional significance up to 1900. Also, the collections are understood to include prints, photographs (including the Landauer collection), and architectural drawings, as well as books, manuscripts, journals, and documents.
2. The library must have sufficient space in the building at 170 Central Park West to allow for storage of collections currently held, the addition of related collections now housed at NYU, and a reasonable amount of future growth.
3. Financial arrangements must be specified that offer the library a realistic opportunity to function effectively and to achieve and maintain financial equilibrium in its operations for the foreseeable future.
4. Responsibility for direction and oversight of the N-YHS library collections must be clearly defined and must rest with an entity that has the requisite professional competence, financial resources, and institutional commitment.

As is customary in the awarding of conditional grants, and at the specific request of representatives of both NYU and the N-YHS, a date was set—February 15, 1994—by which time the conditions would have to be satisfied or the grant would not be awarded. In addition, in the interest of full communication to all interested parties, a letter reporting informally on the action taken by the trustees of the Mellon Foundation was sent to all interested parties, including representatives of NYU, the N-YHS, and the New York Public Library.

Following the Mellon Foundation grant, officers of the Society and NYU began work on a formal contract establishing terms and arrangements for an affiliation. After nine drafts of the contract, NYU and the Society still were unable to reach an agreement, and on February 15, 1994, Rochell wrote to the Mellon Foundation, formally asking for a one-month extension. The Foundation granted the request.

Even with the extension, Rochell and Ross still struggled to come to an agreement. The major points of contention centered around NYU's desire to establish clear lines of authority through the establishment of a library advisory board; NYU's redefinition of the library collections to include the prints, photographs, and architectural drawings; and the inclusion of non–New York colonial materials in NYU's representation of the Society's mission statement. Ross contended that these points would prove unacceptable to government officials, who had agreed to fund "an integrated Society," not a fragmented one. Ross and Winokur planned to present the contract for action at the Society's board meeting set for March 15, 1994, the very day the Mellon Foundation's grant was scheduled to lapse.

On March 14, 1994, Ross and Winokur received a letter from a group of public officials.[24] The letter expressed "dismay at the complete lack of communication regarding the Board's planning for the future of The New-York Historical Society." It also urged the Society's board to table any action regarding the New York University contract until city and state elected officials had been briefed.[25] The letter further stated that "if the Board decides to move ahead with this decision without any public comment our future commitment to the Society will be in jeopardy." The letter concluded: "We hope you reconsider the manner in which you are managing the Society and take steps to address the serious breach of trust that has resulted from your management."

On the morning of March 15, an article appeared in the *New York Times* describing the basic terms of the proposed contract. "The board of the financially starved New-York Historical Society," the article began, "is to vote this morning on an arrangement that would hand over to New York University effective control over nearly all of the Society's holdings other than its art collection. Much of the art collection is expected to be sold later this year to help raise money for the Society."[26] Neither of these first statements was entirely accurate. While it was true that NYU argued in the contract for an independent advisory board to oversee the library, that board was going to report to, and be controlled by, the N-YHS board. Second, the Society did not intend to sell much of its art collection. The tone of the article was to characterize NYU's potential affiliation with the Society as a hostile takeover. This characterization was adopted as fact by many observers of the situation, including most of the important public officials.

In such an environment, it was impossible for the Society's board to act on the proposed contract. Consistent with the letter sent extending the original deadline, the Mellon Foundation's appropriation lapsed. Like the public officials, some members of the Society's board complained that they, too, had not been kept informed regarding negotiations with NYU; however, there was at least some effort to include the board in the deliberations. Board minutes from the Society's December 1993 meeting document a rather detailed discussion regarding terms of a "potential broadening of the existing relationship between the Society and NYU." In the end, whether the board was fully informed was irrelevant. In the wake of the negative characterization of NYU's intentions in the press, several board members took very strong positions against the proposed agreement. These sentiments, which were obviously shared by several important New York City and State officials, doomed the proposal before it came to a vote. There would be no partnership between New York University and The New-York Historical Society.

In early April, having served six months beyond the term of his original contract, "Pug" Winokur resigned his position as the Society's co-chairman and acting chief executive officer. Although he felt that the Society had made great progress—for example, it had hired an effective chief financial officer, it had eliminated hundreds of thousands of dollars of annual waste, and it had planned for and begun to implement the capital renovation of the building—Winokur regarded the NYU-Society partnership as an essential first step in the Society's reawakening. Winokur was in such strong disagreement with the Society's chosen course that he decided to step aside.

The failed attempt to forge a relationship, and the negative publicity associated with it, had clearly hardened public officials against any attempts at affiliation. Whereas the advisory committee had initially stated unequivocally that an affiliation or even several affiliations were necessary if the Society was to survive, it was now the opinion of most observers and many key political officials that the Society's collections had to be kept together. Manhattan Borough President Ruth Messinger, City Councilwoman Ronnie Eldridge, Municipal Arts Society President Kent Barwick, and others demanded "that trustees reaffirm their pledge to preserve the Society's unparalleled trove of Americana . . . and make it accessible to the public. . . . To ensure that there is no further attempt to carve up the Society, . . . state and city officials are . . . getting ex-officio membership on the board of trustees."[27]

The article was also the first to criticize the leadership of Wilbur Ross. "At the center of the latest controversy sits Wilbur Ross, Jr., . . . who until recently was regarded as the Society's smart and conscientious savior. . . . But over the past month, some of the people who once championed Mr. Ross came to see him as a villain. . . . They say he kept them in the dark about the trustees' plans to sell the society's valuable real estate and to deaccession . . . a portion of the Society's $1 billion collection."[28] Regarding the NYU deal, Ross said, "I liked the idea of doing something with New York University, but I didn't like this particular deal. . . . I'd have preferred everything went smoothly, but when you're trying to change how a place relates to the outside world, there are some growing pains, particularly during an interregnum period." A member of the community advisory board provided a counterpoint, saying that "a lot of people put their faith in [Ross]. Now he says he was surprised by the ultimate details of the NYU plan. It's hard to understand, given his business savvy."

With the retirement of Winokur, Ross had assumed the role of chairman, and he declared that he planned to take an active role in running the N-YHS. In addition, Ross disbanded a staff management committee that Winokur had assembled to assist with operating the Society. Ross also directed the library staff to come up with a plan to save $200,000 in recurring operating costs, a demand that library staff considered infeasible. The N-YHS staff responded by refusing to act on directions given to them by Ross.

On April 22, 1994, the Society announced in a press release that its interim chairman, Wilbur Ross, had decided to step down, and that he would be succeeded by Miner H. Warner, who had served on the Society's board since 1985. Warner, president of Public Resources International, an advisory firm to foreign governments on infrastructure finance, stated that "at this point we believe that a new permanent chairman who was not on the front lines during this challenging period of transition should be in place when the new president arrives." Of his abrupt departure, Ross said, "There was a feeling the Society ought to now think through who should be the permanent leadership for the institution. My own attitude is, 'I came on the scene simply to help the place. A lot has occurred. That's fine. I didn't start out life seeking this situation.'"

On May 5, 1994, the New York State Assembly's Committee on Tourism, Arts and Sports Development called a hearing to assess the contribution of state financial assistance toward the financial stability of the Society. The state representatives present at the meeting were Joseph T. Pellittere, chairman; Scott Stringer, assemblyman representing the Upper West Side; Richard Miller, ranking Republican assemblyman on the committee; and Richard Brodsky, assemblyman. As the hearings unfolded, the primary issue of importance to each of the committee members became clear. For Pellittere, it was the feasibility of the Society's financial plan as it was presented to Albany on October 20, 1993; for Brodsky, it was the proper role of deaccessioning; and for Stringer, it was the impact of any real estate development on the neighborhood in his district.

The most important testimony of the hearing was that of Miner Warner, the newly elected chairman. Warner laid much of the blame for the Society's poor performance over the recent past on the fact that there had been no full-time leadership. He enthusiastically reported that the search for a new director had produced six excellent candidates for the job and that a new director would be selected by June 1. Warner discussed plans for deaccessioning and admitted that very little progress had been made on real estate development. He guaranteed that the Society was going to operate in an up-front and open manner and that nothing would be done in secret. "The Society does not want to make the same mistake twice," he said.

The most volatile questioning of the hearing came from Joseph Pellittere, who dissected the Society's 1994–1995 budget, pointing out that it was unrealistic in its revenue projections. Specifically, Pellittere challenged the budget's assumptions regarding interest income from the endowment. The budget projected a total annual interest income of $2.2 million from return on endowment generated by deaccessioning and real estate development. Assuming a 5.5 percent interest rate, Pellittere pointed out that, in order to receive $2.2 million during the year, the Society would have to have $40 million in cash in the bank within two months. Half of the $40 million was to come from deaccessioning proceeds and half from real estate development. Pellittere was especially critical of the real estate assumption since, as Warner admitted, there had been absolutely no progress on that front. James Griffin, the Society's recently reappointed treasurer, admitted that the budget was not realistic and that he was working with Society management to prepare a revised budget that would be made available to the committee within a month.

As Warner had promised, the Society's board moved quickly in its search for a new director, and on June 20, 1994, Betsy Gotbaum was named executive director. Gotbaum's background made her well qualified for the political and fundraising challenges of the job. She was the former commissioner of parks and recreation in the Dinkins administration, had served as the head of three nonprofit organizations, and had worked as an investment banker between 1986 and 1990. Speaking of her own qualifications for the job, she said: "I have good organization skills; I know the city's political system, . . . and I can raise money."[29]

Like her predecessors, however, Gotbaum inherited an institution with morale problems, a board in turmoil, a depleted endowment, and a staggering deficit. She will need all her skills, and some good luck, if the Society is to reestablish itself as an active, financially viable cultural institution.

Notes

1. Honan (1992b).
2. Honan (1993e).
3. Honan (1993e).
4. Honan (1993d).
5. Other members of the advisory committee were Arthur G. Altschul, limited partner in Goldman, Sachs & Co. and vice president of the Yale Art Gallery; Helene L. Kaplan, partner, Skadden, Arps, Slate, Meagher & Flom and chairman of Barnard College; Arthur Ross, president of the Arthur Ross Foundation; and Thomas J. Tisch, managing partner in FLF Associates. Representing the Society's board on the committee were Herbert S. Winokur Jr., recently appointed head of the Society's development and planning committee; Barbara Debs, who had assumed the role of chair of the collections committee following her resignation as president; and Norman Pearlstine, the chairman of the board.
6. Honan (1993f).
7. Honan (1993f).
8. Erikson (1993b).
9. Erikson (1993a).
10. Dunlap (1993).
11. Bagli (1993).
12. Bagli (1993).
13. "Pearlstine's Unsociable Ways" (1993).
14. Kimmelman (1993b).

15. "Cleaning Out New York's 'Attic'" (1993).
16. Honan (1993a).
17. Honan (1993a).
18. "Hearing on a Bill to Limit Sales of Museum Holdings" (1993).
19. Honan (1993c).
20. Honan (1993b).
21. Wallach (1993).
22. Honan (1993b). An additional institution, Lincoln Center, has received support from the city's Department of Cultural Affairs since 1986, but was not a member of the CIG. In 1995, Lincoln Center was added as the thirty-second member of the CIG.
23. Grimes (1993).
24. The letter was jointly signed by Ronnie Eldridge, council member; Franz Leichter, state senator; Ruth Messinger, Manhattan borough president; Manfred Ohrenstein, state senator; Scott Stringer, state assembly member; and Elizabeth Starkey, chair of Community Board Seven.
25. Apparently, an effort to brief public officials had been planned, and a meeting between Ross and a group of politicians had been scheduled for Friday, March 11. Unfortunately, the meeting was canceled at the last minute, although who was responsible for canceling it is a matter of debate. (H. Winokur Jr., personal communication, 1995)
26. Goldberger (1994).
27. Bagli (1994).
28. Bagli (1994).
29. Grimes (1994).

CHAPTER EIGHT

FACING TOUGH CHOICES TODAY

Another New Beginning

The appointment of Betsy Gotbaum as executive director marks yet another "new beginning" in The New-York Historical Society's long and troubled history. At first glance, one cannot help but wonder about the Society's chances for success. Its endowment has dwindled, its donor constituency is narrow, and it has run deficits in twenty of the past twenty-five years. Since 1987 alone, the Society's cumulative operating deficits (including depreciation) have totaled more than $15 million. Ironically, it is the very severity of the Society's situation that has made it possible to try again. The truly dire circumstances, combined with public recognition of the enormous value of the Society's unique collections, have resulted in the first direct and substantial support from the state and city government since well before the turn of the twentieth century.

Unfortunately, however, the $12.6 million appropriation made by the New York State and City governments neither solves the Society's financial problems nor provides the means for the Society to address many of its other programmatic and organizational difficulties. So what is next for the Society? The latter part of this chapter outlines a series of options the Society could consider as it plans for the future. First, however, to frame the various choices the Society's leaders face, it is useful to begin by recapitulating the fundamental threads, themes, and problems that emerge from this study of the Society's 190-year history.

134

The major issues before the Society fall into three broad categories. First, there are the burdens incumbent on any organization responsible for valuable old collections and an aging physical plant. These can be separated into questions of collections management, preservation and conservation, and building maintenance. Second, there are issues associated with the Society's obligation to provide public service. Finally, there are institutional and governance issues, including those arising from the Society's effort to manage and balance the needs of both a museum and a library.

Collections Management

The oldest problem for Society management stems from the undisciplined accumulation of materials during the Society's first 150 years. The steady inflow of tens of thousands of books, boxes of manuscripts, paintings, prints, and ephemera was literally impossible for the Society's tiny staff to keep up with. In addition, during the first seventy-five years of its existence, the Society was on its own, storing and categorizing the items as well as it could, without any established, professionalized standards to guide it. Library and museum norms simply did not exist. By the time professionalized standards for cataloging and sharing collections became widely recognized and used, the Society already faced a hundred-year cataloging backlog.

Today, the backlog remains extremely large. Even for the parts of the collection that have been cataloged, there is no single unified record of the materials, making it difficult for library staff to access the Society's collections with efficiency. Although the exact size of the Society's catalog backlog is uncertain, there is no doubt that to catalog the Society's entire collection would take a very long time, probably decades.

Still, the importance of cataloging the collections cannot be overstated. If an item is not in the catalog, it cannot be found efficiently. If it cannot be found, it might as well not be in the collection. There have been several initiatives to catalog, assess, or rehouse the Society's various library and museum collections over the years, and in each case, there have been numerous "discoveries" of valuable items. In 1985, for example, a gilded chair made for Louis XVI and given to Marie Antoinette was discovered in a Society warehouse. Without a comprehensive catalog, there are bound to remain many such items in this state of "nonexistence." Developing a single up-to-date inventory of the collections will remain a long-range project requiring perpetual investment for the foreseeable future.

Another consequence of the historical lack of a collections management policy is that the Society now owns a collection without clear geographical, chronological, or thematic boundaries. Redefining those boundaries *after* materials are received is extremely difficult. Reasonable people will inevitably disagree on the proper delineation of the boundaries. Debate on whether the Society's updated mission statement ought to include colonial materials not directly related to the New York region, such as the Philadelphia printing of the Declaration of Independence, offers a case in point. Furthermore, even if such decisions could be made, deaccessioning collections has legal ramifications. If a donor stipulated that an item was to be held by the Society in perpetuity, breaking that restriction requires legal action by the state attorney general and the courts—another expensive and time-consuming process.

Conservation and Preservation

At the core of the Society's mission is its responsibility for the millions of items under its care. As one would expect, the Society's most valuable holdings are very old and therefore extremely fragile. Letters and manuscripts were written on paper that will inevitably turn to dust; books were bound with materials and glue that deteriorate; and pictures were created with paints that fade, on canvases that disintegrate. Thus even if elaborate preservation technologies had been available from the Society's earliest days and the Society had actively managed a conservation program, a constant and never-ending portion of the Society's resources would still have to be directed toward the physical maintenance of the collections.

Unfortunately, for much of its history, the Society did little to protect its valuable holdings from the effects of time. The rapid growth of the collections, the lack of resources, and the limited preservation tools available in the early years are all factors that contributed to this neglect. Consequently, a substantial quantity of paintings, manuscripts, drawings, and books are in need of immediate attention. The creation of the painting and paper conservation labs during the late 1980s was an important step forward in addressing this problem, and much progress has been made, but like cataloging, conservation and preservation are unremitting obligations.

Physical Plant

Because of the rapid growth of the collections, the Society has always struggled with the limitations of its physical facilities. In its earliest days, the Society moved several times. After 1904, when it built the central building of the structure it now occupies, the Society dealt with its continuing collections growth by adding the north and south wings. But collections growth did not stop with the 1938 expansion of the building. When it once again found itself short of space, the Society contracted for outside storage. The first record of payments for outside storage appeared in 1969, and for seventeen years such expenditures remained modest. Unfortunately, there was a hidden cost to the inexpensive storage facilities: they did not provide a suitable environment for protection of the collections. The 1988 public controversy about the Society's substandard care of its collections and the subsequent attorney general's investigation were instigated by reports of the conditions in the Society's outside storage facilities. The Society responded to the controversy by moving the collections into a first-rate environment, but at substantial cost. In 1993, the cost of the lease for outside storage was $500,000, nearly 10 percent of the Society's operating budget.

Inadequate storage space is not the only facilities-related problem the Society faces. The building is nearly one hundred years old, and the fixed costs associated with maintaining it are extremely high. Much of the facility is cavernous, with high ceilings that make it extremely expensive to heat in the winter and cool in the summer. In addition, the building is not well designed to provide clear sight lines for guards in the exhibition galleries or to control flow in the library. To safeguard against theft requires substantial security personnel. Finally, and perhaps most important, capital maintenance of the structure, like preservation and conservation of the collections, is an expensive and unceasing job. Unfortunately, for many years, the Society did not spend enough for the regular maintenance of its physical plant. The bill for that deferred maintenance has come due, and it is large. Of the recent $12 million government appropriation, $10 million was for capital improvements, and even that sum has proved insufficient to address all of the structure's problems. Because of the age and condition of the building, substantial funds will be needed annually for plant maintenance and rehabilitation.

Relationship with the Public Sector

In its infancy, the Society was dependent on the public sector for support. It was the state that saved the Society during its first brush with bankruptcy in 1824. In addition, the city made available parcels of land (which the Society did not accept) in the 1860s when the Society had outgrown its Second Avenue home. But after the establishment of the Metropolitan Museum of Art and the New York Public Library, the Society did not petition the public sector for general operating support again until the late 1980s.[1] During that long period, patterns and attitudes were established—both at the Society and in the government—that made it extremely difficult for the Society to appeal successfully for public funds.

In the late 1800s and early 1900s, the Society's emphasis on supporting genealogical organizations and their research drew criticism from people who wanted to see it play a greater public service role. In 1917, the May Van Rensselaer episode brought considerable public attention to the Society's failings in this area. Although some progress was made during the tenure of Alexander Wall, the $4.5 million Thompson bequest in 1934 gave the Society such freedom and independence that for nearly forty years, it was accountable to no one. During this period, the Society's investment proceeds accounted for more than 90 percent of its total annual income. Because it was receiving no government support, Society leadership could congratulate itself when it provided even the most minimal level of service to the public. This attitude affected officials on both sides: the Society's officers, who were proud that their institution accepted no public assistance, and city officials and the public, who came to perceive the Society as elitist and arrogant. When the situation changed in the early 1970s and the Society could no longer live solely off its endowment income, the Society faced a very long climb to rehabilitate its reputation sufficiently to merit public attention. In fact, it was never able to make that climb; government and state support became available only because the Society was near death.

Another major factor that has adversely affected the Society's potential for receiving regular government operating support has been the changing economic and political climate. As the economic environment has grown increasingly difficult for nonprofit institutions generally, more of them have appealed to the city for help. The process for receiving annual support from the city's Department of Cultural Affairs depends on being included in the Cultural Institutions Group. The CIG is composed of thirty-two cultural institutions located in all five boroughs of the city. Because these thirty-two institutions divide up what is a greatly constrained fiscal pie, it is in their interests to prevent new members from being admitted into the group. Furthermore, because of historical patterns, institutions focused on minority issues and institutions in the outer boroughs are underrepresented in the present distribution of members. Together, these factors illustrate why it is very difficult for an institution with an elitist and exclusive reputation, located on the Upper West Side of Manhattan, to qualify for new support today.

Community Outreach

One way for the Society to overcome its stuffy and elitist image would be to provide services to its surrounding community. There is no question that public officials regard such outreach as a prerequisite for any kind of continuing support. What is fascinating is how difficult it has been for the Society to overcome its reputation for arrogance. The generally accepted characterization of the Society as an institution that has made no effort to attract and engage the public with its exhibitions and programs is simply not true. One can argue that its efforts have been unsuccessful, but one cannot assert that no such efforts have been made. Most recently, the Jackie Robinson exhibit, the "Why History?" program, and the educational initiative with O'Shea Junior High are but a few examples of the Society's attempts to open its doors and thereby improve its public image.

The reason for highlighting this distinction between impressions and reality is to show that the process of changing the Society's image has not been, and will not be, easy. A successful public program, whether it is an exhibit, a lecture series, or an educational initiative, is expensive to mount. More important, for such a program to have any chance of fundamentally altering the Society's reputation, it must be sustained. The Society's history is dotted with successful exhibits and programs that were hailed in press articles in which the Society was congratulated for finally opening its doors and shedding its stodgy image. Sadly, when controversy reappears, the positive characterizations disappear, and the Society is relabeled with its traditional and more notorious reputation.

It is clear that an attempt to overcome this bias will require substantial investments over a long period of time, with no guarantee of success. Past efforts have failed. The widely held perception that the Society has not attempted to engage the public is based on the assumption that the problem is one of supply— that the Society has simply not attempted to make available the kinds of programs the public wants. What has not been acknowledged, however, is that the problem may really be more one of demand. Perhaps the Society's collections, no matter how intelligently they are displayed, simply cannot compete with the myriad of options available to tourists and New Yorkers looking for cultural enrichment or other entertainment. After all, how popular is history? If the Society's failings are more a question of demand, substantial investments to improve the Society's reputation carry a very high degree of risk.

Multiple Purposes

Ever since the 1850s, when the first major art collections were donated to the N-YHS, it has been difficult for the Society to achieve a balance between the competing demands of the museum and the library. In the Society's early years, it was a battle for display and storage space. These battles continue even as the Society's building is being renovated. Additional complexity has been added in recent years as the Society has moved to step up its educational and public programming.

In any era, such tensions would be difficult to manage, but it seems that they are even more so today. In the early 1940s, for example, when the costs of running the Society were more modest, Alexander Wall explained that the Society's library could not exist without the museum. He implied that the museum was a kind of cash cow that would pay for the library. He said, "The scholarship part of the historical society's work would be likely to have a bare cupboard if not coupled with a popular museum." Today, there are no cash cows. Museums also struggle to raise the money needed to balance their budgets. No museum would want a portion of the money generated by its exhibits and collections to be siphoned off to finance another programmatic activity (in this case a library) that is unable to sustain itself.

Another complicating aspect of managing the Society's different entities manifests itself when one considers the effects of the change in the career paths of present-day professionals compared to their counterparts in previous generations. Today, professionals are far less likely to spend significant portions of their careers serving a single institution. Mobility tends to increase interdepartmental rivalries as leaders fight to show demonstrable successes that will qualify them for other opportunities.

Finally, and perhaps most important, in a way the Society is a victim of the strength of its collections. One can cite many cases where a library and museum have been folded into a single organization without debilitating difficulty, but in most of them it was quite clear which part of the collection predominates. If an institution's art museum is more renowned, its library collections play a supportive role. The culture has been built around such assumptions, so tension concerning the allocation of resources is minimized. The same is true in cases where it is the library that holds the preeminent collections. In the Society's case, because of the unusual strength of both collections, the Society has never established which entity gets priority. Staffs continue to fight battles over resources, autonomy, and power.

In some ways, it is not surprising that interweaving a library and a museum is so difficult when one considers how different the two institutions have become. Oversimplifying somewhat, a library's central charge is to hold collections and make them accessible for private study by individual scholars. By contrast, a museum is primarily expected to prepare its collections for public display to large groups of people. The two objectives spawn entities with very different personalities: one is introverted; the other is extroverted. Not surprisingly, the cultures that have grown up around these two institutions are very different, and the leaders that come up through the ranks tend to exhibit those differences. Even the cataloging standards used by the two types of entities are different and not transferable. Placing these two cultures together in a single, small organization that is woefully short of resources represents, at best, an extraordinary management and leadership challenge.

Governance

The Society began as a membership organization. For most of its history, it did not have a board of trustees; it had a librarian and a president elected by its members. It was not until 1938 that the Society was reorganized and a self-perpetuating board of trustees was established. Because this reorganization took place after the Society had received the $4.5 million Thompson bequest, the trustees were not called on to play an active role in overseeing the Society's financial affairs. Membership on the board was regarded more as a privilege than as a responsibility. Trustees got together once a month to hear about the Society's new acquisitions, to discuss mutual interests, and to enjoy one another's company. Once elected to the board, a trustee typically served for life.

Examine the following entry in the minutes, which was presented, in December 1967, as the report of the legal committee on the subject of deaccessioning the paintings of Thomas Bryan:

> For several generations we've been tryin'
>
> To ease restrictions set by Bryan;
>
> That is, to loosen up the strictures
>
> Governing our use of his gorgeous pictures.
>
> Now, though our treasury is diminished
>
> We can report the Bryan case is finished!
>
> With blood and tears, and a little fun,
>
> The ghastly lawsuit is finally won!

The purpose of excerpting this entry is not to comment on the appropriateness of selling the Bryan pictures but rather to provide insight into the general tone of Society meetings in simpler times. When the Society's financial situation changed dramatically and abruptly in the early 1970s, circumstances demanded tough, serious, aggressive leadership. That the Society's board proved unable to provide it should not come as a surprise.

In the twenty-five years since 1970, the board has changed, but slowly. Between 1970 and 1980, there was little turnover on the board, and by 1980, the average age of its seventeen members had reached seventy. It was not until the mid 1980s that substantial changes occurred both in the makeup and the organizational structure of the board. Unfortunately, the process was divisive and distracting. When the Society needed leadership, it was preoccupied with issues that should have been resolved years before.

Just as the Society must compete with other New York cultural institutions for visitors, so must it compete for board members. Although the Society has been able to attract well-known and respected business and cultural leaders, too few of them have chosen to make the Society their overriding passion. Without a critical core of powerful and impassioned members, the Society's board has failed to provide either the leadership or the funding to make the Society successful. Establishing such a board remains one of the Society's chief challenges.

Options

What follows is a discussion of alternatives that could be pursued by the Society. The order of presentation is not meant to convey either the desirability or viability of the various options. Instead, purely for organizational purposes, the six alternatives start with the least drastic, maintenance of the Society in essentially its present form. Then, the most drastic alternative, a managed dissolution of the Society, is presented, followed by a series of increasingly less draconian possibilities. This list is not all-inclusive, nor could it be. There are surely options available to the Society that are not discussed here, as well as paths the Society could follow that combine aspects from several or perhaps all of the alternatives. It is hoped that these options and the associated discussion will serve to stimulate the creative thinking needed to overcome the obstacles that have consistently frustrated efforts to maximize the impact of the Society's valuable collections.

Option 1: Continue to Operate as a Freestanding Institution at 170 Central Park West

Because it requires no dramatic change from the Society's traditional mode of operations, perhaps the least controversial course that the Society could follow would be to keep its collections together and remain in its present facility. Such a path carries great risk, however. The Debs administration, aware of the challenges inherent in choosing to try to keep the Society independent, launched a determined effort in 1988. Even though a great deal of money was raised, and much was accomplished programmatically, the effort proved unsuccessful. As had happened before, the Society's capacity for generating revenue, whether in the form of contributions, grants, earned income, or investment income, proved inadequate to address its many needs.

The Ross advisory committee in March 1993 outlined a plan for how the Society could begin to generate a sound capital base through sales of some of its collections and development of a part of its real estate. Whether such a plan can be a success depends on many factors, not the least of which is the time it will actually take to generate money from these initiatives. No one knows whether following these recommendations will allow the Society to remain independent, but regardless of the specifics of its plan for survival, there is one hurdle the Society must clear if it is going to pursue this course.

The Society must balance its budget. For a quarter of a century, Society leadership has justified deficits with claims that excess expenditures were an investment in the future, that they were necessary to show that the Society was an institution worth supporting. The Society is suffering the effects of those investments. Today, not only is the endowment almost gone, but $1.8 million in loans remains outstanding. No single thing the Society can do will go further to restoring public confidence in the institution and its leadership than a balanced budget.

A stable and viable financial plan will require involvement from each and every one of the Society's many constituencies, but the single most important participant is the public sector. Lack of timely public support was one of the key reasons for the failure of the Society's bridge plan in the late 1980s. Significant public support is the one variable that has changed that makes considering an independent path for the Society possible.

It must be understood, however, that the type of public sector support matters a great deal. The Society must convince the city and state to provide *unrestricted* general operating support. What brought the Society to the brink of bankruptcy was not so much lack of support—the Society raised more than $20 million during the Debs administration, much of it in the form of restricted program grants—it was the lack of unrestricted support. As the Society's unrestricted cash balances dwindled, so did its ability to make payroll and pay bills for such basics as utilities. Unfortunately, because of the heightened publicity surrounding the Society, there is some risk that government support could be linked to new programs of community outreach. Such a linkage would be self-defeating; designing and managing such initiatives is expensive and is unlikely to result in any new net income to operate the institution.

Barring significant annual support from the public sector, the Society would once again have to depend on private contributions. Given its recent history, however, it is unlikely that the Society can raise the substantial sums required through annual appeals. If the Society is to be successful in such a scenario, it will require an extremely large donation from a private benefactor to replenish its unrestricted endowment.

Option 2: Dissolve the Society and Distribute the Collections

The most drastic alternative the Society could choose would be to dissolve itself and sell or otherwise distribute its collections. Choosing this option would amount to an admission that the Society does not have a sufficiently broad support base to justify keeping its collections together and in a single independent institution. In addition, to argue for such an alternative, one must put aside one's concern for the institution and instead place more emphasis on the collections and on what maximizes the use of the limited public resources available to care for them. Put simply, it says that the Society as a whole is worth less than the sum of its parts.

If such a conclusion were reached, the mechanism chosen for such a dissolution would, of course, make all the difference. For example, it would be unacceptable to everyone if the Society opted for selling off the collections through private auctions, even if the proceeds were donated to a worthy cause. It would also not be wise to put the Society into receivership, leaving the responsibility for distribution of the collections in the hands of the New York State attorney general. That office does not have the resources, the staff, or the professional expertise to make important and complicated curatorial decisions that following this course would demand. Finally, it would not be appropriate to have other institutions choose what they wanted from the collections. Such a process would lead to a rapid distribution of the most valuable items, leaving the great majority of less renowned yet historically important items orphaned and at great risk.

How, then, could such a transfer of assets be accomplished? One way might be to assemble a temporary full-time team of professionals to oversee the process. The team could be assembled from a combination of people, some, from inside the Society, who know the collections and others, from outside, who understand how the collections fit within the broader context of collections in the region. The first task for the team would be to divide the collections into contiguous parts. After the parts had been established, the team would identify the cultural institutions that would serve as the best homes for the various materials. These decisions would be based on factors such as the complementarity of the collections, the financial stability of the recipient institution, and the recipient institution's desire to house the materials. Once the collection was prepared and its new home had been identified, it would be the responsibility of the dissolution team to work with recipient institutions to raise funds to pay for the transfer and long-term care of the collections. Bundling the collection with an accompanying endowment is an essential element of the plan. Transferring the collections without funds for their care would risk spreading the burden of the Society's many years of deferred care and maintenance to other cultural institutions.

Option 3: Merge with Another Cultural Institution

The concept of a merger with another cultural institution is not new. For example, as explained earlier, extended negotiations took place between the Society and the Museum of the City of New York in 1990. At the time, the merger was deemed to be prohibitively expensive, but there were also political considerations that blocked the deal. Discussions about possible affiliations have taken place with other institutions as well, most notably the New York Public Library in late 1992 and New York University in 1993.

The key issues to consider in contemplating possible mergers are the complementarity of the collections, the allocation of space, how the merger might improve prospects for long-term financial stability, and the division of governance responsibilities between the boards of the combining entities. A discussion of a potential merger partner for the Society best illustrates these issues.

Consider the Museum of the City of New York (MCNY). The museum and decorative arts collections of the Society and the collections of the MCNY complement each other quite well. Thus one key issue, the compatibility of the collections, offers encouragement. Second, a combined entity could lead to cost savings through economies of scale and decreased administrative staff. In addition, the MCNY is already a member of the CIG, so a merged institution could hope to receive significant regular appropriations from the city. If the city is willing to increase appropriations beyond current levels to reflect the increased needs of the combined entity, these factors represent at least a step toward improved financial prospects for the combined collections.

Unfortunately, a merger between the two institutions would not directly solve space problems. To achieve the desired cost benefits and economies of scale, the combined entity must conduct operations from only one of the properties. As has been mentioned, the Society already owns significantly more materials than it can store in-house. The MCNY operates from a building significantly smaller than that of the Society. Although it is likely that some items could be deaccessioned because of redundancies, the number of items would not be sufficient to resolve this question. Even if space were not an issue, the decision over which facility to use would be controversial and painful. The location of an institution goes to the heart of its identity, its traditions, and its history.

Deciding where a combined institution would be located is not the only problem blocking a merger. Designing a new governance structure for the combined entity also involves extremely sensitive negotiations. How many board members from each institution would be on the new board? Would it be balanced? Who would have control? Compromises on such issues are not easily reached; in fact, disagreements in these areas contributed significantly to the breakdown of the merger discussions in 1990.[2]

To effect a merger, whether it is with the Museum of the City of New York, the New York Public Library, or any other institution, will require an outside catalyst. It is hard to imagine two independent institutions resolving such contentious issues without outside help. For these discussions, the key outside entity is the public sector. The New York State and City governments would actively have to support the merger by appropriating sufficient capital to effect a transfer of the collections and by committing to providing continuing annual operating support for the new entity.

Option 4: Save the Society, but Transfer Part of the Collections

A similar but somewhat less extreme option might be to scale back the Society by transferring a major part of its collections. By transferring either its library or museum collections to another institution, the Society could focus its limited resources. Reducing the Society's scale in this way would improve its chances for achieving financial stability. A key question that would have to be addressed clearly and objectively before this option could be pursued is, How much value is there in keeping the library and museum collections together?

If the conclusion reached was that keeping the collections in a single physical location was no longer feasible, deciding on which collection would remain under the auspices of the Society would be an incredibly complex and controversial undertaking. In fact, resolving such a debate may not be possible. However, the key issues in making such a decision should not rest solely on the internal question of what the Society wants to be but rather should take the broader view of what is best for the collective cultural resources of the region.

Independent of whether the Society would want its future to be as a museum or a library, the impact of such a decision should be considered with respect to the many and varied users of the Society's materials. One could ask, for example, if scholars would be better served by transferring the library collections to the New York Public Library. Similarly, one could look into the benefits of joining the Society's collections with the Museum of the City of New York or the Metropolitan Museum. Working through these questions might help the Society determine its comparative strengths and where it ought to focus its resources.

Option 5: Transfer and Merge

As mentioned, there are many possibilities that could combine various elements from these alternatives. One such combination would be the simultaneous pursuit of both a transfer of part of the collections and a merger with another institution.

Given the discussions that have taken place in the past, it is possible to imagine a transfer of the library collections to the New York Public Library or to NYU and a merger with the Museum of the City of New York. The positive aspects of a merger with the MCNY, discussed earlier in this chapter, would continue to apply. In addition, the problem of space might be resolved by moving the library collections to another location, freeing up substantial space for the MCNY collections at the Society's facility on Central Park West. Still, such a move would surely be painful for the constituents of the MCNY, and there would remain the problem of combining and allocating power on a newly constituted board of trustees. The support of the public sector would again be crucial to executing such a plan.

Option 6: Continue to Operate Independently, but Outside New York City

Many people strongly hold to the belief that the truly unique aspect of the Society's collections is its breadth. The Society's collections offer a visitor or researcher the chance to investigate and experience a wide variety of objects from a particular time. For example, while researching the Civil War, a person could read not only books on the War but also the handwritten letters of soldiers, generals, prisoners, and loved ones. One could view prints, photographs, and works of art relating to the topic. One could see the uniforms, weapons, and other materials used in fighting the battles. The collections can provide a comprehensive picture of a moment in time.

One way to retain this breadth would be to keep the collections together but move them out of New York City. The advantages of such a choice are primarily economic. For one thing, the Society could conceivably sell its building and real estate on Central Park West and use the proceeds to begin to bolster its endowment. Second, the Society could substantially reduce its fixed costs of operations, which are exorbitant in its present location. Third, the Society might stand to benefit from leaving the city, where competition for both visitors and donors is intense.

The biggest disadvantage of such an option is removing the collections from the city. For example, keeping the library collections together and in New York is considered especially important because other research libraries in the region have made acquisitions decisions based on the assumption that the Society's library collections would be available nearby. Local library professionals argue that moving the library would leave a hole in the research resources of the city that could not be repaired.

Conclusions

As one steps back to think in broader terms about the future, one must ask what it is that is truly important about The New-York Historical Society. Put another way, what is it that everyone is so eager to save and to protect? Is it the institution or its collections? The answer has profound implications.

If it is the collections of the Society that are preeminent, then the goal should not be to develop a plan that has the best chance of saving the Society in its present form but rather to find the plan that makes the most efficient use of the economic resources available to support cultural institutions. Pursuing such a goal forces one to address difficult, even sacrosanct issues. For example, everyone would like to see the Society's museum, library, and decorative arts collections remain together, but when is the overall cost too high? The Society has already sold parts of its collections to allow it to pursue this objective. How important, really, is it for the collections to be held in a single physical location? With the rapid advance of multimedia computer and communications technologies, how important will it be ten years from now? These are difficult questions, but they are questions the Society's board must begin to answer.

If the board decides to continue to operate the Society in its present form, the challenge is daunting. Perhaps the Society's biggest problem is that it has so many justifiable reasons for spending money. Who can argue if the Society wants to mount a major initiative to catalog every book, print, and manuscript in the library? Or if it plans to add conservation staff to arrest the deterioration of its museum collections? Or if it chooses to mount an aggressive exhibit, lecture series, and marketing campaign to establish itself as a vital and engaged member of the community? Evaluated individually and independently, these initiatives are all justifiable. But the Society has no money. More than anything else, it has been the pursuit of these honorable objectives that has resulted in the extraordinary deficits at the Society over the past seventeen years.

The solution to the Society's problems does not lie in correcting past wrongs or in finally doing the right thing. In fact, there really is no single answer or solution. More than anything else, the Society must face reality. It must find a permanent and sustainable balance among the many worthwhile uses of its limited resources. For the Society to have a chance to find that balance, expectations must be lowered. Problems nearly two centuries in the making are not going to be solved overnight. Observers, both supporters and critics alike, must take the long view and recognize that rehabilitation of the Society will be a very long process, achieved in small steps.

Notes

1. It is important to distinguish between general operating support and restricted program grants. Chapter Ten includes a thorough examination of the subject. The Society has received grants from local, state, and national government agencies to fulfill specific tasks. In general, these grants, which the Society has received intermittently starting in the late 1960s, have been relatively small and have been used to support specific library initiatives and educational programs.

2. Barbara Debs, personal communication, January 18, 1995.

PART TWO

ANALYSES AND LESSONS FOR NONPROFITS

Through an analysis of the Society's long history, Part One of this study revealed many of the reasons for the institution's present difficulties. Events that occurred over a century ago continue to have an impact, as do management decisions made much more recently. But what can other nonprofit institutions learn from the Society's story? Are there general propositions that emerge from an analysis of the Society's situation?

There are obviously dangers in trying to draw general conclusions based on a study of a single institution. Every organization is unique and has its own idiosyncrasies. The discussion that follows will tend to apply more directly to institutions that are similar to the Society or at least share some of its basic

characteristics. Given that premise, it is helpful to list a few of the key attributes that define a relevant universe of comparable institutions. They are

- Older institutions
- Institutions that own valuable fixed assets
- Institutions that own and maintain valuable collections of art, artifacts, or library materials
- Institutions with high fixed operating costs
- Institutions that do not generate significant levels of earned income

The general lessons that emerge from this analysis of the Society fall into three categories. The first has to do with the nature of a nonprofit institution's assets. The second concerns the need for balance between a nonprofit institution's sources and uses of funds. And the third focuses on the signal importance of governance to the long-term health of organizations in the nonprofit sector.

CHAPTER NINE

THE LIABILITIES OF NONPROFIT ASSETS

It is widely acknowledged that The New-York Historical Society owns assets valued at more than $1 billion. The original watercolors for John James Audubon's *Birds of America* are said to be worth nearly $100 million. The Society's building and real estate have been appraised at a value of more than $50 million. The collection of Hudson River School paintings is worth many millions of dollars. The list goes on and on. These estimates raise one of the most common and most perplexing questions asked about the Society: if its collections are so valuable, how can it possibly be in such severe financial distress?

The popular response to this question is to blame management and the board for irresponsible oversight of the Society. Although mistakes definitely have been made, it is important to recognize that there are deeper forces at work. One major source of confusion and misperception regarding the Society's situation stems from the unwitting use of financial terms and concepts developed in the for-profit sector to assess the standing of the Society and its collections. Unfortunately, terms used to describe economic ideas in the corporate realm, where the paramount objective is to maximize economic value, often do not translate directly into the nonprofit world, where objectives are more complex and cannot always be expressed in the one-dimensional terms of present values.

A perfect example of such a failing is the use of the term *asset* to describe the Society's collections. One accounting definition of an asset is "an object, claim [or] other right owned by and having value to an organization . . . either because it can be exchanged for cash or other goods or services . . . or because [it can be used] to increase the amount of cash or other assets at [the organization's] disposal."[1] This definition effectively establishes two tests to determine whether an item owned by an institution is an asset.

The first test considers whether the item is fungible: can it be exchanged for money or other items of value? The majority of the Society's holdings fail this test. For example, in the case of gifts to the collections that have been made with donor-imposed restrictions, the Society is legally bound to retain them. To sell a restricted item requires a special *cy pres* ruling from the courts.

Moreover, even in the case of items in the collection that are free of such direct restrictions, the Society's ability to sell is limited by professional standards regarding deaccessioning. In general, these standards are designed to discourage the sale of art objects. In the occasional instances when professionals would agree that the sale of a work is justified, standards mandate that the proceeds be used only for new acquisitions. The pressure to adhere to these standards is considerable; an institution that chooses to disregard them is regarded as a pariah and is unlikely to receive accreditation from professional associations. Although the Society raised approximately $16 million for its endowment by deaccessioning a portion of its collections in early 1995, this step was highly unusual and required special dispensation from the New York State attorney general's office and other interested parties.

The second defining test to identify an asset is whether the item itself can generate revenue without being exchanged or sold. A small portion of the Society's best-known collections, such as the Audubon watercolors or the Hudson River School paintings, meet this standard. They attract visitors, bringing in admissions income; reproductions of the works can be sold, creating royalty income; and the collections themselves can travel to other museums, producing fee income. The great majority of the Society's holdings, however, do not generate revenue. The Society holds millions of documents, letters, prints, decorative art objects, manuscripts, and ephemera that tell the story of early America and early New York. Viewed as a group, these items do not generate significant revenue, nor can they be sold. Consequently, they are not assets in the strict financial or accounting sense of the word. (Accountants, recognizing this fact, do not require nonprofits to include collections on their balance sheets.)

The fiscal reality is even more ominous: from a purely financial standpoint, the sum total of the Society's collections resemble liabilities more than they do assets. As was explained in Chapter Eight, the Society's collections are actually a net drain on its resources. Incumbent with ownership of those collections is an unremitting obligation to catalog, conserve, protect, and make accessible millions of items. Although not shown on a nonprofit institution's financial statement, the present value of this future stream of expenditures represents a very real financial liability.

The Value of Nonprofit Assets

If these collections cannot be called assets, does that mean that they are not valuable? Of course not. It is precisely the inherent value of these collections that is at the heart of the Society's reason for being. But how does one express that value, if not in dollar terms? Do we have any other way to keep score? What should we call the Society's collections, if not assets?

Many years of deficits under various leaders provide evidence that the Society's collections cost more to maintain than they can possibly generate directly. Were it a for-profit business, it could not survive in its present form; it would be insolvent. So why does the Society continue to exist? And why should it continue to expend substantial resources to preserve and maintain millions of items that most people will not pay to see?

The answer, of course, lies in our belief in the Society's broader purposes. The Society and similar nonprofit institutions are offered some protection from the harsh disciplines of the market because our culture attaches a value to their mission. This "cultural value," which is quite separate from quantifiable economic value, is, by extension, also applied to a nonprofit institution's collections. Thus even though the *financial* value of a "cultural asset" may be negative, it is still considered valuable if it belongs to and is being cared for by an institution with a mission that the community has deemed worthy of support and protection. In the nonprofit realm, that cultural value becomes monetized through contributions, public appropriations, and private grants. But donors and grantors typically provide these resources based on an assessment of a variety of factors, some of which are independent of the asset itself, such as the worthiness of the institution and its mission, the quality of its leadership, and its long-term financial viability. The value of a *cultural* asset, then, is not determined through a net present value calculation of the future cash flow it can generate; rather, it is determined by the relevance of that asset to the broader cultural purposes and capacities of the institution to which it belongs.

Such a proposition has profound implications for the collections management policies of nonprofit entities responsible for large collections. Most important, it implies that these institutions must be extremely careful about collecting items that are not centrally related to their missions. Holding peripheral collections does not add to the cultural value of the entity. In fact, because owning nonprofit assets results in a long-term financial cost, not a benefit, maintaining collections that are not directly related to an institution's mission diverts resources from the care and sustenance of the assets the institution values most.

The concept of cultural value influences not only what an institution should acquire but also what it should keep. The Society's history provides a dramatic illustration of what can happen when the relationship between an institution's mission and its collections is not carefully managed. The uncritical accumulation of materials for many, many years played a major role in creating financial obligations that far exceed the Society's present capacity to meet them.

Acquisitions Policy

Because cultural assets are costly, even when a potential acquisition is judged to be relevant to an institution's mission, care must be taken to ensure that resources will be available for its long-term maintenance. In some cases, it may even be prudent to decline to accept a gift, even if it is enormously valuable. An analogy will help illustrate the point. Suppose that a person with a modest income appears on a television game show and wins a car, a brand new Jaguar. After driving home, the contestant discovers that with the Jaguar comes a whole host of expenses for taxes, insurance, gas, and maintenance. Without the requisite income to afford the new expenses, the contestant becomes increasingly late in making house payments or has trouble paying for regular living expenses. Even a moderate unforeseen expense could drive the person into bankruptcy. In this case, the winner must be smart enough to know not to accept the "free" gift. The admonition is clear: "Don't take the Jaguar!"

Of course, the contestant in this Jaguar example always has the option of selling the car. As has been mentioned, nonprofit institutions do not typically have that option. Consequently, when offered a gift that is relevant to its mission, nonprofit leaders should also ask the donor to help pay for its ongoing maintenance. After all, the nonprofit institution is not receiving a financial benefit from the donor; rather, it is taking on a financial obligation. If the donor is unwilling or unable to provide supplemental financial resources, the institution should either be confident that it can raise the funds in other ways or it should decline the gift.

The inherent cost of cultural assets also suggests that nonprofit managers should attempt to retain flexibility in what they do with the gifts that their institutions do accept. Whenever possible, terms of gifts should be structured to be for the benefit of the institution, not to achieve a specific objective of the donor. Circumstances change, and flexibility must be retained to allow the governing board to use and deploy the institution's resources in the most efficient manner.

Again, an example will help illustrate the point. A wealthy alumnus chooses to donate a valuable painting to the art museum at his alma mater. When it accepts the gift, the university should take steps to protect its right to sell the painting under appropriate conditions. If, as a stipulation to the gift, the donor demands that the university exhibit this painting in the museum forever, a decision to accept the painting should be made very carefully. Accepting the painting with that restriction is justified only if the painting meshes with the museum's other collections and if exhibiting it furthers the museum's fundamental mission. Even then, who can predict whether that situation will continue to exist indefinitely? In such a case, a decision to accept the painting must balance the importance of the painting to both the museum and the broader purposes of the university with the cost of incorporating the painting into the museum's collections, paying for curatorial and restoration work that may be needed, and again, providing funds for its long-term preservation and care.

Deaccessioning

This examination of the nature of nonprofit assets would be incomplete if it overlooked deaccessioning, an issue of great concern not just to observers of the Society but to all parties interested in culturally important collections and the institutions that manage them. The New-York Historical Society has been heavily criticized for its deaccessions over the years, most notably its sales of the Bryan collection of European paintings, the final stage of which took place in January 1995. The issues and controversy surrounding the topic are sufficiently complex that even a cursory assessment is beyond the scope of this study; a proper analysis would constitute a separate project. Still, this investigation of the Society's history has uncovered issues and questions that should be considered carefully as part of the continuing debate.

First, it is clear that some way must be found to destigmatize deaccessioning. Feelings are so strong about the topic that a popular and uncompromising theology has evolved that is used to attack any institution that even considers selling part of its collections. It is generally assumed that an institution engaged in deaccessioning is doing so to raise money and that its board is searching for an easy way out of a financial bind. This assumption may be true in too many cases—but it is not always true. There are situations in which it is sensible to deaccession portions of a collection for reasons that have nothing to do with finances. Redundant items in a collection represent such a case. The nonprofit community would be better served if less energy were expended on attacking deaccessioning on principle and more effort were spent identifying the circumstances that define when deaccessioning is—and is not—a proper course of action.

The case of the Society presents an interesting illustration of the complexities of the deaccessioning issue. For well over one hundred years, the Society had virtually no acquisitions policy. Its accepted whatever was given to it without considering whether the gift was appropriate or relevant to its mission. Should the simple fact that an item was given to an institution in the past commit that institution to caring for it forever? Putting aside the Society's recent efforts to narrow its mission, what if the assets never were relevant to even a tolerably broad interpretation of the Society's mission? Should current management and trustees be saddled with the acquisitions mistakes of their predecessors? Independent of any desire to raise funds, a decision to sell irrelevant collections seems justified.

The linkage between an institution's mission and the value of its cultural assets offers another perspective on the deaccession debate. Up to this point, this inquiry into the value of cultural assets has asserted that the financial value of a cultural asset is generally negative. The reasons are that cultural assets consume resources and cannot be sold. Introducing the possibility of deaccessioning changes these assumptions by making the asset fungible. The total value of that asset now has two components: one continues to be cultural, determined by the broad importance of the asset to society, but the other now becomes financial, determined by the estimated market price of the asset. Unfortunately, once the asset has a financial value attached to it, its cultural value can be obscured. It is very difficult for most people to value what cannot be measured. It is this disregard for the cultural value of a nonprofit asset that critics of deaccessioning properly decry.

Even in cases where it is accepted that deaccessioning of collections is warranted, a second controversy revolves around the proper use of the financial proceeds from those sales. For the simplicity of this discussion, consider the question of selling paintings from a museum.

The generally accepted practice among museum professionals is that proceeds from deaccessioning should be used only for new acquisitions. In fact, for some museum professionals, it seems that almost any deaccession decision is justified if proceeds are used to purchase more art. Although this logic is both understandable and appealing, it raises an important question: if it is acceptable to trade one painting for another, why is it unacceptable to trade one capital good, a painting, for another capital good? It is clearly irresponsible to sell a painting and then use the proceeds for operations; that would be liquidating capital. But what if the value—cultural, financial, or a combination of the two—that resides in a piece of art is transferred to another capital item like endowment, the principal of which must be held in perpetuity? If investment proceeds from that endowment were used to fund an important curatorial position, would that be a misuse of funds? Which use of the capital goes further toward allowing the institution to fulfill its basic mission? Presumably the mission of an art museum is more than just amassing paintings. It has to do something with them.

In the final analysis, the decision about whether an item should be deaccessioned depends on many factors. The nonprofit community would benefit greatly from a thorough and objective investigation of the complexities. As part of such an assessment, one useful framework for identifying both when deaccessioning is appropriate and what should be done with the proceeds might be to focus on the source of the cultural component of a nonprofit asset's value, that is, its relevance and importance to the mission of the nonprofit entity.

Conclusion

There are dangers in translating terms and concepts between the for-profit and nonprofit sectors. For example, the for-profit definition of *assets* is misleading when applied to collections held by nonprofit institutions. Due to restrictions on the fungibility of those collections and their limited capacity to generate revenue, most of these "cultural assets" are actually long-term financial *liabilities* to their owners. Knowing that, when one hears that the Society owns an important and valuable collection of more than six million cultural assets, one should not be surprised that the Society faces a present and future of financial hardship.

In addition, there are also concepts that are important in the nonprofit sector but have no direct counterparts in the for-profit realm. For example, the notion of the cultural value of an asset has little, if any, meaning in a profit-maximizing economic environment. It is therefore a concept that is difficult for most people to understand. That is why, when a nonprofit asset is considered for deaccessioning and is tagged with a dollar value, the emphasis on its cultural value is often lost. Retaining focus on the cultural value of collections requires a thorough understanding of the mission of the nonprofit "owner" and the relevance of the asset to it.

There is little doubt that the financial environment surrounding nonprofit institutions with large collections is becoming increasingly difficult. If nonprofit leaders are to be successful in guiding their institutions through the difficult times that lie ahead, they will need to have a clear understanding of the distinctive characteristics of "cultural assets"—and to recognize them as financial liabilities.

Note

1. Shillinglaw and Meyer (1986, p. 4).

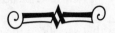

CHAPTER TEN

THE COMPLEXITIES OF NONPROFIT FINANCING

Simply stated, an operating deficit is the result of a shortage of current income relative to operating expenditures during a fiscal year. The actions required to reverse a deficit—either cutting expenditures or raising additional revenue—are never easily accomplished, but they are especially difficult for nonprofit institutions. Cutting expenditures is problematic because nonprofit operating costs tend to rise at an unremitting rate. Increasing operating income is difficult because a significant portion of a nonprofit's revenues often comes from contributors who choose to restrict the use of gifts and grants to specific purposes. These restrictions force nonprofit institutions to do more than just balance the flow of funds into and out of their overall accounts. They must match various sources of funds with specific uses and carefully manage the growth of unrestricted income to ensure that there are adequate funds to pay for general operating expenses.

The financial struggles of The New-York Historical Society provide a rich and dramatic illustration of these complex issues. Expenditures at the N-YHS have risen steadily since World War II, and at a rate consistently higher than inflation. Revenue growth did not keep pace, and by the late 1960s, the Society was having difficulty balancing its budget. In the twenty-four years between 1970 and 1994, the Society suffered deficits nineteen times. These deficits put pressure on what had traditionally been the Society's largest and most reliable revenue stream, the income from its endowment, resulting in policies that sacrificed the endowment's future revenue-generating potential. This chapter reviews the key aspects of this evolution in an effort to draw out lessons of general importance to nonprofit managers and board members.

Expenditures

Since 1960, the total operating expenditures of the Society have increased at a nominal rate of 9.7 percent per year, which is equal to a real rate of 4.6 percent per year. This rate of growth is surprisingly high when one considers that the average annual growth in GDP over the same period was just 2.7 percent. By no means all of this growth in expenditures was the result of programmatic expansion. For example, between 1960 and 1970, operating expenditures at the Society more than doubled, from approximately $402,000 to $887,000,[1] even as the salaried administrative staff at the Society declined from forty to thirty-one persons.

Other than expansion, what else could account for the Society's high expenditure growth rate? Research has shown that costs for institutions with labor-intensive processes for producing "output" tend to rise at a rate faster than the overall price level. This phenomenon, often referred to as Baumol's disease or Bowen's law, is caused by the fact that productivity in labor-intensive industries does not increase as fast as productivity in capital-intensive industries. If wage rates and the prices of other inputs remain in relative balance throughout the economy, the unit costs for institutions with low productivity growth will rise relative to unit costs in general.[2] The Society's activities are unquestionably labor-intensive, and hence Bowen's law offers one explanation for the Society's persistent growth of expenditures over the years.

Although it is possible that there are purely internal explanations for the Society's rising costs, it is likely that the causes are primarily external. The strongest evidence for this is the fact that other nonprofit institutions share this tendency toward inexorable expenditure growth. A recent study of thirty-two prominent nonprofit institutions found that total expenditures rose at a nominal rate of 10.6 percent between 1972 and 1992.[3] Similarly, a study of five major independent research libraries (institutions very similar in many ways to the Society) showed that between 1960 and 1993, their total expenditures rose at an average nominal rate of 9.9 percent per year.[4] The data clearly testify to significant upward pressure on costs at these types of institutions. Given such pressures, it is unlikely that these organizations can hope to balance their budgets through sustainable decreases in total expenditures without significant reductions in services.

Further evidence supporting this assertion emerges from the Society's 1992–1993 financial crisis. Facing mounting deficits and a growing threat of bankruptcy, the Society cut operating expenditures by 17 percent in fiscal 1992 and by 20 percent in fiscal 1993. To accomplish these cuts, the Society reduced its total workforce from a peak of 125 employees in the 1980s to a skeleton staff of just 35 employees in early 1993. The Society closed its galleries and suspended all public programs. There is a limit, however, to how much an organization can cut, year after year. For organizations with valuable collections and fixed assets, overhead and other fixed costs exist that cannot be avoided. Even though the Society had drastically reduced programs and services, its total operating expenditures in 1993 were still $5.3 million.

Such austerity measures have consequences. Most important, it is extremely difficult, if not impossible, for an institution like the Society to generate significant contributed income while it is inactive. Such institutions are expected to offer exhibitions, public education programs, and community outreach services. After a certain point, reductions in expenditures decrease the capacity to generate revenue, both earned and contributed. In the case of the Society, the 1992 and 1993 cuts did not balance the budget; in fact, the deficit actually increased in 1992 and was still $1.5 million in 1993.

The implication of the unremitting pressure on costs is clear: if institutions like the Society are to remain financially viable for the long term, their revenues must grow steadily—and presumably faster than the overall inflation rate.

Revenues

Generating revenues that keep pace with an ever-expanding expenditure base is made more complicated by the fact that all nonprofit revenues are not created equal. Unlike the for-profit sector, where dollars received can be used for whatever purposes management and the board may choose, nonprofit revenues often come with strings attached. A donor may stipulate that funds given to an institution be used only for a specified purpose, spent over an established period of time, or retained in perpetuity as capital. The types of revenues generated by a nonprofit institution can be as important as the absolute dollar values, especially in a time of crisis.

To recognize donor-imposed restrictions in the financial statements of nonprofit entities, a special form of accounting called fund accounting, which links resources and their intended use, was developed. Although straightforward in concept, fund accounting can be extremely confusing in practice. An attempt to clarify the mysteries of fund accounting would take us too far afield; however, there are two issues of broad importance that are illuminated by the Society's accounts. First, the distinction between restricted and unrestricted revenues is a fundamental fund accounting concept that, if misunderstood, can lead to serious confusion concerning the financial health of an organization. Second, the difference between current and capital financial flows, particularly as it intersects with principles of endowment management, continues to perplex not only observers of the nonprofit sector but also many nonprofit administrators and board members.

Restricted Versus Unrestricted Revenues: The Debs Dilemma

In 1988, Barbara Debs took over an institution in acute financial crisis. The Society had run deficits in eleven of the previous thirteen years, and its fiscal 1988 deficit was its largest ever: $3.7 million on a total budget of approximately $7 million. During her four years in office, Debs, her staff, and the Society's trustees managed to raise over $23 million—an extraordinary accomplishment. That success notwithstanding, the Society still ran significant deficits in each year. In fact, when Debs stepped down in September 1992, the Society was financially worse off than it had been when she assumed office. Although annual deficits had been reduced, endowment available to help pay for general operating expenses had declined, and the Society had incurred an external debt of $1 million.

The Society's fiscal 1990 financial records exemplify the complexities involved in trying to ascertain the financial condition of a nonprofit. In that year, the Society brought in approximately $11.1 million, while it spent only $8.2 million. Nevertheless, the Society had an operating *deficit* of $1.8 million. How did this happen?

The answer lies in the nature of the funds flowing into the Society and the fact that only a portion could be used to pay for ongoing operating activities. Of the $11.1 million raised, $2.4 million was a capital inflow, designated for the endowment. Since only investment income from an endowment can be used to pay for current operating expenditures (and then only if the expenditures match any restrictions), very little new money actually flowed to the operating account. Although the remaining $8.7 million could be categorized as current revenues, $4.1 million was restricted to specific uses. These funds were dedicated to such purposes as the Society's "Why History?" program, public outreach initiatives, library and museum collections conservation, and museum exhibitions. Only $4.6 million, 42 percent of the total funds raised, remained to pay for the Society's general unrestricted operations. Operating expenditures (including administrative salaries, building maintenance, utilities, insurance, security, consulting fees, and general administration) amounted to approximately $6.2 million. Hence the nearly $2 million operating deficit.

The relatively low percentage of revenue available to pay for unrestricted general operating expenditures in this instance is not at all unusual for a modern nonprofit institution. In recent years, funders have increasingly tended to make restricted grants, and often only to fund new programs and initiatives. As all nonprofit managers and trustees know, this trend is fraught with danger.

First, it can be difficult to ensure that total expenditures on a restricted program do not exceed the amount of money provided by a grant. Managing a restricted grant will use time and facilities that may not be fully covered, even if there is an allowance for indirect costs. Sophisticated cost accounting allocation estimates are required to get it right. Anything short of superior management of such a grant can end up costing an institution more money than it brings in.

Even if an institution is extremely well managed and has tight financial controls, restricted grants can encourage institutional growth or special projects that cannot be sustained. A recent report on the Society's library documented numerous examples of cataloging and preservation initiatives that had been started with targeted grants but could not be completed due to lack of funds.[5] It is difficult to rebuild enthusiasm for projects that are left only partially completed, no matter how important they may be. More dramatic are situations in which a new program is initiated for which staff must be hired. When the term of the grant expires and the funder has moved on to other priorities, the nonprofit institution has to deal with the task of either releasing employees or finding a way to continue the initiative with funding from other sources (including some unrestricted funds).

The Society has also exhibited clearly the most profound problem related to the distinction between restricted and unrestricted income: when funders want to provide only restricted grants, there may be no way to pay for the basic costs that keep an institution alive. This problem generally becomes even more pronounced when an institution begins to encounter financial difficulty. Typically, donors are unlikely to offer unrestricted funds to institutions perceived to be in trouble because of a very real fear that the funds will serve no long-run purpose. Of course, this sequence of events represents a vicious circle: the institution got into financial trouble in the first place because of a lack of unrestricted resources.

Cash Is King

This study has documented numerous ways in which nonprofits differ from their for-profit cousins, but a fundamental need they both share is the need for cash. In the corporate world, it is not losses that put companies out of business but rather a lack of cash to pay creditors. For nonprofits, it is usually a lack of unrestricted funds to pay employees that closes the doors. For nearly a year leading up to the closing of the Society in February 1993, its leaders desperately searched for cash that would enable it to stay open. First, a $1 million loan was secured from a private foundation, funds subsequently rolled over into a debt assumed by several members of the board. Later, a $1.5 million loan was negotiated with Sotheby's. Meanwhile, the Society removed all board-designated restrictions from funds and applied for *cy pres* relief from the courts in order to use certain special funds. As long as the Society was able to find cash, it could remain open. The Society's story implies that nonprofit institutions need to be every bit as expert, if not more so, at managing cash flow as their for-profit counterparts.

The fact that the Society delayed its closing by finding cash through loans and other means was by no means an entirely positive development. These loans were obtained even as the Society continued to run significant operating deficits. The natural consequence was that the Society continued to dig itself into a deeper financial hole. Simply put, it is one thing to borrow money to cover temporary shortages of cash when one can predict future receipts with confidence; it is quite another to borrow cash simply because one has run out of it.

Sources of Unrestricted Income

Beyond the distinction between restricted and unrestricted revenue streams, there are also different types of unrestricted income. The major sources of nonprofit operating income can be broken down into four categories: earned income, government appropriations, private contributions, and investment income.[6] Is there a proper balance among the various forms of unrestricted revenue for particular types of institutions? If so, what are the implications for the "marketing" strategies that should be pursued?

Over the course of its history, the Society has depended almost exclusively on private contributions to support its activities. As was explained in Chapter Nine, the Society's collections do not generate revenue, so earned income has never played a major role. Earned income from such things as admissions, contributions, royalties on publications, gift shop sales, and facility rentals have averaged only 8 percent of total revenues since 1960. As for government support, except for $2.6 million in transitional funding appropriated following the Society's 1993 crisis, the public sector has provided essentially no unrestricted support in recent times. The responsibility for supporting core operations of the Society has fallen on private giving. The annual revenues from these gifts break down into two different forms: (1) investment income earned on previous endowment gifts and (2) unrestricted contributions.

Before discussing the implications of these two types of income streams, it is important to point out that when private contributions are received by an organization, its board may have some discretion in determining whether each gift should be categorized as a current gift or a capital gift. For the most part, unrestricted gifts are spent when they are received; however, when an organization receives a large one-time gift or bequest, the board should consider categorizing the gift as capital and adding it to the endowment. After all, the large bequest is not truly operating income; it will not be received in subsequent years.

An example will help emphasize the importance of this point. Over the course of eighteen months in 1985 and 1986 (the Society converted to a June 30 fiscal year in 1986), the Society received more than $2 million from the estate of Clara Peck. The cash received from this gift was recognized by the Society as current unrestricted operating income. Consequently, in the year-end statements for 1985 and 1986, the Society registered a significant surplus.

Technically, there is nothing wrong with representing the gift in this way; however, this characterization of the Society's financial activity can have undesirable consequences. From an internal perspective, the additional income can relieve the pressure on Society staff, thereby lessening their resolve to control expenditures and maximize other revenue sources. From the standpoint of an uninitiated outside observer, such a representation could lead to the erroneous conclusion that the Society had finally brought its recurring expenditures in line with revenues. As soon as the Peck bequest had been spent, the Society was running large deficits once again.

The decision about the proper way to treat large one-time gifts comes down to a question of timing. By spending the Peck bequest in its entirety, the Society chose to emphasize current spending over future revenue-generating potential. A similar question of timing must be faced by a board as it contemplates how best to manage its endowment, an important issue to be addressed later in this chapter.

Although investment income and unrestricted contributions both come from essentially the same source (private benefactors), maximizing the value and growth of these revenue streams involves distinctly different management processes and depends on different factors for success. For example, once an endowment has been established, the revenue stream derived from that financial base should be relatively predictable. If the endowment is invested and managed wisely, it has a good chance of growing at a rate exceeding inflation. Unrestricted contributions, by contrast, are a far more volatile revenue source. If an institution somehow falls out of favor, contributions can decline precipitously. Moreover, increasing these contributions on an annual basis requires extraordinarily loyal supporters, perseverance, and fundraising skill.

Obviously, other things being equal, all nonprofit managers would like to have a large endowment base to support their operations. This is rarely possible. Moreover, looked at from the broad perspective of the well-being of the nonprofit sector, it may not be desirable. For some institutions, their characteristics and the nature of their missions make having an endowment important; in other situations, this is less appropriate. It is in the best interest of society to concentrate the limited capital resources available in those institutions that need endowments the most.

Compare, for example, The New-York Historical Society and a dance company run by its founding choreographer. The dance company's principal asset is the creative gift of its founder. Though it is possible that the founder can institutionalize his or her talent through training young dancers and choreographers, in many cases, this does not happen. The "product" is more ephemeral and is validated by the contributed support it receives on an annual basis, as well as through ticket sales and other forms of earned income. By contrast, the Society's library and museum collections are not ephemeral; they are material objects that constitute an irreplaceable resource. Although few people question the cultural value of the millions of manuscripts, books, prints, and other historical documents and artifacts held by the Society, they are not the kinds of assets that inspire and excite contributors. The effort of the Society to generate private contributions, especially over the past five or six years, illustrates that fact. An institution like the Society needs a source of support that both matches the inert nature of its collections and has the potential to grow at least as fast as its expenditures. It must have an endowment.

Endowment Management

The importance of endowment to the Society's long-term financial viability makes the events of the past twenty-five years especially tragic. In 1969, the market value of the Society's unrestricted endowment was $15.7 million, a figure 21.5 times larger than that year's total operating expenditures. Investment proceeds from the endowment exceeded the Society's total operating expenditures. Even if the Society had not generated a single dollar of contributed or earned income, it would have had an operating surplus.

By 1989, the Society's endowment base had been almost totally eradicated. Nominal endowment had fallen to just $5.5 million, *$1 million less than that year's annual total expenditures.* Whereas investment income accounted for 91 percent of total revenues in 1969, it represented just 13 percent of the total in 1989. Obviously, the magnitude of this decline has the most profound implications for the Society. Documenting the causes of that decline offers a classic illustration of the complex and sometimes confusing issues that endowed institutions face as they strive to balance the need for current income with the desire to protect the real value of their endowments over time.

The growth of an endowment depends on three primary elements: investment performance, the addition of capital gifts, and the amount of investment income spent on operations or otherwise drawn down. Before addressing the Society's experience in each of these categories, it is helpful first to summarize briefly some basic principles of endowment management.

Total Return

The return on a capital investment has two fundamental components. The first component, the current return or yield, usually comes in the form of dividends and interest and can be spent without affecting the nominal value of the capital base that generated it. The second component, capital appreciation, is not fungible unless some part of the underlying capital asset is liquidated. Selling units of capital generates realized gains or losses, which are the difference between the selling price and the price at which each unit of the capital in question was purchased (or if a gift, the market value at the time it was received).

In the 1960s, most institutions, including the Society, operated under the assumption that it was inappropriate to "invade" the principal of the endowment by spending realized capital gains. Only dividends and interest generated by the portfolio could be spent. As operating costs rose, so did pressure to generate more current spendable income. For many institutions, maximizing current yield became their investment managers' primary objective. This emphasis on current returns led many managers to sacrifice the long-term growth of their investment capital.

In 1967, the Society adopted a "total return" investment policy for its endowment. The primary objective of this policy is to maximize the total return on the portfolio, independent of whether that return comes in the form of interest, dividends, or gains from capital appreciation. A total return approach is based on the premise that the decision regarding how much of the total return should be spent in a given year can and should be separated from the decision about what assets the portfolio should be invested in.

A total return investment policy must always be paired with a spending rate, a formula that governs what percentage of the market value of the endowment can prudently be spent on operations in a single year. Established by an institution's board of trustees, the spending rate should strike a balance between short-term spending needs and long-term capital growth. In order to increase the predictability and reduce the volatility of the investment income stream, spending is usually determined by multiplying the spending rate by a multiyear moving average of the value of the endowment or by using some other smoothing mechanism.

The failure of the Society to protect its endowment can be attributed to a mix of factors. The following analysis reviews the Society's performance in each of the three areas of endowment management.

Return on Investments

The Society was a leader among institutions of its kind in adopting a professional approach to the management of its investments. In 1964, during the presidency of Frederick B. Adams Jr., the Society hired Fiduciary Trust International, Inc., to manage its investments. Fiduciary Trust remains the Society's investment manager today. Overall, the performance of the Society's investments has been in line with market indexes. Since 1980, the Society's total fund has earned a compound annual return of 12.4 percent. This figure compares with a compound annual return of 13.5 percent for the Standard & Poor's 500 and a 15.1 percent return on the Dow Jones Industrial Average.

Table 10.1 shows the Society's annual investment performance from 1981 through 1993 as compared to total annual return benchmarks published by Cambridge Associates.[7] The table reveals that the performance of the Society's portfolio was quite respectable. It is clear that the erosion of the Society's endowment during the 1980s was not due to poor management of the investments.

Capital Gifts

The second element of a comprehensive endowment management policy is capital fundraising. New gifts provide a boost to an institution's financial base when investment returns are good and help it maintain that base when they are not.

For institutions dependent on endowment, the 1970s were extremely difficult. The loss of endowment principal in the early part of the decade, coupled with high inflation, fundamentally altered the budgetary equation. Investment returns were falling just as costs were rising, and deficits became the rule. The historical narrative presented earlier documents not only the Society's mounting deficits but also its poor record of private fundraising. Capital fundraising was no exception.

Given the struggle to balance the operating budget, it should come as no surprise that the Society did not raise capital gifts during this period. Except for 1977, when capital gifts totaled $259,000, the Society raised a total of just $85,000 in sixteen years, an average of just $5,300 a year.[8]

Spending Rate

The final element of endowment management concerns the use of investment returns to help pay operating expenses. When the Society adopted a total return philosophy in 1967, the spending rate established by the board of trustees was 5 percent of the three-year moving average of the market value of the unrestricted endowment.

TABLE 10.1. INVESTMENT PERFORMANCE, 1981–1993.

Year	N-YHS Total Return (%)	Cambridge Equity Return (%)	Cambridge Bond Return (%)	Cambridge Mix (%)
1981	−0.3	−5.0	−1.3	−4.1
1982	18.0	21.5	42.5	26.8
1983	20.1	22.4	6.3	18.4
1984	7.2	6.1	16.9	8.8
1985	28.1	31.6	30.1	31.2
1986	20.5	18.6	19.9	18.9
1987	3.2	5.1	−0.3	3.8
1988	11.8	16.6	10.7	15.1
1989	24.3	31.7	16.2	27.8
1990	2.0	−3.1	6.8	−0.6
1991	21.1	30.5	19.9	27.9
1992	5.2	7.6	9.4	8.1
1993	12.2	10.1	13.2	10.9
Compound return	12.4	14.3	14.1	14.3

Sources: Fiduciary Trust International, Inc.; Kennedy and Schneider (1994). Used by permission of Cambridge Associates, Inc.

An example will help illustrate how a spending rate works in practice. At the end of 1971, the three-year moving average of the market value of the Society's endowment for 1969, 1970, and 1971 was $13.88 million. At a spending rate of 5 percent, the Society was authorized to spend $694,000. Dividend and interest income, however, amounted to only $450,000. To make up the difference, the Society spent an additional $244,000 of realized gains and thereby reached the authorized spending limit.

An estimate of the Society's total return in 1971 is 16.4 percent. Couldn't the Society have spent more than 5 percent of the endowment's market value during the year? If its goal were simply to maintain the real purchasing power of the endowment for that single year, the answer is yes. The inflation rate in 1971 (calculated from the growth in GDP) was 5.4 percent. Consequently, the Society could have spent an additional 6.0 percent (16.4 percent minus 5 percent minus 5.4 percent), or $833,000, and exactly maintained the real value of its endowment.[9] However, the purpose of a spending rate is to maintain the real value of the endowment *over the long term.* There will invariably be years, such as 1981 (see Table 10.1), when the total return on the endowment does not exceed the sum of inflation and the spending rate. By accepting the discipline of a responsible long-term spending rate, an institution counters the volatility of the markets and increases the likelihood that investment income can continue to provide its required share of the total revenue pool.

For a period, the Society kept its spending from the endowment within the 5 percent constraint; however, in 1974, pressured by a variety of financial factors, the Society spent 7 percent of the market value of its endowment. That action set a very bad precedent. By the mid 1980s, the Society appeared to ignore entirely the maximum spending rate established as part of the total return policy.

Without an enforced spending limit, the total return concept is not an endowment management philosophy; it becomes an improper justification for liquidating endowment principal. In 1985, the Society withdrew a total of $2.7 million from the endowment to pay for operations, an astounding 24.7 percent of the endowment's total market value. In 1986, it spent 15.5 percent. And in 1987, the Society spent an amazing 28.1 percent of its total endowment portfolio.[10]

During this period, the extraordinary level of spending from the endowment was hidden by the tremendous performance of the equity markets. In 1985, for example, the average total return in the equity markets was 31.6 percent.[11] Consequently, even though the Society had spent huge sums from the endowment, in nominal terms the value of the portfolio at the end of the year was still higher than it had been at the beginning of the year. Without a thorough understanding of these concepts and a detailed knowledge of what had transpired, it might have appeared that the Society's spending decisions were justified. After all, the endowment had grown. But this spending plan is like a Ponzi scheme: the deception works only as long as it is fueled by new money. In this case, the new money came in the form of extraordinary investment returns, which were a temporary phenomenon. The October 1987 stock market crash ended the delusion.

Because of the importance of endowment to an institution like the Society, the deleterious impact of its 1980s endowment spending record cannot be exaggerated. During the period between 1974 and 1988, realized gains spent by the Society exceeded the 5 percent spending rate by more than $11 million.

Figure 10.1 shows the cumulative impact of the Society's spending policy on the growth of the endowment since it first exceeded the 5 percent spending rate in 1974. The assumptions of the model are as follows:

1. Spending is limited to 5 percent of the moving average of the end-of-year market value of the endowment for the three previous years.
2. Because the timing of flows into the endowment (in the form of spending) and out of the endowment (in the form of capital gifts) are unknown, it is assumed that the Society earned the benefits of capital appreciation on half of those funds during the year.
3. Between 1981 and 1993, actual annual investment returns as reported by Fiduciary Trust International, Inc., are used to calculate annual appreciation. Those figures are not available for the period between 1975 and 1980. For those years, total return is estimated using a weighted combination of average stock and

FIGURE 10.1. PROJECTED GROWTH OF THE ENDOWMENT WITH 5 PERCENT SPENDING LIMIT IMPOSED, 1975–1993.

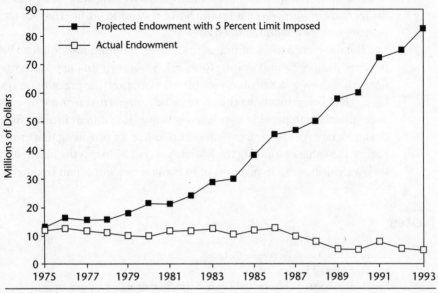

Source: Table C.10 in Appendix C.

bond annual returns published by Cambridge Associates.[12] The ratio of equities to bonds in the weighted average is 75 percent to 25 percent.

This model isolates the impact of the Society's spending from the endowment since 1975. It uses the Society's actual investment performance and the actual capital gifts received, and it follows the board-designated spending policy. It reveals that had the Society operated within the 5 percent spending policy, by the end of 1993 the market value of its endowment could have been nearly $84 million, instead of the actual value of approximately $5 million. Under this scenario, the justifiable 5 percent spending from the endowment in 1993 would have been $3.5 million![13]

Conclusion

The total dollar value of gifts, grants, and contributions in a report from the development office represents only a small part of the revenue picture of a large nonprofit. Is that grant restricted? Can it all be spent this year? Which grants are for endowment? Is the income from that endowment unrestricted? These questions illuminate just a few of the many issues that must be taken into account because nonprofit donors can direct their gifts to specific purposes. Managing these distinctions requires close administrative control to ensure that sources of support are matched with intended uses.

But the complexities of managing a large nonprofit institution go beyond the restrictions on gifts and grants. Research has shown that expenditures at many nonprofits grow at a rate in excess of inflation, exerting pressure on revenues to keep pace. For institutions that cannot rely on earned income or government appropriations to provide significant revenue, investment income from the endowment emerges as the most important source for providing that growth. Sadly, part of the value in studying the Society's recent history is the fact that it provides such a clear illustration of how not to manage this important resource.

Notes

1. See Table C.4–1 in Appendix C.
2. Baumol and Bowen (1966).
3. Bowen, Nygren, Turner, and Duffy, (1994, p. 168).
4. Bergman (1995).
5. McCorison (1995).
6. Investment income is actually a subset of private contributions—it is the current return on a previous capital gift. The importance of investment income to nonprofit institutions like the Society warrants its being analyzed as a separate category.
7. Kennedy and Schneider (1994, pp. 19, 23, 25). The column headed "Cambridge Mix" is a weighted average with an assumption that the benchmark investment portfolio is comprised of 75 percent equities and 25 percent bonds.
8. See Tables C.4–2 and C.5–2 in Appendix C.
9. For the sake of simplicity in this discussion, GDP growth is used as the targeted growth rate for the endowment. As has been shown, the Society's expenditures typically grow at a rate exceeding the general price level; consequently, it could be argued that it would be more precise to estimate the Society's higher expenditure growth rate and use that as a target.
10. See Table C.6–2 in Appendix C.
11. Kennedy and Schneider (1994, p. 19).
12. Kennedy and Schneider (1994).
13. For an explanation of the calculation used for this estimate, along with the underlying data, see Table C.10 in Appendix C.

CHAPTER ELEVEN

THE IMPORTANCE OF GOVERNANCE

It is hard to imagine an institutional history that would provide a richer illustration of the difficulties that nonprofit organizations face than that of The
New-York Historical Society. Major issues already discussed in the second part of
this study include the unique character of nonprofit assets, the distinctions between restricted and unrestricted income, and the importance of careful endowment management. But perhaps no lesson manifests itself more clearly than
the critical importance of governing boards to the long-term health and viability
of organizations in the nonprofit sector. After all, the Society's trustees are ultimately accountable for the decisions and policies, pursued over many years,
that brought the institution from a position of relative financial stability to near
insolvency.

Exactly what are the responsibilities of a nonprofit board? There has been
considerable research on this subject.[1] In brief, the primary responsibilities include
hiring (and firing) the chief executive, setting and updating the organization's basic
mission, overseeing strategic planning, ensuring that the necessary resources are
available to achieve the organization's objectives, and building and sustaining the
diversity and effectiveness of the board itself.

Unfortunately, the Society's board cannot be said to have fulfilled these responsibilities. Over most of its history, the Society did not reexamine or update
its mission, even though its operating environment had changed drastically. In
addition, the long string of operating deficits serves as clear evidence of the

board's failure to ensure that the institution had sufficient resources to meet its objectives. Most important, there is little evidence to suggest that prior to the crisis of 1988, the board faced up to the problems besetting the Society and then set a strategic direction for the institution.

But the purpose of this chapter is not to affix blame for the Society's predicament on its board; rather, it is to highlight what might be learned from this board's struggles. More specifically, it is hoped that delineating the issues the board faced during the Society's decline might help other nonprofit leaders recognize the warning signals of impending trouble.

The Society's saga demonstrates that recognizing trouble and taking steps to overcome it in a timely way are enormously important. If the stature and health of a nonprofit institution are allowed to slip, a loss of board autonomy often follows. What are the steps that signal this loss of control?

When a stable institution first encounters operating deficits, the board has many options for responding to the problem, both in terms of managing short-term cash flow and making longer-term revenue and expenditure adjustments. As deficits mount, however, either financial assets are depleted or debts are incurred, and financial flexibility is sacrificed. If the situation does not turn around, the institution is then forced to look to outside parties to help it avert a financial crisis, a step that sacrifices strategic control. Fundamental decisions about the mission and long-term direction of the institution can end up largely in the hands of outsiders. If the situation devolves further into public controversy played out in the press, the attorney general's office, or politicians' public hearings, the board's ability to direct or even to frame the debate concerning important questions will be lost. The implication of this progression is clear: trustees of institutions facing difficulty must resist the very real temptation to wait for circumstances to improve; they must take action while they still have the power to be effective.

The Importance of Nonprofit Boards

None of what has been discussed thus far is unique to the nonprofit sector. Corporate boards are also accountable for the long-term stability of their organizations. In addition, the cycle of decline toward bankruptcy for a for-profit corporation passes through stages quite similar to those just enumerated. What makes the nonprofit situation unusual, however, is the singularly important role played by the board in safeguarding against starting down the slippery slope.

Compared to their for-profit cousins, nonprofit institutions have fewer external forces working to exert discipline on their activities. A nonprofit tends to pursue a wider variety of objectives, many of which are unrelated to the proverbial bottom line, and so it is more difficult to assess performance. Even if performance were measurable, and quantifiable objectives set, few outside agencies have an interest in forcing a nonprofit to meet them. There are no nonprofit departments in investment banks tracking the decisions of management or publishing research reports on organizational performance. Even the Internal Revenue Service devotes far less time to scrutinizing nonprofits than for-profits, for the simple reason that there is so little tax revenue to be claimed.[2] The only outside agencies that will step in to investigate nonprofits are state attorneys general, but they generally do so only when there is a strong suspicion of illegal activity. They do not have the resources to ensure that nonprofit organizations in their jurisdictions are well managed or have sound governance policies.[3]

In addition to the lack of external market forces, many nonprofits have relatively few internal stakeholders who possess the leverage to challenge top management and the board. In the for-profit sector, owners and shareholders provide this discipline; they monitor net income and demand a return on equity. But nonprofits have no owners, although certain types of nonprofit organizations have active and critical constituencies. For example, at a college or university, the board and administration must respond to the concerns of alumni, faculty, and students, all of whom have a vested interest in the institution. These kinds of institutions are watched very closely. But for the great many nonprofit organizations that, like the Society, serve a relatively narrow constituency, there are few voices to alert the board and management when things are headed in the wrong direction. For these entities, long-term success is almost exclusively dependent on the effectiveness of their trustees.

It Is Easy to Get into Trouble

When an institution has a capital base that is at risk of being eroded to finance unsustainable deficit spending, the importance of the board's oversight role grows larger still. Unfortunately for nonprofit board members, the difficulty of this role may even exceed its importance. The very essence of what justifies an organization's nonprofit status, that is, the primacy of its mission, makes it more complex to govern for the long term. A for-profit board's first obligation to the shareholders is, for the most part, quantifiable. It can evaluate the success of a project on the basis of its profitability and the return on investment. But how does the Society's board quantify the importance of cataloging the collections or conserving a particular group of paintings? When should it pull the plug on important projects that are costing more to manage than they generate? These questions defy formulaic answers.

If nonprofit boards are not extremely vigilant, they can easily fall into a pattern of authorizing, perhaps even for justifiable reasons, levels of activity that are not financially sustainable. In December 1974, when the Society's board was debating a significant operating deficit, its third in a row, it decided, according to the minutes, that "it would be most unfortunate to lose the present momentum of the Society by cutting back activities." Ten deficits later, in 1984, President Goelet wrote in the annual report of the need "to increase our care for [the] collections and for our building . . . [and] to expand further our public programs." The Society's operating deficit in 1984, excluding depreciation, was $833,000, or 33 percent of total expenditures.[4] Looking back on this era, management explained that the 1980s deficits were regarded as investments in the future, as temporary losses necessary to upgrade the museum to make the institution more attractive to potential contributors.[5] But deficit followed deficit until the Society was nearly out of money.

Putting the importance of mission over means leads to another phenomenon common among nonprofit leaders that increases the likelihood that their organizations will encounter financial difficulty. Nonprofit leaders tend to think in terms of the costs of operations first—"this is what we must spend to fulfill our mission"—and then to think about revenues—"this is what we need in terms of support." At least in part, this expenditures-first approach is probably a legacy from the days when managing a nonprofit institution was a simpler endeavor. As one leader of a large cultural institution put it, "Art museums used to be run privately. At the end of the year, you would do your books, there was a deficit, you would sit down with your trustees, they would pass the hat, and that was that. But that isn't possible anymore."[6]

Nevertheless, there remain many organizations in which expenditure levels drive revenue projections. This approach may work perfectly well for stable institutions with predictable revenue streams, but for more inconstant entities, it can result in plans that depend on meeting unattainable fundraising goals. The Society's 1988–1992 bridge plan, which was explicitly based on an effort to increase revenues to meet a preset level of expenditures, offers a case in point. After the plan resulted in deficits in three consecutive years, Society leaders acquiesced, stating at a 1992 meeting that "as we have not been able to achieve the goal of raising revenue sufficiently to meet expenses, . . . we must now examine whether it is feasible to reduce expenses to match assured revenues." A more balanced approach might have held more promise. During the planning process, nonprofit leaders need to think less in terms of what their organizations *must* do and more in terms of what they realistically *can* do.

If tendencies such as these make it easy to get into trouble, how can a nonprofit board best guard against them? The most reasonable answer is through the development of an overall financial and strategic plan with realistic objectives and clearly defined expected outcomes. Only then can an institution's progress be monitored. If deficits must be incurred, the board must identify what is being purchased with those deficits, how large those deficits can be, and how long the institution can afford to run them. Then, if the institution is not achieving desired results, the board can pursue alternate courses of action before it is too late.

Once in Trouble, It Is Difficult to Escape

If a nonprofit board authorizes operating deficits for too many years, financial flexibility will be sacrificed. Deficits must be paid for, and it is likely that either the institution's capital reserves or its endowment will be depleted. As reserves are spent, the chances that any path out of trouble will succeed are diminished. There will always be mistakes, bad luck, and delays that have to be overcome. As every manager knows, having the financial resources to reduce the impact of such unforeseen events very often means the difference between success and failure.

A compelling illustration of the consequences of decreased financial flexibility is the Society's 1988 bridge plan. This plan, though overly optimistic in its revenue projections, was in other respects very well conceived. It was thoroughly evaluated and endorsed not only by Society management and the board but also by an outside advisory group of experts from relevant fields. It included both an overarching strategy and shorter-term objectives that were carefully monitored. As the plan unfolded, the board was kept fully informed about progress made toward those objectives. In all major respects, the plan and its execution met reasonable standards of sound governance. Yet it failed.

Had it been enacted earlier in the Society's history, the bridge plan would have had a much better chance of carrying the Society to financial stability. Barbara Debs and her staff made great strides in raising awareness of the Society and broadening its sources of support, but by the time the plan was put in place, the Society's financial resources had been eroded to such an extent that there was virtually zero margin for error. The Society could not afford even the slightest misfortune or surprise.

Unfortunately, barely a year into the bridge plan, management discovered that the roof urgently needed over $10 million in repairs. If the Society had had sufficient reserves, perhaps it could have patched the roof, buying time for an appeal to the state and city governments for capital funding. But the Society did not have the money or the time. The board was forced to conclude that the Society could no longer exist as an independent entity without substantial annual appropriations from the public sector or a huge private capital gift. Since neither was immediately forthcoming, the board began to assess more drastic solutions to the Society's difficulties, including possible mergers or affiliations with other entities.

The proposed merger between the Society and the Museum of the City of New York (MCNY) further illustrates, however, how difficult it is for an institution, once it has slipped, to get back on its feet. It can become impossible to move beyond the financial exigencies of a situation to evaluate the benefits of proposed solutions. Although the merger of these two complementary collections had (and still has) great appeal, negotiations never got started. Not only did the Society have insufficient resources to help effect the merger, but because its cash flow problems were well known, the Society's bargaining position was extremely weak. Regarded as needy by its potential partner, the Society found it impossible to reach an agreement with the MCNY that would recognize the fair value of the Society's resources.

A lack of cash impedes a board's freedom to make choices in another way as well: timing can become the single dominant factor in decisions of profound importance. Optimum solutions, especially if they involve protracted negotiations between institutions, may simply not be possible. If the other institutions are also nonprofit organizations, the chances of a productive resolution are even more remote. Nonprofit institutions have a fiduciary duty to protect the resources and collections that they hold in public trust. Properly discharging that duty extends the time needed to craft such agreements. For institutions under siege, that kind of time is likely to be an unaffordable luxury.

Consider the Society's attempt to borrow $1.5 million from the New York Public Library in December 1992. One of the most promising aspects of the loan was that it would establish an official link between two institutions with highly complementary collections that could potentially lead to a more permanent relationship. As negotiations proceeded, however, the Society's cash flow situation grew increasingly grim. Society leadership had very real fears that they would not have the cash necessary to issue paychecks in January. Even though both institutions were eager to conclude an arrangement and were aware that time was of the essence, it was impossible, given its fiduciary obligations, for the public library to negotiate an agreement that quickly. It proved to be far easier for the Society to reach an agreement with Sotheby's, which, as a for-profit institution, was not bound by the same kinds of obligations to donors and public constituencies (including city government). Instead of embarking on a new course that could have led to a mutually beneficial relationship between two New York institutions with important collections, the Society added a $1.5 million creditor.

Public Scrutiny Leads to Loss of Control

If a nonprofit institution's difficulties become a matter of public debate and controversy, the board will invariably lose control over the institution. Because the nature of any organization's problems are more complex than can be encapsulated in a newspaper article, some issues will be oversimplified, and others will be exaggerated. When there is criticism, there will be an effort to identify a chief villain, even when none exists. The net result is that important observers can be led to conclusions that are based on insufficient and sometimes inaccurate information. Once a situation is publicly defined in this way, it is extremely difficult, if not impossible, to change that definition. As the situation degenerates, it is absolutely essential that key stakeholders—including members of the board—be kept well informed about developments. If there is a potential path out of such trouble, an institution's top leadership will have to prepare the way.

The Society's attempt to establish a formal affiliation between its library and the library of New York University (NYU) offers a telling example of the impact of public controversy on the options available to an organization. The nature and timing of negative publicity, which appeared on the morning the Society's board was to vote on a contract formalizing a long-term relationship between the two institutions, made a discussion of the agreement on its merits impossible. Particularly damaging was the characterization of NYU as some kind of "corporate raider" intent on a takeover of the Society's most valuable collections. Although not factually correct (no change of title for any of the Society's collections was proposed), this negative characterization was accepted by pretty much everyone not fully briefed on the months of complex negotiations that had led to the proposed contract.

Because of the sensitivity of the negotiations, it is not surprising that only a few people were directly involved; however, not enough work was done to ensure that key stakeholders were adequately informed. Important local political officials, some of whom had been instrumental in passing the $12.6 million appropriated to the Society in 1992, claimed that they were not consulted, and they were angry. They protested the "complete lack of communication" and asserted that the state and city governments' future commitment to the Society would be in jeopardy if the contract were ratified. The proposed agreement never had a chance.

An additional consequence of swirling public controversy is that nearly everyone assumes the role of expert. People lose faith in management and the board, and rather than working to help find solutions, they seek to assign blame for past failures. Grievances are voiced—and must be heard. As the experience of the Society illustrates so well, politicians, scholars, schoolteachers, neighbors—everyone becomes involved in the governance process. In such an environment, institutions are pressured to pursue solutions that aggravate no one—with predictable results.

In effect, public attention reduces the ability for a board to evaluate options, assign priorities, and make choices. One of the Society's largest current financial obligations is a ten-year lease for outside storage that costs $500,000 per year. Some critics argue that many of the items stored in that warehouse are not worth the money that is being expended to store them. They wonder how the Society could have gotten itself into such an expensive agreement for so long a term.

In 1986, Bryant Tolles issued a report criticizing the condition of many of the Society's collections stored in a Paterson, New Jersey, warehouse. Soon after receiving the report, the Society moved the collections out of the warehouse and into safer surroundings in Manhattan. In the summer of 1988, the Tolles report was leaked to the press. The resulting exposé described in great detail the environment from which the Society's collections had been removed two years before. The fact that most of the paintings in storage were of relatively little curatorial or financial value was not addressed in the article. Instead, the article focused on the horrible conditions of the storage environment. The resulting controversy led to the resignation of the Society's director, the convening of a special advisory committee, and an attorney general's investigation.

As the Society struggled to recover, the predominant issue before the board, set by the public debate, was quite naturally the storage conditions for its off-site collections. No expense was spared in finding a top-of-the-line storage facility. Representatives of the press, the attorney general's office, and others were brought to the new facilities to see how the Society had cleaned up its act. The new facilities truly were impressive, and a long-term lease was signed.

No consideration could be given, however, to the quality of the paintings and whether it was necessary or appropriate to store them in such an expensive way. Nor could consideration be given to how the terms of the lease would affect the Society's financial standing over the long term. Most important was responding to public criticism as forcefully as possible.

Conclusion

The New-York Historical Society is not the typical nonprofit organization. Few institutions have the privilege of worrying about caring for over $1 billion worth of irreplaceable collections. Nor do most have to be concerned about how articles in the *New York Times* portray their activities. But that does not make this case unrepresentative; it just makes the lessons it yields more dramatic. The experience of the Society supports the proposition that it is easy for nonprofits to get in financial trouble and that detailed planning processes are essential at nonprofit institutions of all types and sizes. It also shows quite clearly how declining financial stability erodes board autonomy.

In the final analysis, perhaps the most dramatic lesson documented by the Society's long struggle has been the change in the nonprofit operating environment. There was a time when managing and overseeing a nonprofit institution was a far simpler process. To be elected to a board, particularly of a large cultural institution, was to become a member of a prestigious club. Membership was, in a sense, a reward for professional achievement and a recognition of valuable associations. Times have changed. Over the past twenty-five years, many intelligent people, with the best of intentions, have worked heroically in attempts to turn the Society around, only to leave with their reputations tarnished. And still the Society remains on the brink of bankruptcy. Serving on this nonprofit board of trustees has been no sinecure; it has been, rather, an excruciatingly difficult tour of duty.

Notes

1. The National Center for Nonprofit Boards, an organization dedicated to "improving the effectiveness of nonprofit organizations by strengthening their governing boards," recently published a guide that identifies ninety key resources on nonprofit boards.
2. Bowen (1994, p. 16).
3. Bograd (1994).
4. Limiting investment income to 5 percent of the endowment's market value, the 1984 operating deficit would have been nearly $1.3 million, or 48 percent of total expenditures.
5. McGill (1988h).
6. McGill (1988j).

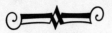

APPENDIXES

APPENDIXES

THE ORIGINAL CONSTITUTION OF THE NEW-YORK HISTORICAL SOCIETY

(ADOPTED DECEMBER 10, 1804)

I. This Society shall be denominated "The New-York Historical Society."

II. The object of the Society shall be to discover, procure, and preserve whatever may relate to the natural, civil, literary, and ecclesiastical history of the United States in general, and of this State in particular.

III. The Society shall consist of resident and honorary members; the former to be persons residing in the State of New-York; the latter persons residing elsewhere.

IV. The officers of the Society, to be elected annually and by ballot, shall be,
A President,
A first Vice-President,
A second Vice-President,
A Treasurer,
A Recording Secretary,
A Corresponding Secretary,
A Librarian,
A Standing Committee of seven Members.

V. It shall be the duty of the Standing Committee to solicit and receive donations for the Society; to recommend plans for promoting its objects; to digest and prepare business; and to execute such other duties as may, from time to time, be committed to them by the Society. They shall meet once at least in every three months; and at each annual meeting they shall make a report to the Society of the principal acquisitions and transactions of the preceding year.

VI. All members (honorary members excepted, with whom it shall be optional) shall pay, on admission, the sum of ten dollars, and an additional sum of two dollars annually, or the sum of thirty-five dollars as a commutation for the annual payment.

VII. The Society shall meet quarterly, to wit, on the second Tuesdays in January, April, July, and October; but the President, or, in his absence, either of the Vice Presidents, may call a special meeting, on giving eight days' notice thereof, to be published in at least two public newspapers printed in the city of New-York. The election of officers shall be at the meeting on the second Tuesday in January, and by a majority of ballots.

VIII. The admission of members shall be by ballot; and there shall be a previous nomination of the persons at the last preceding quarterly meeting.

IX. The constitution may be amended, from time to time, as the Society shall deem proper; but a motion for an amendment shall not be received unless a notice thereof shall have been given, and entered on the Journals of the Society at the last preceding quarterly meeting.

APPENDIX B

TO THE PUBLIC

THE ADDRESS OF THE NEW-YORK HISTORICAL SOCIETY (ISSUED FEBRUARY 12, 1805, AND SEPTEMBER 15, 1809)

Having formed an association, for the purpose of discovering, procuring, and preserving whatever may relate to the natural, civil, literary, and ecclesiastical history of our country, and particularly of the State of New-York, we solicit the aid of the liberal, patriotic, and learned, to promote the objects of our institution.

The utility of societies for the advancement of science, has been so fully proved by the experience of the most enlightened nations of Europe, and by that of our own country, that there can be no need, at this time, of any formal arguments in support of their claim to public patronage. But it may be observed, that, in this State, if we except the Agricultural Society, there is no association for the purposes of general knowledge; and the want of a regular, minute, and authentic History of New-York, renders the combined efforts of individuals for that object more peculiarly necessary.

It is well known that many valuable manuscripts and papers relative to the history of our country remain in the possession of those who, though unwilling to entrust them to a single person, yet would cheerfully confide them to a public institution, in whose custody they would be preserved for the general benefit of society. To rescue from the dust and obscurity of private repositories such important documents, as are liable to be lost or destroyed by the indifference or neglect of those into whose hands they may have fallen, will be a primary object of our attention.

The paucity of materials, and the extreme difficulty of procuring such as relate to the first settlement and colonial transactions of this State, can be fully perceived by those only who have meditated on the design of erecting an historical monument of those events, and have calculated the nature and amount of their resources: for without the aid of original records and authentic documents, history will be nothing more than a well-combined series of ingenious conjectures and amusing fables. The cause of truth is interesting to all men, and those who possess the means, however small, of preventing error, or of elucidating obscure facts, will confer a benefit on mankind by communicating them to the world.

Not aspiring to the higher walks of general science, we shall confine the range of our exertions to the humble task of collecting and preserving whatever may be useful to others in the different branches of historical inquiry. We feel encouraged to follow this path by the honorable example of the Massachusetts Society, whose labors will abridge those of the future historian, and furnish a thousand lights to guide him through the dubious track of unrecorded time. Without aiming to be rivals, we shall be happy to co-operate with that laudable institution in pursuing the objects of our common researches; satisfied if, in the end, our efforts shall be attended with equal success.

Our inquiries are not limited to a single State or district, but extend to the whole Continent; and it will be our business to diffuse the information we may collect in such manner as will best conduce to general instruction. As soon as our collection shall be sufficient to form a volume, and the funds of the Society will admit, we shall commence publication, that we may better secure our treasures by means of the press, from the corrosion of time and the power of accident.

That this object may be sooner and more effectually attained, we request that all who feel disposed to encourage our design will transmit, as soon as convenient, to the Society,

Manuscripts, Records, Pamphlets, and Books relative to the History of this Country, and particularly to the points of inquiry subjoined;

Orations, Sermons, Essays, Discourses, Poems, and Tracts; delivered, written, or published on any public occasion, or which concern any public transaction or remarkable character or event;

Laws, Journals, Copies of Records, and Proceedings of Congresses, Legislatures, General Assemblies, Conventions, Committees of Safety, Secret Committees for General Objects, Treaties and Negotiations with any Indian Tribes, or with any State or Nation;

Proceedings of Ecclesiastical Conventions, Synods, General Assemblies, Presbyteries, and Societies of all denominations of Christians;

Narratives of Missionaries, and Proceedings of Missionary Societies;

Narratives of Indian Wars, Battles, and Exploits; of the Adventures and Sufferings of Captives, Voyagers, and Travellers;

Minutes and Proceedings of Societies for the Abolition of Slavery, and the Transactions of Societies for Political, Literary, and Scientific Purposes;

Accounts of Universities, Colleges, Academies, and Schools; their origin, progress, and present state;

Topographical Descriptions of Cities, Towns, Counties, and Districts, at various periods, with Maps and whatever relates to the progressive Geography of the Country;

Statistical Tables—Tables of Diseases, Births and Deaths, and of Population; of Meteorological Observations, and Facts relating to Climate;

Accounts of Exports and Imports at various periods, and of the progress of Manufactures and Commerce;

Magazines, Reviews, Newspapers, and other Periodical Publications, particularly such as appeared antecedent to the year 1783;

Biographical Memoirs and Anecdotes of eminent and remarkable Persons in America, or who have been connected with its settlement or history;

Original Essays and Disquisitions on the Natural, Civil, Literary, or Ecclesiastical History of any State, City, Town, or District.

As the Society intend to form a Library and Cabinet, they will gratefully receive specimens of the various productions of the American Continent and of the adjacent Islands, and such animal, vegetable, and mineral subjects as may be deemed worthy of preservation. Donations also of rare and useful books and pamphlets relative to the above objects, will be thankfully accepted, and all communications duly noticed in the publications of the Society.

Queries as to Those Points on Which the Society Requests Particular Information

1.   Can you give any information concerning the first settlement of your Town or District by white people, the number and condition of the first settlers— the names of the principal persons—the circumstances attending the settlement, and motives which led to it?

2.   Do you know any thing, more particularly, respecting the first settlement of New-York by the Dutch—the number of the settlers—the time of their arrival— their general character—their condition with respect to property—the authority and encouragements under which they came—or any other circumstances attending the first attempt at colonization?

3. Can you communicate any documents which will throw light on the first organization of civil government in any part of the United States—or which will give authentic information concerning the names, general character powers, salaries, &c. of the principal civil officers appointed at different periods? Especially, when did the first regular organization of a colony in New-Netherlands take place? What was the nature of the government established? Who was the first Chief Magistrate, his title, powers, and character?

4. Is there any thing known concerning Wouter Van Twiller or William Kieft, who preceded Governor Stuyvesant in the Chief Magistracy of New-Netherlands? How long did each remain in office? What stations or offices did they fill prior to their appointment here? Were they removed by death or resignation, or for ill behavior? If in either of the latter ways, how were they disposed of afterwards?

5. In what years were the first Forts built at Albany (then called Fort Orange), and at New-York (then called New-Amsterdam?) Of what numbers did the respective garrisons consist, as well at first as at different periods afterwards? And who were the commanding officers in each previous to the arrival of the first Governor, or Director General?

6. What proportion of the first settlers in New-Netherlands appear to have attached themselves to agriculture, and what proportion to trade? In what districts did these two classes chiefly reside? To what objects of cultivation did the former chiefly devote themselves? And what were the principal objects of the trade in which the latter engaged?

7. Can you communicate any facts which will throw light on the state of Commerce in any particular portion of our country, at different times, and especially at early periods—the number of ships belonging to particular ports—the amount of exports and imports for a series of years—the principal articles exported and imported, and from whence brought?

8. At what period do the most common and simple Manufactures appear to have been commenced in your district? And what facts can you furnish respecting the progress of manufactures since that period?

9. Can you give any information concerning the number of houses and inhabitants in your town, at different periods, since the first settlement?

10. What information do you possess respecting the state of the Militia in your district, especially at the early periods of its history, particularly their numbers, organization, mode of equipment, &c.?

11. Can you communicate any books, or other documents which will give authentic information concerning any of the numerous territorial disputes which have taken place between different portions of the United States, especially between the Colony and State of New-York and the surrounding Colonies and States?

12.   Is it in your power to furnish any information concerning the Indian tribes which formerly inhabited your district, or which may now occupy any portion of it; concerning their numbers and condition when first visited by the whites, their trade disputes, wars and treaties, either among themselves or with the white people; their character, customs, and general history, together with their present numbers and state?

13.   What were the Indian names of the mountains, valleys, rivers, lakes, springs, caverns, or other remarkable places in your neighborhood? And what do well informed people suppose to be the import of those names?

14.   Are you in the possession of any records which will tend to elucidate the ecclesiastical history of any portion of our country? Can you give any information concerning the erection of churches, and the establishment of congregations in your district of every different denomination, from the earliest periods of settlement; the names of all the Ministers who have had pastoral charges, the dates of their settlement and removal, whether by death or otherwise; the changes, either progressive or retrograde, which congregations have undergone with respect to numbers, property, &c., ecclesiastical disputes, or any remarkable persons or events which pertain to ecclesiastical history?

15.   When were schools and other seminaries of learning first instituted in your town? What have been their numbers at different periods since that time? Can any information be had concerning their funds, number of scholars, and general character at different times from the first settlement to the present day?

16.   When was the first Printing-press established in your town, and by whom? When was the first book, pamphlet, or newspaper printed? Who was the first bookseller in your town? And what have been the number of printing presses and book stores, at different periods, to the present time?

17.   Have you any public Libraries? If any, when were they first instituted, by whom, and what is the number of volumes in each?

18.   Can you furnish any information concerning the progress of luxury? Do you possess any records or anecdotes respecting the introduction of the most conspicuous articles of elegant indulgence, such as wheel-carriages, &c. &c.?

19.   Can you give any information which will throw light on the state of morals in our country, at different periods, such as the comparative frequency of drunkenness, gaming, duelling, suicide, conjugal infidelity, prostitution, &c., &c.?

20.   What remarkable laws, customs, or usages, either local or general, at early periods of our colonial establishments, have come within your knowledge?

21.   Can you furnish descriptions, drawings, or other communications concerning mines, mineral springs, ancient fortifications, caverns, mountains, rivers, lakes, or any other natural curiosities, together with minute information concerning

the dates of their discovery, or of other remarkable events respecting them, and in general every fact which may throw light on their origin and history?

22.   What information can you give concerning the dates and progress of the various improvements which have taken place in the departments of politics, commerce, manufactures, agriculture, literature, or humanity?

23.   Do you possess any records concerning seasons remarkable for the extremes either of heat or cold, scarcity or plenty, sickness or health? Can you communicate bills of mortality, histories of epidemic diseases, &c.?

FINANCIAL ANALYSIS: NOTES AND TABLES

A critical component of this story has been the Society's evolving financial condition. Because of that fact, a detailed analysis of the Society's financial statements was conducted that reaches back to 1935, the year the Society received the $4.5 million Thompson bequest. There are certain problems in studying a time series of such length. Most significant, because the analysis uses data from the Society's annual reports and audited financial statements, it changes with the formats chosen by the Society's accountants and managers at the time. Occasionally, these changes make it difficult to keep presentation of the information consistent over time. To alleviate this problem, this analysis focuses on major financial categories only. From 1935 to 1974, the statements were, for the most part, comparable; however, in 1975, the Society converted from cash-based accounting to an accrual accounting system using complex (and very different) fund accounting concepts. Because of that change, the analysis of the tenure of James J. Heslin has been divided into two parts, 1960–1974 and 1975–1981.

The data shown in the tables that follow differ from what was originally presented in the Society's statements. The chief difference involves distinguishing between operating and capital activity. Unfortunately, nonprofit institutions are not required to prepare operating statements. Consequently, activities that are capital in nature, such as the receipt of endowment gifts or sales of real property, are often shown as part of the current operating performance of the institution. Inclusion of such cash inflows as operating income does not provide an accurate picture of an institution's operating stability, and every effort has been made to exclude such capital activity from the operating data.

What follows are brief summaries of the most significant assumptions, along with adjustments that have been made to the results, for the tables that follow.

Table C.3–1

1937: The Society included certain expenditures for the construction of its building. These amounts, totaling $51,000, were excluded from total operating expenditures.

1939: The Society borrowed approximately $25,000 from the endowment to cover a deficit, but it was shown as revenue. $25,000 was deducted from total operating revenue. The interfund loan was repaid in 1950.

1943: The Society purchased a neighboring lot at 15 West Seventy-Sixth Street for $25,000. That amount was deducted from total operating expenditures.

Table C.3–2

1950: The Society transferred $25,000 from operations to the endowment to retire the interfund loan taken in 1939 (no interest was paid). $25,000 was deducted from total operating expenditures.

1954: Several changes took place in the Society's accounts in this year. First, there were several capital transfers from operations (including a $15,000 transfer to a publications fund) totaling approximately $24,000, which has been deducted from total operating expenditures. The Society also established three board-designated funds, the accumulated surplus fund, a pension fund, and an accessions fund.

1955: After 1955, the Society began making transfers to fund its board-restricted pension account. In the Society's statements, the total amount of these transfers was shown as expenditure. This analysis adjusts the expenditure by deducting only the amount actually spent to pay benefits.

Tables C.4–1 and C.4–2

1966: $266,000 from the operating account was spent on the Society's building renovation. This amount has been deducted from total operating expenditures.

1967: Prior to 1967, investment income included only dividends and interest received. After 1967, when the Society adopted the total return investment policy, capital gains were realized to bring the investment income up to the spending limit.

1974: For the first time, the Society exceeded its 5 percent spending limit. Investment income, total income, and the operating surplus (deficit) are shown both with and without the 5 percent spending limit imposed. This presentation continues for the rest of the financial tables.

Tables C.4–3 through C.6–2

1975: After 1975, the data shown are compiled from audited financial statements (using accrual fund accounting) instead of from annual reports (using cash accounting) as had been done previously. (1979 and 1980 are exceptions; the audited financial statements were not available.)

1986: This "year" lasted only six months because the Society converted to a fiscal year ending June 30.

Table C.10

This table shows how the calculation was done to show what the value of the Society's endowment would be if it had held to a 5 percent spending limit. The table works as follows:

At the beginning of 1975, the market value of the Society's endowment stood at $10,455,000 (see upper left portion of table). The three-year-moving-average market value of the Society's endowment for 1974, 1973, and 1972 was $10,805,000. Using the spending rule of 5 percent, the Society would be allowed to spend $699,000 in 1975 (lower left part of table). Assuming that spending was spread out evenly over the course of the year, the equivalent of half of that amount, or $349,000, would appreciate during the year. Similarly, one-half of the $2,000 in capital gifts, $1,000, would earn a return over the course of the year. Summing the beginning-of-the-year market value, one-half of the funds spent, and one-half of the funds received results in a market value base of $10,805,000.

The market value base is used to calculate the amount of appreciation in the Society's investments during the year. Using a composite average return of 31.6 percent (calculated from average returns published by Cambridge Associates), the market value after appreciation but before spending and gifts received is estimated as $14,214,000. The Society's assumed 5 percent level of spending is then subtracted and actual gifts received are added, yielding an estimate of the year-end market value of the Society's endowment of $13,565,000 for 1975 if spending had been limited to 5 percent. The same sequence of calculations is then repeated through 1993.

TABLE C.3–1.   OPERATING RESULTS AND ENDOWMENT FUND BALANCES, 1935–1943 (THOUSANDS OF DOLLARS).

	1935	1936	1937	1938	1939	1940	1941	1942	1943
Operating Income									
Gifts, grants, and contributions	9	55	4	1	2	2	3	1	2
Investment income	65	139	147	159	160	173	186	199	201
Earned income	0	0	0	0	0	0	0	0	0
Other income	5	6	4	3	4	7	8	6	8
Total income	79	200	154	163	166	182	196	207	211
Operating Expenditures									
Compensation and benefits	40	50	53	63	117	122	123	130	125
Acquisitions	4	19	13	9	17	13	15	8	2
Building maintenance	3	6	5	14	21	17	17	19	17
Storage	0	0	0	0	0	0	0	0	0
Other expenditures[a]	17	25	23	26	29	25	29	26	24
Total expenditures	64	100	94	112	183	178	184	182	168
Surplus/Deficit									
Excluding depreciation	15	100	60	51	(17)	4	12	25	43
Endowment									
Nominal book value	3,502	5,949	5,586	4,454	4,524	4,426	4,419	4,478	4,311
Spending rate[b]	1.8%	2.3%	2.6%	3.6%	3.5%	3.9%	4.2%	4.5%	4.7%

[a]Includes binding, subscriptions, equipment, printing, legal expenses, and insurance.

[b]Calculated as the percentage of the endowment value (at the beginning of the year) recognized as investment income in a single year. For a detailed explanation, see Chapter Ten.

Source: New-York Historical Society annual reports.

TABLE C.3–2. OPERATING RESULTS AND ENDOWMENT FUND BALANCES, 1944–1959 (THOUSANDS OF DOLLARS).

	1944	1945	1946	1947	1948	1949	1950	1951
Operating Income								
Gifts, grants, and contributions	3	5	4	8	4	5	5	4
Investment income	192	163	199	232	278	280	311	298
Earned income	0	0	3	3	4	3	3	6
Other income	26	27	25	30	31	23	10	9
Total income	221	195	231	274	316	312	329	316
Operating Expenditures								
Compensation and benefits	126	135	162	165	191	198	204	235
Acquisitions	2	3	4	4	4	6	2	6
Building maintenance	18	19	21	22	24	22	21	25
Storage	0	0	0	0	0	0	0	0
Other expenditures[a]	43	43	39	55	66	57	44	59
Total expenditures	189	200	226	246	284	283	272	325
Surplus/Deficit								
Excluding depreciation	31	(5)	5	27	31	29	57	(9)
Endowment								
Nominal book value	4,346	5,141	5,580	5,585	5,612	5,515	5,645	5,762
Nominal market value[b]	N.A.	N.A.	N.A.	5,012	4,905	5,370	5,979	6,319
Spending rate	4.4%	3.2%	3.6%	4.6%	5.7%	5.2%	5.2%	4.7%

Table C.3–2, cont.

Operating Income	1952	1953	1954	1955	1956	1957	1958	1959
Gifts, grants, and contributions	4	12	8	7	12	23	17	14
Investment income	291	292	305	324	358	367	353	362
Earned income	5	4	4	5	5	6	7	6
Other income	13	14	14	14	15	18	14	14
Total income	313	322	331	350	390	413	391	397
Operating Expenditures								
Compensation and benefits	223	240	236	239	263	284	288	290
Acquisitions	1	2	9	4	6	9	17	13
Building maintenance	24	23	23	24	28	27	29	29
Storage	0	0	0	0	0	0	0	0
Other expenditures[a]	56	59	58	59	53	55	41	52
Total expenditures	305	324	326	326	350	375	376	384
Surplus/Deficit								
Excluding depreciation	8	(2)	6	24	41	38	14	12
Board-Designated Restricted Funds								
Accumulated surplus	N.A.	N.A.	N.A.	216	233	238	233	221
Pensions	N.A.	N.A.	N.A.	10	20	32	54	66
Accessions	N.A.	N.A.	N.A.	3	6	17	12	8
Endowment								
Nominal book value	5,900	5,926	6,164	6,497	6,765	7,212	7,879	8,065
Nominal market value	6,697	6,420	8,110	9,150	9,338	8,307	10,583	10,723
Spending rate	4.3%	4.5%	3.8%	3.5%	3.8%	4.4%	3.3%	3.4%

Note: N.A. indicates "not available."

[a]Includes binding, subscriptions, equipment, printing, legal expenses, and insurance.

[b]Prior to 1947, the Society did not report the market value of its endowment.

Source: New-York Historical Society annual reports.

TABLE C.4–1.   OPERATING RESULTS, 1960–1974 (THOUSANDS OF DOLLARS).

	1960	1961	1962	1963	1964	1965	1966	1967
Operating Income								
Gifts, grants, and contributions	5	5	6	9	25	25	19	32
Investment income	385	384	407	440	473	480	509	753
Earned income	8	11	9	14	17	16	17	22
Other income	15	15	15	15	14	14	14	14
Total income	412	414	437	478	529	535	558	820
Operating Expenditures								
Compensation and benefits	302	290	311	327	379	394	395	422
Acquisitions	14	13	13	14	31	26	23	25
Building maintenance	24	31	34	36	40	40	40	91
Administration	0	0	0	0	18	17	19	21
Professional services	0	0	0	0	13	17	47	69
Storage	0	0	0	0	0	0	0	0
Other expenditures[a]	62	80	77	89	34	41	41	39
Total expenditures	402	413	435	465	515	536	565	667
Surplus/Deficit								
Excluding depreciation	10	1	2	13	14	(1)	(7)	154
Board-Designated Restricted Funds								
Accumulated surplus	219	215	217	216	0	0	0	0
Pension reserve	87	96	103	126	136	128	115	120
Accessions	13	17	23	17	15	16	15	27
Building reserve	0	0	0	216	215	220	0	0
Development fund	0	0	0	0	194	369	52	204

Table C.4–1, cont.

	1968	1969	1970	1971	1972	1973	1974
Operating Income							
Gifts, grants, and contributions	58	29	50	103	113	140	127
Investment income	736	771	710	694	729	740	948
Earned income	23	27	28	28	31	47	68
Other income	0	16	23	23	23	23	23
Total income	817	844	811	848	895	950	1,166
Operating Expenditures							
Compensation and benefits	479	503	617	578	580	622	646
Acquisitions	25	22	27	43	45	35	80
Building maintenance	97	104	98	116	130	151	206
Administration	18	26	26	45	33	19	21
Professional services	26	19	57	36	32	39	43
Storage	0	5	5	31	5	5	7
Other expenditures[a]	50	52	56	22	49	110	140
Total expenditures	696	732	887	871	875	981	1,143
Surplus/Deficit							
Excluding depreciation	122	112	(76)	(23)	21	(31)	23[b]
Board-Designated Restricted Funds							
Accumulated surplus	0	0	0	0	0	0	0
Pension reserve	127	128	52	41	42	38	27
Accessions	31	20	19	42	107	171	205
Building reserve	0	0	0	0	0	0	0
Development fund	239	310	302	327	197	0	0

[a]Includes subscriptions, equipment, printing, public relations, and insurance.

[b]With 5 percent spending rate limit, deficit comes to –$227,000.

Source: New-York Historical Society annual reports.

TABLE C.4–2. RESTRICTED AND ENDOWMENT FUND BALANCES, 1960–1974 (THOUSANDS OF DOLLARS).

	1960	1961	1962	1963	1964	1965	1966	1967
Restricted Funds								
Special funds	101	118	128	147	750	751	745	738
Harper Fund	0	0	38	77	616	627	647	632
Bryan Fund	0	0	0	0	0	0	0	0
Total restricted funds	101	118	165	224	1,366	1,378	1,392	1,370
Endowment								
Nominal book value	8,216	8,845	8,525	9,251	8,860	9,759	10,320	10,514
Nominal market value[a]	10,868	12,250	11,523	12,139	N.A.	N.A.	N.A.	N.A.
Spending rate	3.5%	3.1%	3.5%	3.6%	N.A.	N.A.	N.A.	5.0%

Table C.4–2, cont.	1968	1969	1970	1971	1972	1973	1974
Restricted Funds							
Special funds	753	779	792	997	1,057	797	807
Harper Fund	633	615	577	564	574	568	551
Bryan Fund	0	0	0	0	0	245	192
Total restricted funds	1,386	1,394	1,368	1,561	1,631	1,610	1,550
Endowment							
Nominal book value	11,474	11,768	12,915	13,133	11,964	11,162	11,216
Nominal market value[a]	N.A.	N.A.	13,279	14,770	17,546	13,928	10,455
Spending rate	4.8%	4.9%	4.8%	4.8%	4.9%	4.8%	6.8%

Note: N.A. indicates "not available."

[a]Between 1963 and 1969, financial tables in the annual reports did not report the market value of the endowment; after 1967, market values shown are drawn from board minutes.

Source: New-York Historical Society annual reports.

TABLE C.4–3.   OPERATING RESULTS, 1975–1981 (THOUSANDS OF DOLLARS).

	1975	1976	1977	1978	1979	1980	1981
Operating Income							
Gifts, grants, and contributions	117	205	139	151	155	67	107
Investment income	835	903	833	835	1,031	922	1,035
With 5% limit imposed	699	602	587	612	605	563	531
Earned income	124	111	89	113	180	112	136
Other income	11	2	15	16	9	4	5
Total income	1,087	1,221	1,076	1,114	1,374	1,105	1,284
With 5% limit imposed	951	921	830	891	949	745	779
Operating Expenditures							
Compensation and benefits	700	683	749	835	879	814	1,003
Collections and exhibits	29	310	64	39	39	40	80
Building maintenance[a]	36	46	48	44	77	81	57
Utilities	171	226	190	195	239	267	319
Administration	48	50	68	78	104	144	156
Professional services	49	48	50	54	70	77	47
Storage	7	7	7	7	8	10	10
Other expenditures[b]	66	36	73	57	45	18	29
Total expenditures	1,104	1,406	1,250	1,309	1,462	1,451	1,702
Surplus/Deficit							
Excluding depreciation	(17)	(185)	(174)	(195)	(87)	(347)	(419)
With 5% spending rate limit	(153)	(485)	(420)	(417)	(513)	(706)	(923)

[a]Prior to 1975, included utilities.

[b]Includes printing, education, public programming, and interest.

Source: Audited financial statements of The New-York Historical Society.

TABLE C.4–4. RESTRICTED AND ENDOWMENT FUND BALANCES, 1975–1981
(THOUSANDS OF DOLLARS).

	1975	1976	1977	1978	1979	1980	1981
Restricted Funds							
Special funds[a]	343	290	255	257	209	189	274
Harper Fund	565	605	641	596	612	637	672
Bryan Fund	87	91	62	66	22	1,141	1,177
Total restricted funds	995	986	959	918	843	1,967	2,123
Endowment							
Nominal book value	11,712	11,634	11,697	11,496	10,442	10,058	10,491
Nominal market value[b]	11,758	12,990	11,971	11,346	10,442	10,058	11,696
Spending rate	6.9%	7.7%	6.8%	6.9%	9.2%	8.7%	9.6%
Capital inflows	22	31	259	9	0	0	8

[a]In 1975, the Society's statements were converted from a cash basis to an accrual basis. Several reclassifications were made, including a transfer of more than $570,000 from Special Funds to Endowment.

[b]Audited financial statements were not available for 1979 and 1980. Figures from the annual reports were used instead. Market values of the endowment were not listed in the annual report.

Source: Audited financial statements of The New-York Historical Society.

TABLE C.5–1. OPERATING RESULTS, 1982–1988 (THOUSANDS OF DOLLARS).

	1982	1983	1984	1985	1986[a]	1987	1988
Operating Income							
Gifts, grants, and contributions	95	87	233	1,048	1,320	874	1,573
Investment income	1,889	1,696	1,033	2,687	1,685	3,402	825
With 5% limit imposed	537	559	595	581	587	605	588
Earned income	164	276	430	349	250	531	583
Other income[b]	11	7	27	271	107	213	331
Total income	2,159	2,067	1,714	4,354	3,362	5,021	3,312
With 5% limit imposed	806	929	1,275	2,249	2,264	2,223	3,075
Operating Expenditures							
Compensation and benefits	1,203	1,399	1,508	1,757	1,095	2,850	3,686
Collections and exhibits	70	392	174	181	38	141	267
Building maintenance[c]	58	95	83	476	256	681	725
Utilities	316	397	318	0	0	0	0
Administration	132	325	308	227	178	534	690
Professional services	63	168	110	297	294	639	625
Storage[d]	11	13	13	N.A.	N.A.	N.A.	N.A.
Other expenditures[e]	37	104	38	273	168	763	813
Total expenditures	1,891	2,894	2,552	3,211	2,027	5,608	6,806
Surplus/Deficit							
Excluding depreciation	268	(827)	(838)	1,143	1,335	(587)	(3,494)
With 5% spending rate limit	(1,084)	(1,965)	(1,277)	(962)	237	(3,384)	(3,731)

[a]In 1986, the Society converted to a fiscal year ending June 30. Data shown for 1986 cover only six months.

[b]After 1984, gross sales of photos, duplicates, and so on are included as Other Income rather than Earned Income.

[c]After 1984, utilities and maintenance were not reported separately.

[d]After 1984, storage expenditures were not reported separately.

[e]Includes printing, education, public programming, and interest.

Source: Audited financial statements of the New-York Historical Society.

TABLE C.5–2.   RESTRICTED AND ENDOWMENT FUND BALANCES, 1982–1988 (THOUSANDS OF DOLLARS).

	1982	1983	1984	1985	1986[a]	1987	1988
Restricted Funds							
Special funds	470	497	754	1,332	1,212	1,587	1,764
Harper Fund	763	803	852	852	1,201	1,506	1,637
Bryan Fund	1,391	1,456	1,420	1,420	1,915	2,378	2,441
Total restricted funds	2,624	2,755	3,026	3,605	4,328	5,471	5,843
Endowment							
Nominal book value	10,515	10,299	9,493	10,629	10,916	8,902	8,033
Nominal market value	11,761	12,214	10,896	12,116	13,284	9,862	7,994
Spending rate	16.9%	14.3%	8.9%	22.9%	13.9%	28.9%	8.0%
Capital inflows	4	10	2	0	0	375	198

[a]In 1986, the Society converted to a fiscal year ending June 30. Data shown for 1986 cover only six months.

Source: Audited financial statements of the New-York Historical Society.

TABLE C.6–1. OPERATING RESULTS, 1989–1992
(*THOUSANDS OF DOLLARS*).

	1989	1990	1991	1992
Operating Income				
Gifts, grants, and contributions	2,751	3,788	4,520	3,150
Investment income	530	680	582	829
With 5% limit imposed	519	390	315	308
Earned income	386	545	523	422
Other income	405	374	213	278
Total income	4,073	5,388	5,838	4,679
With 5% limit imposed	4,062	5,097	5,572	4,158
Operating Expenditures				
Compensation and benefits	3,223	4,017	4,397	3,774
Collections and exhibits	203	253	346	281
Building maintenance	654	805	1,094	1,008
Administration	590	675	656	563
Professional services[a]	1,274	706	757	484
Other expenditures[b]	571	551	746	523
Total expenditures	6,514	7,007	7,996	6,633
Surplus/Deficit				
Excluding depreciation	(2,441)	(1,619)	(2,158)	(1,954)
With 5% spending rate limit	(2,452)	(1,909)	(2,424)	(2,475)

Note: Accounting statements were kept on an accrual basis.

[a]Includes legal fees resulting from New York State attorney general's investigation.

[b]Includes printing, education, and public programming.

Source: Audited financial statements of the New-York Historical Society.

TABLE C.6–2. RESTRICTED AND ENDOWMENT FUND BALANCES, 1989–1992 (THOUSANDS OF DOLLARS).

	1989	1990	1991	1992
Restricted Funds				
Special funds	1,926	4,293	4,818	4,841
Harper Fund	1,755	1,567	1,714	1,926
Bryan Fund[a]	2,687	2,912	1,098	1,110
Total restricted funds	6,367	8,772	7,629	7,876
Endowment				
Nominal book value	5,328	4,943	7,415	5,336
Nominal market value	5,553	5,344	7,573	5,496
Spending rate	6.8%	10.8%	9.4%	13.5%
Capital inflows	1,734	2,360	400	44

[a]In 1991, the Society transferred $1.95 million from the Bryan Fund to operations "representing reimbursement of past cumulative expenditures made from the Operating Fund for the care and conservation of the Bryan Collection."

Source: Audited financial statements of the New-York Historical Society.

TABLE C.10. PROJECTED ENDOWMENT VALUE WITH 5 PERCENT SPENDING LIMIT IMPOSED (THOUSANDS OF DOLLARS).

	1975	1976	1977	1978	1979	1980	1981	1982	1983
Beginning-of-year market value	10,455	13,517	16,347	15,525	15,921	17,579	21,402	20,890	24,247
3-year moving average	13,976	12,633	13,440	15,130	15,931	16,342	18,300	19,957	22,180
+½ outflows to spending at 5% (3-yr)	349	316	336	378	398	409	458	499	554
+½ inflows from capital gifts	1	16	125	5	0	0	4	2	5
Market value base	10,805	13,848	16,808	15,908	16,319	17,987	21,863	21,391	24,807
Stock allocation	75.0%	75.0%	75.0%	75.0%	75.0%	75.0%			
Bond allocation	25.0%	25.0%	25.0%	25.0%	25.0%	25.0%			
Average 1-year stock return	37.2%	23.6%	−7.4%	6.4%	18.2%	32.3%			
Average 1-year bond return	14.6%	18.7%	1.7%	−0.1%	−4.2%	−2.8%			
Weighted average composite return	31.6%	22.4%	−5.1%	4.8%	12.6%	23.5%			
Total return	N.A.	N.A.	N.A.	N.A.	N.A.	N.A.	−0.3%	18.0%	20.1%
Market value after capital appreciation	14,214	16,947	15,947	16,668	18,375	22,219	21,797	25,242	29,793
Projected spending at 5% of 3-yr market value	699	632	672	756	797	817	915	998	1,109
Capital gifts	2	31	251	9	0	0	8	4	10
End-of-year market value	13,517	16,347	15,525	15,921	17,579	21,402	20,890	24,247	28,694

Table C.10, cont.

	1984	1985	1986	1987	1988	1989	1990	1991	1992	1993
Beginning-of-year market value	28,694	30,191	38,177	45,360	46,462	51,298	57,724	61,172	73,602	75,969
3-year moving average	24,610	27,711	32,354	37,909	43,333	47,707	51,828	56,731	64,166	70,248
+½ outflows to spending at 5% (3-yr)	615	693	809	948	1,083	1,193	1,296	1,418	1,604	1,756
+½ inflows from capital gifts	1	0	0	187	99	36	1,180	200	20	0
Market value base	29,310	30,884	38,985	46,495	47,645	52,526	60,199	62,790	75,226	77,725
Stock allocation										
Bond allocation										
Average 1-year stock return										
Average 1-year bond return										
Weighted average composite return										
Total return	7.2%	28.1%	20.5%	3.2%	11.8%	14.3%	2.0%	21.1%	5.2%	12.2%
Market value after capital appreciation	31,420	39,562	46,977	47,983	53,267	60,038	61,403	76,039	79,138	87,208
Projected spending at 5%										
of 3-yr market value	1,231	1,386	1,618	1,895	2,167	2,385	2,591	2,837	3,208	3,512
Capital gifts	2	0	0	375	198	71	2,360	400	39	0
End-of-year market value	30,191	38,177	45,360	46,462	51,298	57,724	61,172	73,602	75,969	83,695

Note: N.A. indicates "not available."

Source: Calculated from audited financial statements of The New-York Historical Society.

APPENDIX D

1959 LIBRARY ACQUISITIONS POLICY

The suggestions contained in this report are proposed as a statement of policy in determining future library acquisitions.

Two factors have particularly influenced decision in this matter (1) the strength of collections at present in the library, and (2) the proximity of two large libraries (Columbia University Library and The New York Public Library) in this area.

Before considering the collections in The New-York Historical Society Library, however, it seems proper here to mention two aspects of general acquisition policy. It has been the practice in instances of purchases of material for $100.00 or more, to await action by the Library Committee and the Board, or in cases where immediate action was necessary, to refer decision to the President of the Society. It is suggested that this practice be continued. When gifts of library material are offered it is suggested that such material be accepted with the understanding that if it does not complement already existing collections this material can be offered for exchange or otherwise used to benefit the library. Thus, the thoughtfulness of donors may be rewarded by the knowledge that the gifts which they have presented have been, in one way or other, of benefit to the library.

Limitations concerning primary material in the following report are not designed to eliminate the acquisitions of material principally concerning New Yorkers or of distinct New York interest.

In the report which follows, the expression "Primary material" shall be construed to mean diaries, journals, and letters in manuscript form, official documents and "rare books."

The following material briefly described constitutes the major collections in the library.

1. Slavery Collection

This collection includes thousands of books and pamphlets concerning slavery and reconstruction. Among the pamphlets are sermons, tracts, etc., in defense of, or against slavery. The collection is used regularly and will be used even more, it is safe to say, in view of the great interest in the background of the Civil War.

Some idea of the strength of this collection may be ascertained from the following statistics, relating to the number of titles listed under *Slavery* in the three major research libraries in the area:

New York Public Library	5,000
Columbia University Library	3,000
The New-York Historical Society Library	9,135

a. It is suggested that the Library continue to collect primary material relating to slavery in the United States.
b. It is suggested that secondary material in the field noted above, be purchased only selectively on the basis of reviews in the outstanding historical journals.

2. California Gold Rush and Early Southwest Exploration Period

The bulk of our California Gold Rush material was originally collected as a result of the interest of a former librarian who migrated to California during the Gold Rush days. The collection consists of newspapers, pamphlets, early guides to California, etc.

Our material relating to the Southwest exploration period is a collection essentially of historical society reprints, general histories, etc. Its value to the researcher consists in the general material which would supplement more detailed studies.

a. It is suggested that no primary material relating to the California Gold Rush be acquired in the future. It is suggested that secondary material be purchased only selectively on the basis of reviews in the outstanding historical journals.
b. It is suggested that no primary or secondary material relating to Early Southwest Exploration be acquired in the future.

3. Early Florida Period (18th Century)

This collection was donated to the Society in the nineteenth century by the historian J. Buckingham Smith. The material relates primarily to early Florida but there is also material dealing with Central America and Spanish rule in the area. A large part of this collection—consisting of manuscript maps and printed items pertaining directly to Florida—was microfilmed some years ago for the University of Florida. We no longer add to this collection since other libraries pursue the subject more extensively.

It is suggested that no further additions of primary or secondary material be made to this collection.

4. American Indian Captivities

This is a good collection of the accounts and record of prisoners captured by American Indians. The collection, instituted in 1809, has been added to as opportunity presents. (It may be of interest to note that the largest collection of this material is owned privately by the Deering family of Saco, Maine. This collection consists of some 750 copies, which include various editions of the same titles.) The Newberry Library in Chicago has some 650 titles, the largest of the collections in any library open to the public. Many of these are also various editions of the same titles. The New York Public Library and the American Antiquarian Society Library have large collections. Our library has some 150 copies which also include various editions of the same titles.

It is suggested that we continue to add primary material to this collection but that no secondary material be added.

5. Newspapers

Our collection of 18th century newspapers is the fourth largest in the country. We collect U.S. newspapers through 1820, with particular emphasis on the Eastern Seaboard. We attempt to obtain procurable New York State newspapers in the nineteenth century, especially for the first twenty-five or forty years of a particular community when such material, generally scarce, is of greater historical value. In this connection, it is worth noting that except for sporadic collecting by the New York State Library there appears to be little planned collecting, by institutions, of New York State newspapers of the nineteenth century.

Outside of New York State our collecting is chiefly confined to early newspapers, as noted above. Where exceptions exist the material has generally come by gift. We have however been successful in exchanging out-of-state later nineteenth century newspapers for New York State newspapers of a similar period.

The newspaper collection is used constantly and is, in every sense, an active collection. The emphasis placed on the newspaper as a source of social history accounts, undoubtedly, for the steady use of our holdings.

It is suggested that the present practice of adding to our collection of 18th century newspapers and for the first twenty-five years or so of a particular community in New York State be continued.

6. Local Histories

Our collection of local histories is comprehensive. This is especially true for the New York State and Eastern Seaboard area. These histories, especially those written during the nineteenth century, are invaluable for biographical, political and geographical data. Local histories of middlewestern, far western states, etc., are confined chiefly to county histories and are used as general reference material.

a. It is suggested that every city, town and county history of New York State be acquired.

b. It is suggested that county histories of New England, New Jersey, Pennsylvania, and the following states: Ohio, Indiana, Illinois, Michigan, Wisconsin and Minnesota be acquired.

c. It is suggested that we should have, for general reference use, at least one good state history for each state, and add any outstanding new state history which might be published in the future.

7. Circus Material

Our circus material—posters, pamphlets, route books, biographies, memoirs, etc.—is unusually comprehensive. Much of the material relating to the circus in America has come by gift (e.g., the Leonidas Westervelt Collection) and the rest has been purchase over the years.

It is suggested that this Collection be added to as opportunity presents.

8. Naval History

The Naval History Society gave its library to our Society and, in addition, also donated funds for the purchase of more material (Naval History Fund). The Naval History Society Collection, accompanied by catalog, covers the United States Naval History from the Revolution through World War I. It includes biographies of naval leaders, accounts of naval campaigns, histories of naval vessels, etc. We continue to purchase, through the funds provided, naval histories prior to

World War I, but we have not attempted to collect naval historical and campaign material relating to World Wars I and II, except for some official government publications in the field of naval historical and campaign material. This material is used by researchers in our library and the collection is an active one.

It is suggested that the Library should actively collect primary material in U.S. Naval History through the Spanish-American War. This terminal date seems practical because of the large Lathrop C. Harper Collection of Spanish-American War material. It is suggested that for the period after 1898 the Society should accept primary material offered as gifts and should continue to purchase primary material related to New York City and State. It is further suggested that the purchase of secondary material should be limited to outstanding histories on the basis of reviews in selective historical journals.

9. Military History (Including Military Manuals)

As in the case of our naval history collection we received the libraries of two organizations interested in military history. The libraries of *The Seventh Regiment— New York National Guard* and *The Military Order of the Loyal Legion of the United States* were given to us. Funds were not provided, however, by either of these organizations for the purchase of further material and we add to our collection of military history from regular special funds. Spanish-American War material was donated five years ago by Mrs. Lathrop C. Harper, together with funds, later added, for purchase in this field.

Our collection of military history contains army lists, orderly books, muster rolls, adjutant generals' reports, related journals and periodicals. Our area of collecting in military history extends from the Colonial period through the Spanish-American War, and to a certain degree, through World War I; with emphasis only on official campaign documents for World War II. We are unusually strong in the Colonial Wars, Revolutionary War, War of 1812, Civil War, and Spanish-American War material. Our Mexican War material is less strong than that of other wars but it is, nonetheless, an adequate collection. This collection of printed pamphlets and books is supplemented by broadsides and posters in the Map and Print Room and by material in the Manuscript Collection.

The collection of military manuals which we have consists of field exercise instructions, cavalry tactics, etc., and while it extends through the Civil War we make special efforts to obtain Revolutionary War and War of 1812 data.

It is suggested that the Library pursue an acquisition policy similar to that suggested in connection with the naval history collection, i.e., for the period after 1898 the Society should accept primary material offered as gifts and should continue to purchase primary material related to New York City and State. It is further suggested that the purchase of secondary material should be limited to outstanding military histories on the basis of reviews in selective historical journals.

10. Civil War

In view of the strong collection of Civil War material we have it seems advisable here to discuss this material in more detail. The range in this area is very much wider than that of other wars. We have over 11,000 titles, and these titles touch on every aspect of the Civil War, i.e. economic, political, social, industrial, etc. The Civil War collections include regimental histories (not only of New York but of other states), official records, memoirs, prison life accounts, reminiscences, rosters, histories of battles and campaigns, etc. The size and scope of this collection apparently are due to systematic collecting in the past by our Trustee, Daniel Parish, Jr., and others. In so far as the other two major libraries in the city are concerned (Columbia University Library and The New York Public Library) the New-York Historical Society Library has the largest collection of Civil War material [As of February 7, 1958: 4,000 titles at Columbia; 8,120 at New York Public Library].

There are differences, however, in the three collections (Columbia, N-YHS, NYPL). Columbia has a good collection of standard secondary material and some primary material, but in effect, it is a college and university 'working' library. (As evidence of this Columbia graduate students come to our library and to the NYPL to pursue some intensive research.) It is the least comprehensive and helpful *from a research point of view*, of the three collections.

The NYPL, however, has an outstanding Civil War collection. Among the material are regimental histories which comprise all possible histories of Northern and Southern regiments (although Southern regimental histories in any case are less common than for those of the Northern states). In fact, so comprehensive is this collection of regimental histories that the present Chief of the American History Division stated recently that it is difficult to acquire any more regimental histories because the collection is so complete.

On the other hand, The N-YHS Library has a larger collection—in comparison with the NYPL—of memoirs, reminiscences and recollections of the war, as seen by various participants. It is safe to say that the two libraries (N-YHS and NYPL) are about equal in the *number* of accounts of prison life, both North and South. They are not necessarily equal in the sense that we duplicate one another since we have material they do not have, and vice versa. The New York Public Library is stronger in economic histories of the Civil War, which include accounts of financial developments, currency fluctuations and the like. At the same time, the NYPL's diplomatic records of the war—i.e., relation with foreign countries and vice versa—is more complete than ours. It is also stronger in Confederate imprints.

It might be advisable to concentrate on New York material (which we do not overlook in any event) and also to attempt to collect primary material outside of the areas in which the NYPL is strongest (political, economic, and diplomatic aspects of the war).

In any case, the collections in the NYHS and the NYPL do not constitute complete duplication in Civil War material. It is currently the policy at the New York Public Library to purchase almost all Civil War material now published. In one area, for example, the purchase of regimental histories relating to regiments outside of New York State we might, in view of the NYPL collection, consider discontinuing such purchases.

a. It is suggested in view of the survey above that we continue to purchase Civil War regimental histories. It is suggested, particularly that we include regimental histories of New England and the other Middle Atlantic states.
b. In view of the large collection of accounts of prison life diaries, memoirs and reminiscences—of Union troops—it is suggested that this material be added to when possible.
c. It is suggested, in view of the large Confederate Collections of reminiscences, memoirs, diaries, etc., in the outstanding Southern universities (e.g., University of North Carolina) that we do not attempt to collect this material for our library.
d. It is suggested, because of the general histories cf the period and the specific material which we already have adequately dealing with this area, that we do not attempt to collect additional material relating to the diplomatic and economic aspects of the Civil War. A further consideration in this field, worthy of note, is the fact that the NYPL and Columbia are particularly strong in this area.
e. It is suggested, since our strength is essentially in Union material and also because of present inflated prices, that we do not attempt to build a collection of Confederate imprints, *as such*, beyond what we already have.
f. It is suggested that we collect primary material relating to slavery, anti-slavery and Reconstruction in view of the outstanding pamphlet collection which we have at present in this field.
g. It is suggested that military history of the Civil War, *per se*, be purchased when it is of a primary nature or of such outstanding value as to complement the material in our Reference Library. In this area, as a suggestion, we might include such items as battle accounts, campaign recollections of military figures, etc.
h. It is suggested, because of the flow of secondary accounts currently published dealing with the Civil War, that this material be purchased only on the basis of reviews in the outstanding history periodicals. It is also suggested, in this connection, that the purchase of secondary material might also be determined by the worth of its bibliographies and new source material.

11. Songsters, Sheet Music Through 1910–1916

Our collection of sheet music is based, essentially, on the illustrations which appear on the covers of early sheet music. In most cases the illustrations portray scenes no longer existing, and, in other instances, provide the only illustrations available of buildings or streets or views of a city. The emphasis in this collection is on New York City and State material. We also have a collection of Civil War sheet music, for example, which is valuable in view of the great interest in this period. Mrs. Landauer purchases sheet music for her collection which frequently eliminates the necessity for using regular library funds.

Our collection of songsters is an old one which was begun in the late nineteenth century and is added to from time to time. The emphasis is basically on New York City and State material.

It is suggested, in view of the holdings of the NYPL in which there is a comprehensive collection of American sheet music and songsters, that no further additions be made to this collection.

12. Hotel Material for U.S. Including Contemporary Hotel Material

Our hotel material was donated to us. In the case of contemporary hotel material, the collection consists of indexed clippings, photographs and press releases (which are given to us) and the collection at present is kept up to date by the voluntary efforts of the widow of the donor. The emphasis here is on New York City hotels but, since many of the New York hotels are parts of nation-wide chains, the collection in some instances covers hotels outside of New York.

The earlier hotel material consists largely of engravings, photographs, etc., of early hotels in New York City and in some of the major Eastern Seaboard cities. Requests for reproductions of this material come to us by mail and telephone and it has useful reference value. In general, it is correct to state that we add very little by purchase since the collection attracts material from interested donors. [As of this writing our material is in use in connection with a forthcoming history of the Hotel Association of New York City.]

a. It is suggested that no further purchases be made in this area.
b. It is suggested that hotel material (relating to New York State) which is donated, be added to the collection.

13. Menus for U.S. Restaurants, Including Contemporary Restaurants

The nucleus of our menu collection is the Arnold Shircliffe menu collection of 10,000 items, which was donated to us by Mr. Shircliffe's son. There are some 18th century menus, but the bulk of the collection consists of 19th and early 20th (to approximately 1940) menus. These items are from restaurants all over the United States.

Supplementing the collection above are menus received by gift, or those which come to us from the public relations departments of contemporary restaurants. It is seldom that we add material, through purchase, to this collection. We receive almost all menus as gifts.

There is always an interest in menus either from the point of view of social history or for commercial purposes on the part of magazines and other restaurants. This collection is used regularly.

It is suggested that no further additions, except as relating to New York State, be made to this collection.

14. Biographies of National Importance

Our collection of biographies is unusually good in the field of American history. In general, these are biographies of national figures: political, military, etc. We have also acquired biographies of persons prominent in New York City and New York State who may not, necessarily, have achieved national prominence.

This is a working reference collection which supplements our other material.

a. It is suggested that important biographies of persons nationally prominent before 1865 be added to this collection. It is suggested that only biographies of figures of outstanding national importance *after* 1865 be purchased.
b. It is also suggested that biographies of New Yorkers after 1865 be added to the collection. It is further suggested that these purchases be based on selective book reviews in scholarly historical journals.

15. Latin American Collection

This collection consists of general histories of the Spanish exploration period. We do not add to it with any regularity since there are strong collections in the city. It is suggested that no further material be added to this collection.

16. Travels in the United States, Colonial Era to Present

This collection consists of an unusual group of American travel accounts with emphasis on *early American travels*. Included in these printed books are descriptions of localities and events which are invaluable records of history as it happened. Only relatively outstanding accounts of contemporary travels are purchased since this field is crowded with innumerable superficial or 'picture-book' volumes of little worth.

It is suggested that we continue to buy accounts of travel in America undertaken prior to 1850. For the period 1850 to 1900 it is suggested that secondary material be purchased only selectively on the basis of reviews in the outstanding historical journals.

17. Trials in the United States up to 1860

Our collection of early trials—the majority prior to 1850—is unusually strong. These reports of trials range from crudely printed pamphlets and leaflets to more detailed legal accounts. The emphasis, however, is on the social aspect of American history, rather than on the legal history of the period before 1850. These trials were often not reported in the press of the time because of the absence of newspapers in the vicinity of the trials.

The collection, which is well known, has been in the library and added to when possible, for many years. Additions to it are fairly uncommon, however since this material is rare and does not often appear for sale.

It is suggested that we do not purchase accounts of trials after 1850.

18. Drama

This collection represents American drama up to 1860, with emphasis on late 18th and early 19th century drama. We do not purchase late 19th or 20th century drama, a field adequately covered by the larger university libraries. (As a supplement to this collection we have some special material relating to artists such as Jenny Lind and the concert singer Emma Thursby.)

Supplementing the collection further are a number of standard reference works relating to the theatre of the 18th and 19th centuries.

It is suggested that only material of special interest relating to New York and New York State be added for the period up to, and including, 1900.

19. American Fiction, Poetry and Belles-Lettres to 1850

This is a strong collection, well publicized, whose beginnings can be traced to gifts received from donors during the 19th century. [Frequent letters from faculty members in colleges, both within and outside of New York, demonstrate the value of these volumes. In this connection a fairly recent bibliography of early American fiction by Lyle Wright (*American Fiction: A Contribution toward a Bibliography, 1744–1850*. San Marino: 1948) lists many of our titles. It should be noted that only in rare instances is this collection added to by purchase beyond the 1850 date. Exceptions occur only in the case of works by minor New York City or New York State authors whose works would probably not be collected by the average public or university library.]

It is suggested that only American fiction, poetry and *belles-lettres* of especial New York City and New York State interest be acquired through 1900.

20. Genealogies

The library has a large collection of collective and family genealogies. There is strong emphasis on New York City and State families. Genealogies of southern and western families are no longer collected, except in so far as they bear directly on families prominent in the eastern seaboard states during the 18th century. Many of these genealogies have come to us as gifts and the practice is still fairly common. They are frequently of value to the biographer and historian as well as the genealogist.

It is suggested that except for New York City and State families, no genealogies be added to this collection. This suggestion is offered in view of the statement of the Chief of the American History division of The New York Public Library who advises that it is now the policy of that library to acquire a copy of every printed genealogy relating to families in the United States. At the same time The New York Public Library pursues a policy of selective purchase of British (including Canadian) genealogies. Added to the above is the existence of The New York Genealogical and Biographical Society Library in the city.

21. Professional Literature

Under this category may be classed early United States histories and reference books relating to art and architecture (for museum research). Much of this material, over the years, has been donated. We have endeavored to purchase only such books and pamphlets as complement areas in which we have strong collections. Certain basic reference books are properly classed in this category (directories, lists, etc.). Under this category also may be classed such printed material relating to 18th and early 19th centuries as religious history; medical histories including such items as accounts of epidemics in early New York City and State; histories of early business and industrial firms; political histories, and some economic histories of the 18th and 19th centuries.

It is suggested that only material which has a specific reference tool value to the Library and/or to the Museum be purchased for the period after 1850.

22. New York City Records

This collection includes a complete list of Directories (including business Directories) and Guides. In addition, there are indexes to vital records, wills, newspaper records, etc., as well as early reports of New York City religious, benevolent, charitable, social, fraternal, patriotic, etc., organizations. The collection comprises partial files of early city departmental reports (health, fire, education, police, etc.) together with printed records of the Minutes of the Common Council, Proceedings of the Board of Aldermen, etc. Added to the maps and atlases in the Map and Print Room the collection of New York City material, through the 19th century, is most comprehensive.

It is suggested that this material be added to whenever possible.

23. New York State Records

Sets of official documents of colonial and state legislative journals, laws and executive documents, regional, county, city and town guides and directories and various institutional publications (large colleges and universities, local historical societies, etc.) comprise a cross-section of our New York State records.

It is suggested that this material be added to whenever possible.

24. Map and Print Collections

The map and print collections may be divided into eight general categories.

A. BROADSIDES

We have an unusually strong collection of broadsides through 1865. These items rarely come to the Library through donation and, as a result, must be acquired when possible through purchase. The broadsides we have, or buy supplement material in the field of printed books, e.g., War material, 18th century New York City proclamations, announcements, etc.

It is suggested that purchases in this area be determined on the basis of the field in which the broadsides belong. These fields might be determined according to the suggestions already listed in the foregoing paragraph.

B. POLITICAL CARICATURES AND POSTERS TO 1900–1910

This is a large and useful collection of material relating to political campaigns, both of New York and the nation, through 1910. The posters relate to such varied fields as the circus in America, outstanding events in the history of New York and items relating to the Spanish-American War. Unlike the broadside collection we frequently receive gifts of material in this area.

It is suggested that we add to this collection as opportunity presents.

C. STEAMBOAT COLLECTION

This collection consists of nine albums of photographs (the George Murdock Collection) of steamboats which traveled the Hudson River and Long Island Sound in the 19th century. Supplementing this collection are illustrations—in one form or other—of famous steamboats of the 19th century.

a. It is suggested that illustrations of American steamboats through 1920 be added to this collection.
b. It is also suggested that illustrations of steamboats identified with New York waters be added when available; irrespective of date.

D. MAPS AND ATLASES

This is a collection—strongest in 18th and early 19th century material—of maps of New York and the Eastern Seaboard. Included also are early railroad maps, atlases of the Civil War period, street maps of New York City, etc.

a. It is suggested that we add manuscript maps of the 18th and 19th centuries when available.
b. It is suggested, whenever possible, we add state and county atlases of the 18th and 19th centuries to supplement our present collection.
c. It is suggested that we continue to add some current maps which are necessary for general reference use.

E. SILHOUETTES

This is a general collection of silhouettes from the Colonial period through 1844. Strongest in New York City material, and for the years 1790–1844, the collection also includes the work of silhouettists outside of New York,

It is suggested that no purchase of material later than 1844 be added to this collection.

F. DAGUERREOTYPES

Primarily this collection is for the years 1850–1860 and the emphasis is on New Yorkers.

It is suggested, except for daguerreotypes of New Yorkers, that the terminal date for purchase of this material should be 1860.

G. ENGRAVED PORTRAITS, PHOTOGRAPHS AND LITHOGRAPHS

Our large collection of engraved portraits, photographs and lithographs consists of illustrations of prominent Americans with emphasis on the period up to 1920.

a. It is suggested that engraved portraits, photographs and lithographs of nationally prominent Americans be added to this collection; irrespective of date.
b. It is also suggested that engraved portraits, photographs and lithographs of New Yorkers (City and State) be added; irrespective of date.

H. VIEWS OF AMERICAN CITIES—18TH–19TH CENTURY

As the classification indicates, this collection consists of illustrations of American cities as they appeared in those centuries and the emphasis is usually on early views of American cities. Our New York City collection is exceptionally strong.

In this connection the following comments and statistics relating to the holdings of four institutions in the city, including ours, may be of interest.

Early Views of New York City

New York Public Library	500: It should be noted that the New York Public Library is not pursuing an active policy of acquiring New York City Views.
Columbia University Library	The holdings of this library are not significant in number or quantity.
The New York Historical Society Library	660: This figure includes material in the Museum Collection.
Museum of The City of New York—J. C. Davies and Arnold Collections	There are no figures available from this institution but the two collections cited are important sources for early views of New York and other American cities.

The statistics relating to Early American cities, *outside* of New York City, *to 1850* are as follows:

The New York Public Library	560
Columbia University Library	The holdings are not outstanding in this area.

The New-York Historical   741 (This figure includes material in the
Society Library   Museum Collection)

a. It is suggested on the basis of holdings of Columbia University Library, The New York Public Library and The New-York Historical Society Library that we continue to acquire views of New York City and New York State.

b. It is suggested that we continue to acquire views of cities *outside* of New York City and State up to 1850. It is suggested for the period 1850 to 1880 only scenic and city views of historical significance outside of New York City and State be purchased. It is further suggested, however, that only such material as engravings, lithographs, pen and ink sketches, photographs and water colors (Museum acquisitions) be added.

25. The Landauer Collection

The Landauer Collection consists primarily of thousands of 19th century business cards, professional advertisements, catalogues, souvenirs used by 19th century business firms, etc. This material, because of its pictorial nature, is especially in demand by commercial photographers, magazine editors and the like.

Included in this collection are the early and later 19th century bookplates collected by Mrs. Landauer, which are supplemented, in turn, by two collections of bookplates of the late 19th and early 20th century donated to the Library.

[Mrs. Landauer adds to this collection from her own funds.]

26. Manuscript Collection

The Manuscript Collection is one of the oldest in the Library. In 1813, only nine years after the Society was founded, fifty-one manuscripts were listed in the Society's Catalogue of its library. The collection now consists of over 300,000 single manuscripts and hundreds of bound volumes. Among these are papers of the Colonial and Revolutionary War periods, account books, diaries, journals, etc., of New York and early New Yorkers. The Manuscript Collection is particularly cohesive and is enriched, almost equally, by gift and purchase.

It is suggested that only material be purchased which has special relevance to material already in the collection.

27. Periodicals

As of March 1958 we received a total of 398 periodicals. Of these 222 were paid subscriptions and 289 were received "by exchange." This is explained by the fact that some of these "exchanges" are to individuals or to institutions in which we desire to have our *Quarterly* represented.

Of the 398 different periodicals which were received some arrive annually, some quarterly, etc.

a. In order to reduce the flow of this material, with its attendant handling and storage problems, it is suggested that the paid subscriptions—66 in number—listed below be discontinued.

b. It is suggested that the "exchange" items—32 in number—listed below be discontinued.

c. It is suggested that the exchange list be reviewed annually in order to avoid receiving extraneous material and at the same time to assure ourselves that our *Quarterly* is received by those who welcome it.

d. It is suggested that new subscriptions and exchanges be based on the suggestions put forth in the previous pages.

PRESIDENTS, LIBRARIANS, AND DIRECTORS OF THE NEW-YORK HISTORICAL SOCIETY

Presidents

Egbert Benson, LL.D.	1805–1815
Gouverneur Morris	1816
DeWitt Clinton, LL.D.	1817–1819
David Hosack, M.D., LL.D.	1820–1827
James Kent, LL.D.	1828–1831
Morgan Lewis	1832–1835
Peter Gerard Stuyvesant	1836–1839
Peter Augustus Jay, LL.D.	1840–1842
Albert Gallatin, LL.D.	1843–1849
Luther Bradish, LL.D.	1850–1863
Frederic De Peyster, LL.D.	1864–1866
Hamilton Fish, LL.D.	1867–1869
Thomas DeWitt, D.D.	1869–1871
Augustus Schell	1872
Frederic De Peyster, LL.D.	1873–1882

Augustus Schell	1883–1884
Benjamin Hazard Field	1885–1886
John Alsop King	1887–1900
Eugene Augustus Hoffman, D.D., LL.D.	1901–1902
Samuel Verplanck Hoffman	1903–1912
John Abeel Weekes	1913–1939
George A. Zabriskie, LL.D.	1939–1947
Fenwick Beekman, M.D.	1947–1956
Leroy E. Kimball, LL.D.	1956–1962
Irving S. Olds	1962–1963
Frederick B. Adams Jr.	1963–1970
Robert G. Goelet	1970–1987
Albert L. Key	1987–1989
Norman Pearlstine	1989–1993
Herbert S. Winokur Jr. and Wilbur L. Ross Jr.	1993–1994
Miner H. Warner	1994–

Librarians

John Forbes	1805–1809
John Pintard, LL.D.	1810–1811
John W. Francis, M.D.	1812–1818
Frederick C. Schaeffer, D.D.	1819–1820
Henry M. Francis, M.D.	1821
Matthew C. Patterson	1822
Henry W. Ducachet, M.D.	1823
Robert Greenhow, M.D.	1824–1826
Richard Ray	1827
James A. Hillhouse	1828
John Delafield Jr.	1828–1830
Samuel Ward III	1831–1835
Joseph Blunt	1836–1839
George W. Folsom	1840–1841

George Gibbs	1842–1847
Jacob B. Moore	1848
George H. Moore	1849–1876
John Austin Stevens	1876–1878
Jacob B. Moore	1879–1887
Charles Isham	1888–1892
William Kelby	1893–1898
Robert H. Kelby	1898–1921
Alexander J. Wall	1921–1937

Directors

Alexander J. Wall	1937–1944
R.W.G. Vail, Litt.D., L.H.D.	1944–1960
James J. Heslin	1960–1982
James B. Bell	1982–1988
Barbara Knowles Debs	1988–1992
Betsy Gotbaum	1993–

POSTSCRIPT

Part One of this book concluded with the summer of 1994 and the appointment of Betsy Gotbaum as executive director. As was explained in the preface, it did not seem appropriate to write a historical review while events were still unfolding. Although I continue to believe this to be true, it would be misleading to leave the reader with the impression that the Society is in the same position it was at the conclusion of this book's historical narrative. As one would expect, a great deal has happened since Gotbaum took over. This brief postscript does not attempt to analyze the first year of Gotbaum's tenure; rather, its purpose is simply to bring the reader up-to-date on significant events that have occurred during this time.

Not surprisingly given the Society's history, almost immediately after assuming her new position Gotbaum faced controversy. As if installing a new management team, building a strong relationship with her board, and reviving an institution in a state of financial crisis were not enough, one of Gotbaum's first major tasks was to oversee deaccessioning of approximately $20 million worth of Society collections. The plans for this process, which had been put in place prior to Gotbaum's appointment, called for the auctioning of three separate parts of the collections: "Important Old Master Paintings," which was composed of most of the remaining paintings from the Bryan collection; "Important Paperweights," a large collection of European paperweights; and "Americana and Decorative Arts," which was made up of various general materials in addition to items from the decorative arts collection. Even though the Society negotiated a special agreement with New York Attorney General Oliver Koppell to allow New York cultural institutions to preempt other bidders and purchase auctioned items at a discounted price, there was considerable criticism from the arts community. Nevertheless, beginning with the sale of the Bryan collection on January 12, 1995, and continuing through the sale of the decorative arts collections on January 29, 1995, the Society raised a net total of just under $16 million. The Society is currently preparing to sell the remaining items identified during the original deaccessioning process, including a large number of items from the library collections. All deaccessioning proceeds are being placed in permanent endowment restricted to care and maintenance of the remaining collections.

In addition to deaccessioning, another major project Gotbaum undertook early in her administration was renovating the Society's aging building. This step, long overdue, had been made possible by the joint New York city and state special capital appropriation of $10 million in 1993. Although much of the funding went toward building repairs, especially of the Society's roof and its heating and ventilation system, funds were also allocated to make other improvements to the facility. Gotbaum and her staff oversaw this important work, which resulted in substantial reconstruction of the Society's first-floor gallery spaces, enlargement and relighting of the first-floor hallway to create a brighter, more open environment for visitors, and a reorientation of the Society's primary entrance to 77th Street, facing the Museum of Natural History.

During the course of the building repair work, the Society's museum remained closed and its library was open just three days a week. The skeletal staff focused on developing and installing the first exhibition that would announce the Society's reopening. On May 11, 1995, the Society opened its doors to the public with "Treasury of the Past." The exhibit, designed to highlight the Society's museum and library collections, explores two hundred years of American history from 1750 to 1950. Each year in that time period is represented by an item from the collections, some of which are well known, like a Tiffany lamp or a Hudson River School painting, while other items speak of ordinary life, such as letters, household items, and toys.

Unfortunately, in spite of the efforts of the Society to reach out to a broader audience, the reopening of the Society has not resulted in a dramatic increase in visitors. The Society has averaged approximately three thousand visitors per month since the opening. It would seem that, at least for the short term, there is little potential for the Society to generate significant amounts of income from admissions, gift shop sales, and other forms of earned income.

As had been the case prior to Gotbaum's arrival, financial pressures have continued to be the top challenge for Society management. Gotbaum has committed the institution to balancing its budget and has cut expenditures substantially. The fiscal 1995 to 1996 budget calls for the Society to spend a total of just $5.2 million. Because of the Society's high fixed costs, such a frugal budget makes it very difficult for the Society to mount a regular series of exhibitions or to expand its public programming.

When the advisory committee chaired by Wilbur Ross issued its report in 1993, it asserted that the success of its recommendations depended on the generation of funds from three sources: deaccessioning, real estate, and public appropriations. In the opinion of the committee, the plan could not be successful unless all three components were simultaneously and quickly achieved. The Society has implemented successfully a difficult deaccessioning plan. It has also received and managed a capital appropriation that has substantially improved the building and facilities. However, the Society has made little progress on the difficult task of monetizing its real estate assets. In addition, thus far at least, government officials have been unable or unwilling to commit annual unrestricted operating support to the Society. Without these two components of the Ross committee's plan, especially a continuing commitment from the public sector, the Society's future remains uncertain.

Despite the trials, Gotbaum and her staff have persevered. Their continuing efforts were rewarded when, on June 23, 1995, the Society received a $7.5 million five-year grant from the Henry Luce Foundation. This grant is to be used to install an open study/storage center on the fourth floor of the Society's facility on Central Park West. The installation of the Henry Luce III Center for the Study of American Culture will not only make the Society's valuable collections more accessible to the public, it will also significantly reduce the annual expenditures on outside storage of museum-grade objects, which are approximately $500,000 per year. Furthermore, the size of the grant, the second largest ever made by the Luce Foundation, is a strong vote of confidence in the long-term importance of the Society and its collections.

Clearly, much has been accomplished. Yet there remains much to do. At the time of this writing, the Society still does not have the financial resources necessary to provide public services commensurate with the value and importance of its holdings. Finding a way to structure a sustainable balance between the scale of the collections and the resources available to maintain them—either through substantial new private and public support, or by making the collections more accessible to the public through creative relationships with other institutions—will likely be the primary topic in the next chapter of the Society's long struggle.

REFERENCES

Bagli, C. V. "New-York Historical Society Rattling Toward Disintegration." *New York Observer,* Feb. 22, 1993.

Bagli, C. V. "Politicians Wrestling Trustees over Fate of Historical Society." *New York Observer,* Apr. 18, 1994.

Baumol, W. J., and Bowen, W. G. *Performing Arts: The Economic Dilemma.* New York: Twentieth Century Fund, 1966.

Beekman, F. Speech delivered at the Sesqui-Centennial Dinner, May 3, 1954. *New York Historical Society Quarterly,* July 1954.

Beekman, F. "The Founding and Future of the Society." *New-York Historical Society Quarterly,* Jan. 1955.

Bergman, J. I. *Managing Change in the Nonprofit Sector: Lessons from the Evolution of Five Independent Research Libraries.* San Francisco: Jossey-Bass, 1995.

Bograd, H. *The Role of State Attorneys General in Relation to Troubled Nonprofits.* Report prepared for the Andrew W. Mellon Foundation. New York: Nonprofit Coordinating Committee of New York, 1994.

Bowen, W. G. *Inside the Boardroom.* New York: Wiley, 1994.

Bowen, W. G., Nygren, T. I., Turner, S. E., and Duffy, E. A. *The Charitable Nonprofits.* San Francisco: Jossey-Bass, 1994.

Carroll, M. "New-York Historical Society, Proud of Its Hyphen, Celebrates Its History." *New York Times,* Nov. 19, 1984.

Christiansen, K. "Putting Our Patrimony on the Block." *New York Newsday,* Dec. 7, 1994.

"Cleaning Out New York's 'Attic.'" Editorial. *New York Times,* Mar. 21, 1993.

"Curator's Dismissal Draws Protest." *New York Times,* Mar. 7, 1983.

De Peyster, F. *The Moral and Intellectual Influence of Libraries on Social Progress.* New York: New-York Historical Society, 1865.

"Dry Bones Were Shaken Up." *New York Times,* Jan. 5, 1917.

Dunlap, D. W. "Group Planning a New Building at West 76th St." *New York Times,* Mar. 18, 1983.

Dunlap, D. W. "Museum's Plan to Build Tower Stirs West-Siders." *New York Times,* Jan. 25, 1984.

Dunlap, D. W. "Historical Society Shuts Its Doors, but Still Hopes." *New York Times,* Feb. 20, 1993.

Dunlap, L. W. *American Historical Societies, 1790–1860.* Madison, Wis.: Cantwell, 1944.

Erikson, C. "Ailing Historical Society Gets Ray of Hope from Cuomo." *Manhattan Spirit,* Feb. 24, 1993a.

Erikson, C. "Historical Society Gets Funds." *Manhattan Spirit,* Mar. 3, 1993b.

Fox, D. R. "The President's Page." *New York History,* Jan. 1937.

Goldberger, P. "Historical Society May Put Holdings in NYU's Control." *New York Times,* Mar. 15, 1994.

Grimes, W. "Historical Society Gets NYU's Help." *New York Times,* Aug. 12, 1993.

Grimes, W. "Betsy Gotbaum Heads Troubled Historical Society." *New York Times,* June 20, 1994.

"Hearing on a Bill to Limit Sales of Museum Holdings." *New York Times,* Apr. 9, 1993.

"Hidden Treasures." *New York Herald,* Jan. 22, 1899.

"Historical Society to Take on New Life." *New York Times,* Jan. 4, 1917.

Honan, W. H. "Manhattan Institutions Reject Merger Idea." *New York Times,* Mar. 4, 1992a.

Honan, W. H. "To Be Rescued, Historical Society May End Up Joining Its Savior." *New York Times,* Nov. 19, 1992b.

Honan, W. H. "Albany Allocates Funds for Historical Society." *New York Times,* Apr. 6, 1993a.

Honan, W. H. "Dinkins Budget Pleases Many Arts Institutions." *New York Times,* May 5, 1993b.

Honan, W. H. "Historical Society Budget Priority in Doubt." *New York Times,* Apr. 27, 1993c.

Honan, W. H. "The Historical Society Is Criticized for Using Artworks as Collateral." *New York Times,* Jan. 28, 1993d.

Honan, W. H. "Historical Society Puts Up Artworks as Loan Collateral." *New York Times,* Jan. 27, 1993e.

Honan, W. H. "Scholars Mourn and Fight Landmark Library's Closing." *New York Times,* Feb. 9, 1993f.

Kennedy, I., and Schneider, C. *Historical Capital Market Returns.* Boston: Cambridge Associates, 1994.

Kimball, L. "The Society Welcomes a New Director." *New-York Historical Society Quarterly,* Oct. 1944.

Kimmelman, M. "A New Spirit at the New-York Historical Society." *New York Times,* Sept. 5, 1990.

Kimmelman, M. "Is This the End for New York's Attic?" *New York Times,* Feb. 21, 1993a.

Kimmelman, M. "Selling Art to Save Historical Society: A Painful Remedy." *New York Times,* Mar. 18, 1993b.

Larson, K. "Plundering the Past: The Decline of the New-York Historical Society." *New York,* July 25, 1988.

McCorison, M. A. "A Brief History of the Society." In N. Burkett and J. Hench (eds.), *Under Its Generous Dome.* Worcester, Mass.: American Antiquarian Society, 1992.

McCorison, M. A. *The Collections of the New-York Historical Society.* Report prepared for the Andrew W. Mellon Foundation, 1995.

McCusker, J. J. *How Much Is That in Real Money? A Historical Price Index for Use as a Deflator of Money Values in the Economy of the United States.* Worcester, Mass.: American Antiquarian Society, 1992.

McGill, D. C. "Art People: History of the Society." *New York Times,* Oct. 14, 1988a.

McGill, D. C. "Criticism Moves Historical Society—a Little." *New York Times,* July 25, 1988b.

McGill, D. C. "Historical Society Cuts Staff in Budget Crisis." *New York Times,* June 30, 1988c.

McGill, D. C. "Historical Society Is Planning Cuts to Meet Crisis." *New York Times,* June 28, 1988d.

McGill, D. C. "Historical Society Reshaping Itself for Survival." *New York Times,* Nov. 30, 1988e.

McGill, D. C. "Hundreds of Art Works Damaged by Mildew in Museum Warehouse." *New York Times,* July 10, 1988f.

McGill, D. C. "Much of Damaged Art at Society Is on Loan." *New York Times,* July 13, 1988g.

McGill, D. C. "Museum's Downfall: Raiding Endowment to Pay for Growth." *New York Times,* July 19, 1988h.

McGill, D. C. "Panel Will Seek Rescue for Historical Society." *New York Times,* Aug. 14, 1988i.

McGill, D. C. "Troubled Museums Try to Master the Fine Art of Survival." *New York Times,* Aug. 28, 1988j.

New-York Historical Society. *Library Acquisitions Policy.* New York: New-York Historical Society, 1959. (Amended in 1971.)

"Pearlstine's Unsociable Ways." Editorial. *New York Observer,* Mar. 1, 1993.

Richards, P. S. *Scholars and Gentlemen: The Library of the New-York Historical Society, 1804–1982.* Hamden, Conn.: Archon Books, 1984.

"Robert Walton Goelet, 61, Dies; Leading City Real Estate Owner." *New York Herald-Tribune,* May 3, 1941.

Robertson, N. "How a Small Museum Puts On Its Big Shows." *New York Times,* Feb. 4, 1983.

"Sale of Very Valuable Books." *New York Commercial Advertiser,* May 24, 1825.

Shillinglaw, G., and Meyer, P. *Accounting: A Management Approach.* Homewood, Ill.: Irwin, 1986.

"Tells Historical Society It Is Dead." *New York Times,* Jan. 3, 1917.

U.S. Bureau of Economic Analysis. *Survey of Current Business.* Washington, D.C.: U.S. Department of Commerce, 1994.

Vail, R.W.G. *Knickerbocker Birthday: A Sesqui-Centennial History of the New-York Historical Society, 1804–1954.* New York: New-York Historical Society, 1954.

Walker, S. A. "The Old Masters of the New-York Historical Society." *Independent,* Oct. 15, 1896.

Wall, A. J. "The Place of the Historical Society and Museum in the United States and Elsewhere." *New-York Historical Society Quarterly,* Apr. 1938.

Wallach, A. "Breathing Life into a Perennial Invalid." *New York Newsday,* Apr. 8, 1993.

Yarrow, A. L. "Historical Society Names New Leaders." *New York Times,* Apr. 13, 1989a.

Yarrow, A. L. "Historical Society Opens Two Conservation Labs." *New York Times,* Jan. 28, 1989b.

INDEX